The History
of American Management

Selections from the
Business History Review

The
History
of
American Management

Selections from the
Business History Review

Edited by
James P. Baughman
Associate Professor of Business History,
Harvard Graduate School of Business Administration
and Editor of the *Business History Review*

Prentice-Hall, Inc.,
Englewood Cliffs, New Jersey

Printed in the United States of America
Library of Congress Catalog Card Number: 69-11205
Current printing (last digit):
10   9   8   7   6   5   4   3   2   1

PRENTICE-HALL INTERNATIONAL, INC., *London*
PRENTICE-HALL OF AUSTRALIA, PTY. LTD., *Sydney*
PRENTICE-HALL OF JAPAN, INC., *Tokyo*
PRENTICE-HALL OF CANADA, LTD., *Toronto*
PRENTICE-HALL OF INDIA PRIVATE LTD., *New Delhi*

Preface

Throughout history, and particularly in the United States, the businessman, his values, his organizations, and his conduct have played dynamic roles. But business, like all mankind, is experiencing change of unprecedented scope and speed: the challenge of space; instantaneous and mass communications; ever-increasing propensities and capabilities for generating, storing, and manipulating information; "predictive" and "life" sciences; automation and increased consciousness of "human" rights; and, over all, the possibility of massive annihilation. How these or other forces may modify the traditional conduct of business enterprise is an open question. What rearrangement of historic relationships among business, labor, and government may emerge is a matter of daily interest.

Informed discussion of current or future business purposes, and appraisals of the values and skills possessed by or to be expected of business managers, are certainly furthered by reference to what has gone before. In this spirit, this anthology presents a handy reservoir of case studies illustrative of the historical evolution of business management in the United States. For the teacher, the student, and the general reader, these essays provide in-depth description and analysis of real-life firms and managers confronting and resolving business problems. These problems range from self-definition of values and purpose, through those of organization and control, to questions of viable strategies and tactics in dealing with competitors, the government, labor, and public opinion.

These essays are intended for those readers and curricula which inquire into the humanistic determinants and processes of economic and social change. They should be relevant to courses in economic and business history, business and society, and to general surveys of the evolution of American institutions and values. They will also complement those studies and curricula which emphasize more impersonal, macroeconomic and social trend analysis. In any context, however, it is hoped that they will contribute to more extended and insightful consideration of the heritage and prospects of American business.

The business firm is but one of the myriad organizational forms employed by human beings engaged in purposeful activity. Internally, it is a system of interacting, but not necessarily compatible, economic, political, and social processes. Externally, it is one of many interest groups whose objectives and actions affect and are affected by the allocation of resources, the possession and exercise of power, and the values of society. Business purposes and behavior may or may not blend with those of other groups, but as action-oriented organizations, firms are dynamic economic, political, and social units.

Amidst these internal and external possibilities of success and failure, it is the task of a firm's proprietors to "manage:" to chose among goals and strategies with varying forms and degrees of risk and uncertainty; to appraise opportunities and deploy resources efficiently, given these goals and strategies; to tune themselves and their organizations to become more perceptive than obtuse, more systematic than intuitive, more imaginative than dull, more harmonious and purposeful than disjointed, and more anticipatory than reactionary.

Thus "management" is as much an ideology as a skill. It is applicable at all levels of the firm and in many contexts, be it in the formulation of an entrepreneurial grand design or in the improvement of the flow of materials through a plant, in the improvement of internal informational flows or in sophistication of the means by which a firm "reads" its environment. And, most important, management is an intensely human process of decision making, which may use whatever technological assistance it can, but which is still greatly affected by human needs and the fortes and foibles of man.

But there are always men seeking to improve their ideologies and skills through experience and experimentation. The readings that follow are concerned with that improvement process as it has evolved in the management of business firms. The selections scan the first century of "modern" American business and focus upon various managerial challenges and styles. They present situations representative of the ways in which management has become more conscious, more informed, more responsible, and more professional. Inevitably, too, they often portray something less than enlightened leadership. Such value judgments as these readings make or imply, however, are always subject to the tender mercies of the reader. The purpose here is to provide informed, insightful appraisals of managerial performance which may serve as the basis for informed and insightful reflection and discussion.

The first selection, "The Beginnings of 'Big Business' in American Industry," considers the historical circumstances surrounding the birth of the "large vertically integrated, centralized, functionally departmentalized industrial organization." It was this type of firm, Professor Chandler argues, that was most important in altering the traditional "internal and external situations in which and about which business decisions were made." How these situations were altered and what managerial responses such change engendered are his concern. In particular, he inquires as to the sequence and nature of innovations in "strategy" and "structure," in purchasing, production, finance, marketing, and control, and asks if a national market was a prerequisite for such change.

The next three selections consider these questions in greater detail by focusing on the experience of three groups of businessmen coping with growth and change. In "The Railroads: Pioneers in Modern Corporate Management," Professor Chandler advances the hypothesis that large and complex operations breed managerial innovation, especially in communication and control, and that American railroads were the first to reach such a critical mass. His conclusions concerning the ways in which the early railroad managers handled such internal problems as data flow and the appropriate lines of authority and responsibility contribute to understanding of larger questions in the evolution of administrative practices. In "Systematic Management: Design for Organizational Recoupling in American Manufacturing Firms," Professor Litterer provides the experience of other groups of managers which can be compared to that of the railroads. Were the problems of the railroads really as unique as Professor Chandler believes? What were the origins and styles of "systematic management" that appeared in manufacturing? Is it useful to distinguish between "entrepreneurial" and "managerial" problems and responses? Were the chronic difficulties internal or external, technological or human, cyclical or random?

At a somewhat later point in time, Messrs. Dale and Meloy examine the managerial learning process within a single, large, complex firm. "Hamilton MacFarland Barksdale and the DuPont Contributions to Systematic Management," epitomizes the evolution in America of conscious "principles" of management and focuses upon the career of a prime mover in that process. The obvious questions are to what extent Barksdale and DuPont were able to benefit from the experience of the earlier generations portrayed by Chandler and Litterer; if Barksdale was dealing with new situations and to what extent he was, indeed, "innovative;" and how truly anticipatory was the state of the managerial art by 1920.

The next three selections shift attention from the internal problems of the firm to the relationship of businessmen and their organizations to society. The purpose is not to be comprehensive, but to present historical situations which illuminate the essence of the process of change. Professor Hawkins, for example, traces the evolution of a particularly crucial aspect of the business-government-public entente. In "The Development of Modern Financial Reporting Practices among American Manufacturing Corporations," he examines the gradual standardization of financial records-keeping within the firm and the internal and external pressures which have produced more public and credible financial disclosure. Here the questions turn upon the criteria relevant to custodial as opposed to managerial accounting; upon what business information is or should be privileged and what public; and upon the varying responsibilities of the manager, the independent auditing profession, and the government administrator in effecting constructive change. Implicit, of course, is the larger issue of self versus public regulation of business practice.

In the selections by Professors Galambos and Fine, conflicts between the interests of the managers of business enterprises and the interests of the public as represented by the government are directly confronted. "The Cotton-Textile Institute and the Government: A Case Study in Interacting Value Systems," portrays businessmen and their representatives negotiating with government officials over the conditions of competition in a key industry. The study deals with the subtle ways in which competing firms coalesced into a concerted trade association; with how, in this case, business values "modified the goals of public policy but at the same time absorbed several new concepts . . . which helped the businessman accommodate himself to an environment in which he was held to be accountable to the public for many of his actions." Professor Galambos' findings also permit careful scrutiny of the stereotypes of a monolithic business "community" and a single-minded government "policy" toward business. Given the maneuvering room between business and government, and given the problems of unifying either side, what sort of managerial skills are relevant; what are or should be their forms and substances; what are or should be their utilities and proprieties?

"The Ford Motor Company and N.R.A." presents a dramatic alternative to the posture adopted by the Cotton-Textile Institute in its dealings with government. Under the stress of the Great Depression, while the whole set of assumptions upon which American business had operated for decades was being searchingly and publicly reappraised, Henry Ford and the President of the United States debated the compatibilities of public economic policy and the interests of private corporations. Again, the essay focuses upon the context in which negotiation took place and the strategies, tactics, and temper of the bargaining process. The larger issue posed is not whether Ford "won" or "lost," but what, in this period of profound social change, was to be the "fundamental American idea" of business and government relationships.

Rounding out the broad view of the changing world of American management begun by Professor Chandler's lead article, the last two selections examine more recent trends. "Management Decentralization: An Historical Analysis" relates administrative structure to the nature of a company's business and suggests the importance of managerial personalities in governing the timing of structural change. The basic management structures of fifty large corporations are examined in historical perspective and in terms of cycles of centralization and decentralization. What companies

have tended toward product decentralization and why? Which companies
have decentralized geographically and why? Why have some companies
not found decentralization a meaningful answer for their prevailing administrative problems? Have structures developed to improve internal efficiency
served well in external situations, and vice versa? Are "company" problems
and "industry" problems always the same?

Professor Newcomer provides a final perspective on the first century
of modern American management by summarizing the evidence of "Professionalization of Leadership in the Big Business Corporation." To the questions raised in the earlier selections concerning the extent to which the
conditions of management have changed, she adds the query whether the
top decision makers of the mid-twentieth century differ from their predecessors. Once again, the broader questions of what constitute "principles"
of management, what comprise the skills of "managers," and what roles
these principles and skills play or should play in society are posed. The
reader, of course, will formulate his own answers, but these brief excursions
into history should aid him in sorting out myth from reality.

JAMES P. BAUGHMAN

Contributors

Alfred D. Chandler, Jr., is Professor of History at the Johns Hopkins University and editor of the Eisenhower Papers.

Ernest Dale is Professor in the Wharton School of Finance and Commerce at the University of Pennsylvania and president of Ernest Dale Associates.

Sidney Fine is Professor of History at the University of Michigan.

Louis P. Galambos is Associate Professor of History at Rice University.

David F. Hawkins is Associate Professor in the Graduate School of Business Administration at Harvard University.

Joseph A. Litterer is Professor in the Graduate School of Business Administration at the University of Illinois.

Charles Meloy is research associate and consultant in Ernest Dale Associates.

Mabel Newcomer is Professor of Economics *emerita* at Vassar College.

Contents

Alfred D. Chandler, Jr.

1

The Beginnings of "Big Business" in American Industry*

CRITERIA FOR SELECTION AND ANALYSIS

The historian, by the very nature of his task, must be concerned with change. What made for change? Why did it come when it did, and in the way it did? These are characteristically historians' questions. For the student of American business history, these basic questions can be put a little more precisely. What in the American past has given businessmen the opportunity or created the need for them to change what they were doing or the way they were doing it? In other words, what stimulated them to develop new products, new markets, new sources of raw materials, new ways of procuring, processing, or marketing the goods they handled? What encouraged them to find new methods of financing, new ways of managing or organizing their businesses? What turned them to altering their relations with their working force, their customers and competitors, and with the larger American public?

The question of what constitutes the dynamic factors in American business history, dynamic in the sense of stimulating change and innovation, can be more clearly defined if the country's land, natural resources, and cultural patterns are taken as given. Land and resources were the raw materials with which the businessmen had to work, and the cultural attitudes and values helped set the legal and ethical rules of the game they had to play. Within this cultural and geographic environment a number of historical developments appear to have stimulated change. These provide a framework around which historical data can be compiled and analyzed.

* This study was supported by the Sloan Research Fund of The School of Industrial Management and the Center for International Studies, Massachusetts Institute of Technology.

The following major dynamic forces are visible in the American business economy since 1815: the western expansion of population; the construction and initial operation of the national railroad network; the development of a national and increasingly urban market; the application of two new sources of power: the internal combustion engine and electricity, to industry and transportation; and the systematic application of the natural and physical sciences, particularly chemistry and physics, to industry through the institutionalizing of research and development activities.

The first, the westward expansion, appears to have provided the primary impetus, except possibly in New England, to business innovation in the years from 1815 to about 1850; the building of the railroads appears to have been the major factor from the 1850's to the late 1870's; the growth of the national and urban market from the 1880's until a little after 1900; the coming of electricity and the internal combustion engine from the early 1900's to the 1920's; and, finally, the growth of systematic and institutionalized research and development since the 1920's.

These five factors are essentially aspects of fundamental population changes and technological advances. There were, of course, other factors that encouraged business innovation and change. The coming of the new machines and mechanical devices may have been a more important stimulant to innovation in New England than the growth of her markets and sources of supply in the expanding South and West. Wars usually precipitated change. The business cycle, flow of capital, government policy and legislation all played a significant part in business innovation. But such political and financial developments appear to have intensified or delayed the more basic changes encouraged initially by fundamental population shifts and technological achievements.

The purpose of making such a list is, however, not to argue that one development was more dynamic than the other. Nor are these five factors to be considered as "causes" for change; nor are they "theses" to be argued as representing reality, nor "theories" to provide an overall explanation of change or possibly of predicting change. They are, rather, a framework on which historical information can be tied and interrelated. They provide a consistent basis upon which meaningful questions can be asked of the data.

This framework and these questions are, it should be emphasized, concerned only with fundamental changes and innovation in the business economy. They do not deal with the day-to-day activities to which businessmen must devote nearly all of their time. They are not concerned with the continuous adaptation to the constant variations of the market, sources of supply, availability of capital, and technological developments. Nor do they consider why some businesses and businessmen responded quickly and creatively to the basic population and technological changes and others did not. But an understanding of the continuous response and adjustment would seem to require first an awareness of the meaning of the more fundamental or "discontinuous" changes.

Since historical compilation and analysis must be selective, it is impossible to undertake any historical study without some criteria either implicit or explicit for selection. Further study and analysis, by indicating the defects of this approach and framework, will suggest more satisfactory ones. In the process, an analysis and interpretation of change in the American business past should come a little nearer to reality.

The purpose of this article then is, by using the framework of basic, dynamic forces, to look a little more closely at the years that witnessed the beginnings of big business in American industry. What types of changes came during these years in the ways of marketing, purchasing, processing, and in the forms of business organization? Why did these changes come when they did in the way they did? Was the growth of the national market a major prerequisite for such innovation and change? If not, what then was? How did these innovations relate to the growth of the railroad network or the coming of electricity and the internal combustion engine?

In addition to secondary works on this period, the data used in seeking answers to these questions have been annual and other corporation reports, government documents, articles in periodicals, histories, and biographies concerning the 50 largest industrial companies in the country in 1909. Nearly all these companies, listed in Table I, had their beginnings in the last years of the nineteenth century.

Major Changes in American Industry at the End of the Nineteenth Century

Between the depression of the 1870's and the beginning of the twentieth century, American industry underwent a significant transformation. In the 1870's the major industries serviced an agrarian economy. Except for a few companies equipping the rapidly expanding railroad network, the leading industrial firms processed agricultural products and provided farmers with food and clothing. These firms tended to be small, and bought their raw materials and sold their finished goods locally. Where they manufactured for a market more than a few miles away from the factory, they bought and sold through commissioned agents who handled the business of several other similar firms.

By the beginning of the twentieth century, many more companies were making producers' goods, to be used in industry rather than on the farm or by the ultimate consumer. Most of the major industries had become dominated by a few large enterprises. These great industrial corporations no longer purchased and sold through agents, but had their own nationwide buying and marketing organizations. Many, primarily those in the extractive industries, had come to control their own raw materials. In other words, the business economy had become industrial. Major industries were dominated by a few firms that had become great, vertically integrated, centralized enterprises.

In the terms of the economist and sociologist, a significant sector of American industry had become bureaucratic, in the sense that business decisions were made within large hierarchical structures. Externally, oligopoly was prevalent, the decision-makers being as much concerned with the actions of the few other large firms in the industry as with overall changes in markets, sources of supplies, and technological improvements.

These basic changes came only after the railroads had created a national market. The railroad network, in turn, had grown swiftly primarily because of the near desperate requirements for efficient transportation created by the movement of population westward after 1815.[1] Except for the Atlantic seaboard between Boston and Washington, the construction of the American railroads was stimulated almost wholly by the demand for better transportation to move crops, to bring farmers supplies, and to open up new territories to commercial agriculture.

By greatly expanding the scope of the agrarian economy, the railroads quickened the growth of the older commercial enters, such as New York, Philadelphia, Cincinnati, Cleveland, and St. Louis, and helped create new cities like Chicago, Indianapolis, Atlanta, Kansas City, Dallas, and the Twin Cities. This rapid urban expansion intensified the demand for the products of the older consumer goods industries—particularly those which processed the crops of the farmer and planter into food, stimulants, and clothing.

At the same time, railroad construction developed the first large market in this country for producers' goods. Except for the making of relatively few textile machines, steamboat engines, and ordnance, the iron and nonferrous manufacturers had before 1850 concentrated on providing metals and simple tools for merchants and farmers. Even textile machinery was usually made by the cloth manufacturers themselves. However, by 1860, only a decade after beginning America's first major railroad construction boom, railroad companies had already replaced the blacksmiths as the primary market for iron products, and had become far and away the most important market for the heavy engineering industries. By then, too, the locomotive was competing with the Connecticut brass industry as a major consumer of copper. More than this, the railroads, with their huge capital outlay, their fixed operating costs, the large size of their labor and manage-

---

[1] The factors stimulating the growth of the American railroad network and the impact of the earlier construction and operation of this network on the American business economy and business institutions is suggested in Chandler, *Henry Varnum Poor—Business Editor, Analyst, and Reformer* (Cambridge, 1956), especially Chaps. 4, 6–9.

ment force, and the technical complexity of their operations, pioneered in the new ways of oligopolistic competition and large-scale, professionalized, bureaucratized management.

The new nationwide market created by the construction of the railroad network became an increasingly urban one. From 1850 on, if not before, urban areas were growing more rapidly than rural ones. In the four decades from 1840 to 1880 the proportion of urban population rose from 11 per cent to 28 per cent of the total population, or about 4 per cent a decade. In the two decades from 1880 to 1900 it grew from 28 per cent to 40 per cent or an increase of 6 per cent a decade. Was this new urban and national market, then, the primary stimulant for business innovation and change, and for the coming of big business to American industry?

Changes in the Consumers' Goods Industries

The industries first to become dominated by great business enterprises were those making consumer goods, the majority of which were processed from products grown on the farm and sold in the urban markets. Consolidation and centralization in the consumers' goods industries were well under way by 1893. The unit that appeared was one which integrated within a single business organization the major economic processes: production or purchasing of raw materials, manufacturing, distribution, and finance.

Such vertically integrated organizations came in two quite different ways. Where the product tended to be somewhat new in kind and especially fitted for the urban market, its makers created their businesses by first building large marketing and then purchasing organizations. This technique appears to have been true of the manufacturers or distributors of fresh meat, cigarettes, high-grade flour, bananas, harvesters, sewing machines, and typewriters. Where the products were established staple items, horizontal combination tended to precede vertical integration. In the sugar, salt, leather, whiskey, glucose, starch, biscuit, kerosene, fertilizer, and rubber industries a large number of small manufacturers first combined into large business units and then created their marketing and buying organizations. For a number of reasons the makers of the newer types of products found the older outlets less satisfactory and felt more of a need for direct marketing than did the manufacturers of the long-established goods.

Integration via the Creation of Marketing Organization

The story of the changes and the possible reasons behind them can be more clearly understood by examining briefly the experience of a few innovating firms. First, consider the experience of companies that grew large through the creation of a nationwide marketing and distributing organization. Here the story of Gustavus F. Swift and his brother Edwin is a significant one. Gustavus F. Swift, an Easterner, came relatively late to the Chicago meat-packing business. Possibly because he was from Massachusetts, he appreciated the potential market for fresh western meat in the eastern cities.[2] For after the Civil War, Boston, New York, Philadelphia, and other cities were rapidly outrunning their local meat supply. At the same time, great herds of cattle were gathering on the western plains. Swift saw the possibilities of connecting the new market with new source of supply by the use of the refrigerated railroad car. In 1878, shortly after his first experimental shipment of refrigerated meat, he formed a partnership with his younger brother, Edwin, to market fresh western meat in the eastern cities.

For the next decade, Swift stuggled hard to carry out his plans, the essence of which was the creation, during the 1880's, of the nationwide distributing and marketing organization built around a network of branch houses. Each "house" had its storage plant and its own marketing organization. The latter included outlets in major towns and cities, often managed by Swift's own salaried representatives. In marketing the product, Swift had to break down, through advertising and other means, the prejudices against eating meat killed more than a thousand miles away and many weeks earlier. At the same time he had to combat boycotts of local butchers and the concerted efforts of the National Butchers' Protective Association to prevent the sale of his meat in the urban markets.

To make effective use of the branch house network, the company soon began to market products other than beef. The "full line" soon came to include lamb, mutton, pork, and, some time later, poultry, eggs, and dairy products. The growing distributing organization soon demanded an increase in supply. So between 1888 and 1892, the Swifts set up meat-packing establishments in Kansas City, Omaha, and St. Louis, and, after the depression of the 1890's, three more in St. Joseph, St. Paul, and Ft. Worth. At the same time, the company systematized the buying of its cattle and other products at the stockyards. In the 1890's, too, Swift began a concerted effort to make more profitable use of by-products.

Before the end of the 1890's, then, Swift had effectively fashioned a great, vertically integrated organization. The major departments—marketing, processing, purchasing, and accounting—were all tightly controlled

---

[2] Swift's story as outlined in Louis F. Swift in collaboration with Arthur Van Vlissingen, *The Yankee of the Yards—the Biography of Gustavus Franklin Swift* (New York, 1928). The United States Bureau of Corporations, *Report of the Commissioner of Corporations on the Beef Industry, March 3, 1905* (Washington, 1905), is excellent on the internal operations and external activities of the large meat-packing firms. There is additional information in the later three-volume *Report of the Federal Trade Commission on the Meat-Packing Industry* (Washington, 1918–1919). R. A. Clemen, *The American Livestock and Meat Industry* (New York, 1923) has some useful background data.

from the central office in Chicago. A report of the Commissioner of Corporations published in 1905 makes clear the reason for such control:[3]

> Differences in quality of animals and of their products are so great that the closest supervision of the Central Office is necessary to enforce the exercise of skill and sound judgement on the part of the agents who buy the stock, and the agents who sell the meat. With this object, the branches of the Selling and Accounting Department of those packing companies which have charge of the purchasing, killing, and dressing and selling of fresh meat, are organized in the most extensive and thorough manner. The Central Office is in constant telegraphic correspondence with the distributing houses, with a view to adjusting the supply of meat and the price as nearly as possible to the demand.

As this statement suggests, the other meat packers followed Swift's example. To compete effectively, Armour, Morris, Cudahy, and Schwarzschild & Sulzberger had to build up similar integrated organizations. Those that did not follow the Swift model were destined to remain small local companies. Thus by the middle of the 1890's, the meat-packing industry, with the rapid growth of these great vertically integrated firms had become oligopolistic (the "Big Five" had the major share of the market) and bureaucratic; each of the five had its many departments and several levels of management.

This story has parallels in other industries processing agricultural products. In tobacco, James B. Duke was the first to appreciate the growing market for the cigarette, a new product which was sold almost wholly in the cities.[4] However, after he had applied machinery to the manufacture of cigarettes, production soon outran supply. Duke then concentrated on expanding the market through extensive advertising and the creation of a national and then worldwide selling organization. In 1884, he left Durham, North Carolina, for New York City, where he set up factories, sales, and administrative offices. New York was closer to his major urban markets, and was the more logical place to manage an international advertising campaign than Durham. While he was building his marketing department, Duke was also creating the network of warehouses and buyers in the tobacco-growing areas of the country.

In 1890, he merged his company with five smaller competitors in the cigarette business to form the American Tobacco Company. By 1895 the activities of these firms had been consolidated into the manufacturing, marketing, purchasing, and finance departments of the single operating structure Duke had earlier fashioned. Duke next undertook development of a full line by handling all types of smoking and chewing tobacco. By the

---

[3] *Report of Commissioner of Corporations on the Beef Industry*, p. 21.

[4] Some information on James B. Duke and the American Tobacco Company can be found in John W. Jenkins, *James B. Duke, Master Builder* (New York, 1927), Chaps. 5–7, 10. More useful was the United States Bureau of Corporations, *Report of the Commissioner of Corporations on the Tobacco Industry* (Washington, 1909).

end of the century, his company completely dominated the tobacco business. Only two other firms, R. J. Reynolds & Company and P. Lorillard & Company had been able to build up comparable vertically integrated organizations. When they merged with American Tobacco they continued to retain their separate operating organizations. When the 1911 antitrust decree split these and other units off from the American company, the tobacco industry had become, like the meat-packing business, oligopolistic, and its dominant firms bureaucratic.

What Duke and Swift did for their industries, James S. Bell of the Washburn-Crosby Company did during these same years in the making and selling of high-grade flour to the urban bakeries and housewives, and Andrew J. Preston achieved in growing, transporting, and selling another new product for the urban market, the banana.[5] Like Swift and Duke, both these men made their major innovations in marketing, and then went on to create large-scale, departmentalized, vertically integrated structures.

The innovators in new consumer durables followed much the same pattern. Both Cyrus McCormick, pioneer harvester manufacturer, and William Clark, the business brains of the Singer Sewing Machine Company, first sold through commissioned agents. Clark soon discovered that salaried men, working out of branch offices, could more effectively and at less cost display, demonstrate, and service sewing machines than could the agents.[6] Just as important, the branch offices were able to provide the customer with essential credit. McCormick, while retaining the dealer to handle the final sales, came to appreciate the need for a strong selling and distributing organization, with warehouses, servicing facilities, and a large salaried force, to stand behind the dealer.[7] So in the years following the Civil War, both McCormick and Singer Sewing Machine Company concentrated on building up national and then worldwide marketing departments. As they purchased their raw materials from a few industrial companies rather than from a mass of farmers, their purchasing departments were smaller, and required less attention than those in the firms processing farmers' products. But the net result was the creation of a very similar type of organization.

Integration via Horizontal Combination

In those industries making more standard goods, the creation of maketing organizations usually followed large-scale combinations of a

---

[5] The story of Bell is outlined in James Gray, *Business Without Boundary, the Story of General Mills* (Minneapolis, 1954), and of Preston in Charles M. Wilson, *Empire in Green and Gold* (New York, 1947).

[6] The early Singer Sewing Machine experience is well analyzed in Andrew B. Jack, "The Channels of Distribution for an Innovation: the Sewing Machine Industry in America, 1860–1865," *Explorations in Enterpreneurial History*, Vol. IX (Feb., 1957), pp. 113–141.

[7] William T. Hutchinson, *Cyrus Hall McCormick* (New York, 1935), Vol. II, pp. 704–712.

number of small manufacturing firms. For these small firms, the coming of the railroad had in many cases enlarged their markets but simultaneously brought them for the first time into competition with many other companies. Most of these firms appear to have expanded production in order to take advantage of the new markets. As a result, their industries became plagued with overproduction and excess capacity; that is, continued production at full capacity threatened to drop prices below the cost of production. So in the 1880's and early 1890's, many small manufacturers in the leather, sugar, salt, distilling and other corn products, linseed and cotton oil, biscuit, petroleum, fertilizer, and rubber boot and glove industries joined in large horizontal combinations.

In most of these industries, combination was followed by consolidation and vertical integration, and the pattern was comparatively consistent. First, the new combinations concentrated their manufacturing activities in locations more advantageously situated to meet the new growing urban demands. Next they systematized and standardized their manufacturing processes. Then, except in the case of sugar and corn products (glucose and starch), the combinations began to build large distributing and smaller purchasing departments. In so doing, many dropped their initial efforts to buy out competitors or to drive them out of business by price-cutting. Instead they concentrated on the creation of a more efficient flow from the producers of their raw materials to the ultimate consumer, and of the development and maintenance of markets through brand names and advertising. Since the large majority of these combinations began as regional groupings, most industries came to have more than one great firm. Only oil, sugar, and corn products remained long dominated by a single company. By World War I, partly because of the dissolutions under the Sherman Act, these industries had also become oligopolistic, and their leading firms vertically integrated.

Specific illustrations help to make these generalizations more precise. The best-known is the story of the oil industry, but equally illustrative is the experience of the leading distilling, baking, and rubber companies.

The first permanent combination in the whiskey industry came in 1887 when a large number of Midwestern distillers, operating more than 80 small plants, formed the Distillers' and Cattle Feeders' Trust.[8] Like other trusts, it adopted the more satisfactory legal form of a holding company

---

[8] The major sources of information on combination and consolidation in the distilling industry are Jeremiah W. Jenks, "The Development of the Whiskey Trust," *Political Science Quarterly*, Vol. IV (June, 1889), pp. 296–319; J. W. Jenks and W. E. Clark, *The Trust Problem* (rev. ed.; New York, 1917), pp. 141–149. The annual reports of the Distilling and Cattle Feeding Company and its various successors provide some useful additional data, as does the Industrial Commission, *Preliminary Report on Trusts and Industrial Combinations* (Washington, 1900), Vol. I, pp. 74–89, 167–259, 813–848, and Victor S. Clark, *History of Manufactures in the United States* (New York, 1929), Vol. II, pp. 505–506. Changes in taxes on liquors also affected the company's policies in the early 1890's.

shortly after New Jersey in 1889 passed the general incorporation law for holding companies. The major efforts of the Distillers Company were, first, to concentrate production in a relatively few plants. By 1895 only 21 were operating. The managers maintained that the large volume per plant permitted by such concentration would mean lower costs, and also that the location of few plants more advantageously in relation to supply and marketing would still reduce expenses further. However, the company kept the price of whiskey up, and since the cost of setting up a distillery was small, it soon had competition from small local plants. The company's answer was to purchase the new competitors and to cut prices. This strategy proved so expensive that the enterprise was unable to survive the depression of the 1890's.

Shortly before going into receivership in 1896, the Distillers Company had begun to think more about marketing. In 1895, it had planned to spend a million dollars to build up a distributing and selling organization in the urban East—the company's largest market. In 1898, through the purchase of the Standard Distilling & Distributing Company and the Spirits Distributing Company, it did acquire a marketing organization based in New York City. In 1903, the marketing and manufacturing units were combined into a single operating organization under the direction of the Distillers Securities Company. At the same time, the company's president announced plans to concentrate on the development of brand names and specialties, particularly through advertising and packaging.[9] By the early years of the twentieth century, then, the Distillers Company had become a vertically integrated, departmentalized, centralized operating organization, competing in the modern manner, more through advertising and product differentiation than price.

The experience of the biscuit industry is even more explicit. The National Biscuit Company came into being in 1898 as a merger of three regional combinations: the New York Biscuit Company formed in 1890, the American Biscuit and Manufacturing Company, and the United States Biscuit Company founded a little later.[10] Its initial objective was to control price and production, but as in the case of the Distillers Company, this strategy proved too expensive. The Annual Report for 1901 suggests why National Biscuit shifted its basic policies:[11]

> This Company is four years old and it may be of interest to shortly review its history. . . . When the Company started, it was an aggregation of

---

[9] *Annual Report of the President of the Distillers Securities Company* for 1903.

[10] The information on National Biscuit comes largely from its annual reports.

[11] *Annual Report of the National Biscuit Company for the Year Ending December, 1901,* January 3, 1902. References to centralizing of manufacturing facilities appear in several early annual reports. As this was written before Theodore Roosevelt had started to make the Sherman Act an effective antitrust instrument and Ida Tarbell and other journalists had begun to make "muck raking" of big business popular and profitable, the Biscuit Company's shift in policy could hardly have been the result of the pressure of public opinion or the threat of government action.

plants. It is now an organized business. When we look back over the four years, we find that a radical change has been wrought in our methods of business. In the past, the managers of large merchandising corporations have found it necessary, for success, to control or limit competition. So when this company started, it was thought that we must control competition, and that to do this we must either fight competition or buy it. The first meant a ruinous war of prices, and a great loss of profit; the second, a constantly increasing capitalization. Experience soon proved to us that, instead of bringing success, either of those courses, if persevered in, must bring disaster. This led us to reflect whether it was necessary to control competition. . . . . we soon satisfied ourselves that within the Company itself we must look for success.

We turned our attention and bent our energies to improving the internal management of our business, to getting full benefit from purchasing our raw materials in large quantities, to economizing the expenses of manufacture, to systematizing and rendering more effective our selling department; and above all things and before all things to improve the quality of our goods and the condition in which they should reach the customer.

It became the settled policy of this Company to buy out no competition. . . .

In concentrating on distribution, the company first changed its policy from selling in bulk to wholesalers to marketing small packages to retailers. It developed the various "Uneeda Biscuit" brands, which immediately became popular. "The next point," the same Annual Report continued, "was to reach the customer. Thinking we had something that the customer wanted, we had to advise the customer of its existence. We did this by extensive advertising." This new packaging and advertising not only quickly created a profitable business, but also required the building of a sizable marketing organization. Since flour could be quickly and easily purchased in quantity from large milling firms, the purchasing requirements were less complex, and so the company needed a smaller purchasing organization. On the other hand, it spent much energy after 1901 in improving plant layout and manufacturing processes in order to cut production costs and to improve and standardize quality. Throughout the first decade of its history, National Biscuit continued the policy of "centralizing" manufacturing operations, particularly in its great New York and Chicago plants.

In the rubber boot, shoe, and glove industries, the story is much the same. Expansion of manufacturing facilities and increasing competition as early as 1874, led to the formation, by several leading firms, of the Associated Rubber Shoe Companies—an organization for setting price and production schedules through its board of directors.[12] This company continued until 1886. Its successor, the Rubber Boot and Shoe Company, which lasted only

[12] The background for the creation of the United States Rubber Company can be found in Nancy P. Norton, "Industrial Pioneer: the Goodyear Metallic Rubber Shoe Company" (Ph. D. thesis, Radcliffe College, 1950), Constance McL. Green, *History of Naugatuck, Connecticut* (New Haven, 1948), pp. 126–131, 193–194, and Clark, *History of Manufactures*, Vol. II, pp. 479–481, Vol. III, pp. 235–237. The company's annual reports provide most of the information on its activities.

a year, attempted, besides controlling prices and production, to handle marketing, which had always been done by commissioned agents. After five years of uncontrolled competition, four of the five firms that had organized the selling company again combined, this time with the assistance of a large rubber importer, Charles A. Flint. The resulting United States Rubber Company came, by 1898, to control 75 per cent of the nation's rubber boot, shoe, and glove output.

At first the new company remained a decentralized holding company. Each constituent company retained its corporate identity with much freedom of action, including the purchasing of raw materials and the selling of finished products, which was done, as before, through jobbers. The central office's concern was primarily with controlling price and production schedules. Very soon, however, the company began, in the words of the 1896 Annual Report, a policy of "perfecting consolidation of purchasing, selling, and manufacturing."[13] This was to be accomplished in four ways. First, as the 1895 Annual Report had pointed out, the managers agreed "so far as practicable, to consolidate the purchasing of all supplies of raw materials for the various manufacturies into one single buying agency, believing that the purchase of large quantities of goods can be made at more advantageous figures than the buying of small isolated lots."[14] The second new "general policy" was "to undertake to reduce the number of brands of goods manufactured, and to consolidate the manufacturing of the remaining brands in those factories which have demonstrated superior facilities for production or advantageous labor conditions. This course was for the purpose of utilizing the most efficient instruments of production and closing those that were inefficient and unprofitable." The third policy was to consolidate sales through the formation of a "Selling Department," which was to handle all goods made by the constituent companies in order to achieve "economy in the distribution expense." Selling was now to be handled by a central office in the New York City headquarters, with branch offices throughout the United States and Europe. Of the three great new departments, actually manufacturing was the slowest to be fully consolidated and centralized. Finally, the treasurer's office at headquarters began to obtain accurate data on profit and loss through the institution of uniform, centralized cost accounting.

Thus United States Rubber, National Biscuit, and the Distillers Securities Company soon came to have organizational structures paralleling those of Swift and American Tobacco. By the first decade of the twentieth century, the leading firms in many consumers' goods industries had become departmentalized and centralized. This was the organizational concomitant to vertical integration. Each major function, manufacturing, sales, purchas-

---

[13] *The Fifth Annual Report of the United States Rubber Company, March 31, 1897*, pp. 6–7.
[14] This and the following quotations are from the *Fourth Annual Report of the United States Rubber Company, May 25, 1896*, pp. 4–5, 7–8.

ing, and finance, came to be managed by a single and separate department head, usually a vice president, who, assisted by a director or a manager, had full authority and responsibility for the activities of his unit. These departmental chiefs, with the president, coordinated and evaluated the work of the different functional units, and made policy for the company as a whole. In coordinating, appraising, and policy-making, the president and the vice presidents in charge of departments came to rely more and more on the accounting and statistical information, usually provided by the finance department, on costs, output, purchases, and sales.

Changes in the Producers' Goods Industries

Bureaucracy and oligopoly came to the producers' goods industries somewhat later than to those making products for the mass market. Until the depression of the 1890's, most of the combinations and consolidations had been in the consumers' goods industries. After that, the major changes came in those industries selling to other businesses and industrialists. The reason for the time difference seems to be that the city took a little longer to become a major market for producers' goods. Throughout the 1880's, railroad construction and operation continued to take the larger share of the output of steel, copper, power machinery, explosives, and other heavy industries. Then in the 1890's, as railroad construction declined, the rapidly growing American cities became the primary market. The insatiable demand for urban lighting, communication, heat, power, transportation, water, sewerage, and other services directly and indirectly took ever-growing quantities of electric lighting apparatus, telephones, copper wire, newsprint, streetcars, coal, and iron, steel, copper, and lead piping, structures and fixtures; while the constantly expanding urban construction created new calls on the power machinery and explosives as well as the metals industries. Carnegie's decision in 1887 to shift the Homestead Works, the nation's largest and most modern steel plant, from rails to structures, symbolized the coming change in the market.[15]

Also the new combinations and consolidations in the consumers' goods industries increased the demand for producers' products in the urban areas. Standard Oil, American Tobacco, Swift and other meat packers, McCormick's Harvesting Machinery and other farm implement firms, American Sugar, Singer Sewing Machine, and many other great consumer goods companies concentrated their production in or near major cities, particularly New York and Chicago.

The changes after 1897 differed from the earlier ones not only in types of industries in which they occurred but also in the way they were promoted and financed. Combinations and vertical integration in the consumer goods

[15] Clark, *History of Manufactures*, Vol. II, Chap. 19.

industries before 1897 had been almost all engineered and financed by the manufacturers themselves, so the stock control remained in the hands of the industrialists. After 1897, however, outside funds and often outside promoters, who were usually Wall Street financiers, played an increasingly significant role in industrial combination and consolidation. The change reflected a new attitude of investor and financier who controlled capital toward the value of industrial securities.[16] Before the depression of the 1890's investment and speculation had been overwhelmingly in railroad stocks and bonds. The institutionalizing of the American security market in Wall Street had come, in fact, as a response to the needs for financing the first great railroad boom in the 1850's.

The railroads, however, had made a poor showing financially in the middle years of the 1890's when one-third of the nation's trackage went through receivership and financial reorganization. The dividend records of some of the new large industrial corporations, on the other hand, proved unexpectedly satisfactory. Moreover, railroad construction was slowing, and the major financial and administrative reorganizations of the 1890's had pretty well stabilized the industry. So there was less demand for investment bankers and brokers to market new issues of railroad securities.

Industrials were obviously the coming field, and by 1898 there was a rush in Wall Street to get in on this new business. The sudden availability of funds stimulated, and undoubtedly overstimulated, industrial combination. Many of the mergers in the years after 1897 came more from the desire of financiers for promotional profits, and because combination had become the thing to do, and less from the special needs and opportunities in the several industries. Moreover, as the financiers and promoters began to provide funds for mergers and expansion, they began to acquire, for the first time, the same type of control over industrial corporations that they had enjoyed in railroads since the 1850's.

The changes in the producers' goods industries were essentially like those in the consumer goods firms before the depression. Only after 1897 the changes came more rapidly, partly because of Wall Street pressures; and the differences that did develop between the two types of industries reflected the basic differences in the nature of their businesses. Like the companies making consumer goods, those manufacturing items for producers set up nationwide and often worldwide marketing and distributing organi-

[16] The story of the shift from rails to industrials as acceptable investments is told in Thomas R. Navin and Marian V. Sears, "The Rise of the Market for Industrial Securities, 1887–1902," *Business History Review*, Vol. XIX (June, 1955), pp. 105–138. Government securities were, of course, important in the years before 1850 and during and after the Civil War, but in the late 1870's and 1880's as in the 1850's, railroads dominated the American security exchanges. As Navin and Sears point out, some coal and mining firms were traded on the New York Exchange, but the only manufacturing securities, outside of those of the Pullman Company, were some textile stocks traded on the local Boston Exchange. The connections between the railroad expansion and the beginnings of modern Wall Street are described in detail in Chandler, *Poor*, Chap. 4.

zations, consolidated production into a relatively few large plants and fashioned purchasing departments. Because they had fewer customers, their sales departments tended to be smaller than those in firms selling to the mass market. On the other hand, they were more concerned with obtaining control over the sources of their supply than were most of the consumer goods companies.

Here a distinction can be made between the manufacturers who made semi-finished products from raw materials taken from the ground, and those who made finished goods from semi-finished products. The former, producing a uniform product for a few large industrial customers, developed only small sales departments and concentrated on obtaining control of raw materials, and often of the means of transporting such materials from mine to market. The latter, selling a larger variety of products and ones that often required servicing and financing, had much larger marketing and distributing organizations. These makers of finished goods, except for a brief period around 1900, rarely attempted to control their raw materials or their semi-finished steel and other metal supplies. They did, however, in the years after 1900, begin to buy or set up plants making parts and components that went into the construction of their finished products.

Except in steel, integration usually followed combination in the producers' goods industries. And for both makers of semi-finished and finished goods, integration became more of a defensive strategy than it was in the consumers' goods industries processing agricultural products. In the latter the manufacturers had an assured supply of raw materials from the output of the nation's millions of farms. In the former, on the other hand, they had to consider the threatening possibility of an outsider obtaining complete control of raw materials or supplies.

Integration and Combination in the Extractive Industries

By the early twentieth century nearly all the companies making semi-finished product goods controlled the mining of their own raw materials. The industries in which they operated can, therefore, be considered as extractive. This was also true of two consumers' goods industries: oil and fertilizer. The experience of these two provides a good introduction to the motives for integration and the role it played in the coming of "big business" in steel, copper, paper, explosives and other businesses producing semi-finished goods.

In both the oil and fertilizer industries, control over raw materials came well after combination and consolidation of groups of small manufacturing firms. The Standard Oil Trust, after its formation in 1882, consolidated its manufacturing activities and then created a domestic marketing organization. Only in the late 1880's, when the new Indiana field began to be developed and the older Pennsylvania ones began to decline, did the

Trust consider going into the production of crude oil. Both Allan Nevins in his biography of John D. Rockefeller and the Hidys in their history of Standard Oil agree that the need to be assured of a steady supply of crude oil was the major reason for the move into production.[17] Other reasons, the Hidys indicate, were a fear that the producers might combine and so control supplies, and the desire of the pipeline subsidiaries to keep their facilities operating at full capacity. Although neither Nevins nor the Hidys suggest that the desire to obtain a more efficient flow of oil from the well to the distributor was a motive for this integration, both describe the committees and staff units that were formed at the central office at 26 Broadway to assure more effective coordination between production, refining, and marketing.

What little evidence there is suggests somewhat the same story in the fertilizer industry. Shortly after its organization in the mid-1890's, the Virginia-Carolina Chemical Company, a merger of many small southern fertilizer firms, began, apparently for the same defensive reasons, to purchase phosphate mines. Quickly its major competitor, the American Agricultural Chemical Company, a similar combination of small northeastern companies formed in 1893, responded by making its own purchases of mines. As the latter company explained in a later annual report: "The growth of the business, as well as the fact that available phosphate properties were being fast taken up, indicated that it was the part of wisdom to make additional provision for the future, and accordingly . . . available phosphate properties were purchased, and the necessary plants were erected and equipped, so the company now has in hand a supply of phosphate rock which will satisfy its growing demand for 60 years and upwards."[18] However, neither of these companies appeared to have set up organizational devices to guide the flow of materials from mine to plant to market; nor did the managers of a third large integrated fertilizer company, the International Agricultural Corporation, formed in 1909.

Defensive motives were certainly significant in the changes in the steel industry. Here the story can be most briefly described by focusing on the history of the industry's leader, the Carnegie Steel Company.[19] That

[17] Ralph W. Hidy and Muriel E. Hidy, *Pioneering in Big Business, 1882–1911* (New York, 1955), pp. 176–188. Allan Nevins, *Study in Power, John D. Rockefeller, Industrialist and Philanthropist* (New York, 1953), Vol. II, pp. 1–3. Nevins adds that another reason for the move into production was "partly to limit the number of active wells and reduce the over-production of crude oil," Vol. II, p. 2, but he gives no documentation for this statement.

[18] *Annual Report of the American Agricultural Chemical Company, August 14, 1907;* also the same company's *Annual Report* dated August 25, 1902. In addition to the annual reports of the two companies, Clark, *History of Manufactures*, Vol. III, pp. 289–291, provides information. There is a brief summary of the story of the International Agricultural Corporation in Williams Haynes, *American Chemical Industry—A History* (New York, 1945), Vol. III, p. 173.

[19] The information on the Carnegie Steel Company is taken from Burton J. Hendrick, *The Life of Andrew Carnegie*, 2 vols. (New York, 1932), George Harvey, *Henry Clay Frick, the Man* (New York, 1928), James H. Bridge, *The Inside Story of the Carnegie Steel Company* (New York, 1903).

company's chairman, Henry C. Frick, had in the early 1890's consolidated and rationalized the several Carnegie manufacturing properties in and about Pittsburgh into an integrated whole. At the same time, he systematized and departmentalized its purchasing, engineering, and marketing activities. The fashioning of a sales department became more necessary since the shift from rails to structures had enlarged the number of the company's customers.

Then in 1896 the Carnegie company made a massive purchase of ore lands when it joined with Henry W. Oliver to buy out the Rockefeller holdings in the Mesabi Range. As Allan Nevins points out, the depression of the 1890's had worked a rapid transformation in the recently discovered Mesabi region.[20] By 1896, the ore fields had become dominated by three great interests: the Oliver Mining Company, the Minnesota Mining Company, and Rockefeller's Consolidated Iron Mines. A fourth, James J. Hill's Great Northern Railroad, was just entering the field. Frick's purchases, therefore, gave the Carnegie company an assured supply of cheap ore, as well as providing it with a fleet of ore ships. Next, Frick and Carnegie bought and rebuilt a railroad from Lake Erie to Pittsburgh to carry the new supplies to the mills.

Yet the steel company's managers did little to coordinate systematically the mining, shipping, and manufacturing units in their industrial empire. These activities did not become departments controlled from one central office but remained completely separate companies under independent managements, whose contact with one another was through negotiated contracts. This was the same sort of relation that existed between the Frick Coke Company and Carnegie Steel from the time Frick had joined Carnegie in 1889. If the Carnegie company's strategy had been to provide a more effective flow of materials as well as to assure itself of not being caught without a supply of ore and the means to transport it, then Frick and Carnegie would have created some sort of central coordinating office.

The steel industry responded quickly to the Carnegie purchases.[21] In 1898, Chicago's Illinois Steel Company, with capital supplied by J. P. Morgan & Company, joined the Lorain Steel Company (with plants on Lake Erie and in Johnstown, Pennsylvania) to purchase the Minnesota Mining Company, a fleet of ore boats, and railroads in the Mesabi and

---

[20] Nevins, *Rockefeller*, Vol. II, p. 252.

[21] The experience of the other steel firms comes primarily from their annual reports and from prospectuses and other reports in the Corporation Records Division of Baker Library. A company publication, *J & L—The Growth of an American Business* (Pittsburgh, 1953) has some additional information on that company. Also, books listed in footnote 26 on the United States Steel Corporation have something on these companies. Two other steel companies listed in Table I made major changes somewhat before and after the period immediately following 1898. One, the Colorado Fuel & Iron Co., established in 1892, quickly became an integrated steel company in the Colorado area. The Bethlehem Steel Corporation was formed in 1904 when Charles F. Schwab, formerly of the Carnegie company and the United States Steel Corporation, reorganized the finances, corporate structure, and administrative organization of the bankrupt United States Shipbuilding Company.

Chicago areas. Again, little attempt was made to coordinate mining and shipping with manufacturing and marketing. In the same year, many iron and steel firms in Ohio and Pennsylvania merged to form the Republic and National Steel Companies. Shortly thereafter, a similar combination in the Sault Sainte Marie area became the Consolidated Lake Superior Company. These three new mergers began at once to set up their marketing organizations and to obtain control by lease and purchase of raw materials and transportation facilities. In 1900, several small firms making high-grade steel did much the same thing by the formation of the Crucible Steel Company of America. In these same years, the larger, established steel companies, like Lackawanna, Cambria, and Jones & Laughlin obtained control of more supplies of ore, coke, and limestone and simultaneously reorganized their manufacturing and marketing organizations. Like Carnegie and Federal, they at first made little effort to bring their mining and coke operations under the direct control of the central office.

In copper, defensive motives for integration appear to have been somewhat less significant. In the 1890's, mining, smelting and refining were combined on a large scale. During the 'eighties the railroad had opened up many western mining areas, particularly in Montana and Arizona; a little later the new electrical and telephone businesses greatly increased the demand for copper. Mining firms like Anaconda, Calumet & Hecla, and Phelps Dodge moved into smelting and refining, while the Guggenheims' Philadelphia Smelting & Refining Company began to buy mining properties.[22] In the copper industry, the high cost of ore shipment meant that smelting and—after the introduction of the electrolytic process in the early 1890's—even refining could be done more cheaply close to the mines. Of the large copper firms, only Calumet & Hecla and the Guggenheims set up refineries in the East before 1898, and both made use of direct water transportation.

After 1898, several large mergers occurred in the nonferrous metals industries. Nearly all were initially promoted by eastern financiers. Of these, the most important were Amalgamated Copper, engineered by H. H. Rogers of Standard Oil and Marcus Daly of Anaconda, the American Smelting and Refining Company which the Guggenheims came to control, and United Copper promoted by F. Augustus Heinze. United Copper remained little more than a holding company. Amalgamated set up a subsidiary to operate a large refinery at Perth Amboy and another, the United Metals Selling Company, with headquarters in New York City, to market the products of its mining and processing subsidiaries. The holding company's central offices in New York remained small and apparently did

[22] Information on the mining companies came from their annual reports and from Isaac P. Marcosson's two books, *Magic Metal—the Story of the American Smelting and Refining Company* (New York, 1949), and *Anaconda* (New York, 1957), also Clark, *History of Manufactures*, Vol. II, pp. 368–369.

comparatively little to coordinate the activities of its several operating companies. The Guggenheims formed a much tighter organization with direct headquarters control of the company's mining, shipping, smelting and marketing departments. On the whole, there appears to have been somewhat closer coordination between mining and processing in the large copper than in the major steel companies.

Lowering of costs through more effective coordination appears to have been a major motive for consolidation and combination in three other businesses whose raw materials came from the ground: explosives, paper, and coal.[23] The mergers that created the Pittsburgh Coal Company in 1899 and greatly enlarged the Consolidation Coal Company in 1903 were followed by a reorganization and consolidation of mining properties and then by the creation of large marketing departments which operated throughout most of the country. The merger of close to 30 paper companies, forming the International Paper Company in 1899, was followed first by consolidation and reorganization of the manufacturing plants, next by the formation of a national marketing organization with headquarters in New York City, and then by the purchase of large tracts of timber in Maine and Canada. These three activities were departmentalized under vice presidents and controlled from the New York office. In all these cases, the central office was responsible for the flow of materials from mine or forest to the customer or retailer.

The explosive industries underwent a comparable sweeping change in 1902 and 1903. Since the 1870's, price and production schedules had been decided by the industry's Gunpowder Trade Association, and almost from its beginning, that Association had been controlled by one firm, the E. I. DuPont de Nemours & Company. However, the member concerns had retained their own corporate identities and managements. In 1902, the DuPonts bought out a large number of these independent companies through exchanges of stock, and then consolidated them into a single centralized organization. In the process, plants were shut down, others enlarged, and new ones built. A nationwide selling organization was created, and centralized accounting, purchasing, engineering and traffic departments formed. Once the new organization was completed, then the company's executives obtained control of their raw materials through the purchase of nitrate mines and deposits in Chile.

---

[23] The story of the leading explosives, paper, salt and coal companies comes from annual reports and also from Charles E. Beachley, *History of the Consolidation Coal Company 1864–1934* (New York, 1934), George H. Love, *An Exciting Century in Coal* (New York, 1955), the company-written, *The International Paper Company, 1898–1948* (n.p., 1948), William S. Dutton, *DuPont—One Hundred and Forty Years* (New York, 1940), and *U.S. V. E. I. DuPont de Nemours & Company et al. in Circuit Court of the United States for the District of Delaware*, #280 *in Equity (1909)*, *Defendants' Record Testimony*, Vol. I, and for the paper industry, Clark, *History of Manufactures*, Vol. III, pp. 245–252. The American Writing Paper Company, though less successful, had many parallels to International Paper.

Except possibly in paper, the control of price and production does not appear to have been a major motive for the initial combinations in the extractive industries making producers' goods. In steel before 1901, and in nonferrous metals and coal, there were several combinations, but none acquired as much as 20 per cent of the market. Nor is there any evidence that the creators of the different mergers, while they were forming their organizations, were arranging with one another to set overall price and production schedules. In explosives, control of competition could not have been a significant reason for the 1902 changes since the DuPont company had enjoyed such control since the 1870's. In coal and explosives, and possibly in copper, the major motive for combination, consolidation, and the integration of supply with the manufacturing and marketing processes seems to have been an expectation of lowered costs through the creation of a national distributing organization, the consolidation of manufacturing activities, and the effective coordination of the different industrial processes by one central office. In steel and possibly copper, the desire for an assured supply of raw materials appears to have been more significant in encouraging combination and integration.

Changes and Integration in the Finished Producers' Goods Industries

Control of price and production was, on the other hand, much more of an obvious motive for combination and resulting consolidation in the industries manufacturing finished products or machinery from the semi-finished materials produced by the extractive firms. Concern over supply, however, was also a cause for change, for after 1898 the users of steel, copper, coal, and other semi-finished materials felt threatened by the growing number of combinations among their suppliers. In any case, between 1898 and 1900 there was a wave of mergers in these industries, largely Wall Street financed, which led to the formation of American Tin Plate, American Wire & Steel, American Steel Hoop, National Tube, American Bridge, American Sheet Metal, Shelby Steel Tube, American Can, National Enameling & Stamping Company and a number of other combinations among steel-fabricating firms.[24] At the same time, there were many amalgamations in the power machinery and implement businesses, such as American Car & Foundry, American Locomotive, Allis-Chalmers, International Steam Pump, and International Harvester. The largest combination among the copper users, the American Brass Company, came a little later, in 1903, after the Guggenheims, Rogers, and Heinze had completed the major copper mergers.

[24] The best brief summary of these mergers and the formation of the United States Steel Corporation is in Eliot Jones, *The Trust Problem in the United States* (New York, 1924), pp. 189–200. The companies' annual reports and prospectuses provide additional material.

Nearly all these combinations quickly consolidated their constituent companies into a single operating organization. Manufacturing facilities were unified and systematized, overall accounting procedures instituted, and national and often worldwide distributing organizations formed. Many set up central traffic and purchasing departments; some even began to assure themselves control over supply by building up their own rolling mills and blast furnaces. As American Wire & Steel and National Tube began to make their own steel, they cancelled contracts with Carnegie and other semi-finished steel producers. This development, in turn, led Carnegie to develop plans for fabricating his own finished products.[25]

The resulting threat of overcapacity and price-cutting led to the formation of the United States Steel Corporation.[26] This giant merger, which included Carnegie, Federal and National Steel, and the first six of the fabricating companies listed above, continued on as a combination. Although the activities of the various subsidiaries were re-formed and redefined, there was no consolidation. United States Steel remained a holding company only, and the central office at 72 Broadway did comparatively little to coordinate the operations of its many subsidiary companies.

After 1901, the fabricators and the machinery manufacturers made little attempt to produce their own steel or copper. Nor did the makers of semi-finished products try, for some years to come, to do their own fabricating. Possibly the metal users realized that even with the formation of United States Steel they were fairly certain of alternative sources of supply. Also they may have found that once they had combined they had enough bargaining power to assure themselves of a supply of steel and other materials more cheaply than they could make it themselves.

While such firms no longer sought to control their basic materials, many, particularly the machinery makers like General Electric, Westinghouse, American Car & Foundry, International Harvester and, a little later, General Motors, began to purchase or set up subsidiaries or departments to make parts and components.[27] Here again the motive was essentially defensive. Since much of their manufacturing had now become mainly assembling, they wanted to be sure to have a supply of parts available at all times. The lack of a vital part could temporarily shut down a plant. However, they expected to take only a portion of the output; a major share was sold to outsiders. One outstanding exception to this pattern was Henry Ford. He came to control his raw materials as well as his parts and compo-

---

[25] Hendrick, *Carnegie*, Vol. II, pp. 116–119.

[26] The beginnings and the operation of the United States Steel Corporation are outlined in Abraham Berglund, *The United States Steel Corporation: A Study of Growth and Combination in the Iron and Steel Industry* (New York, 1907), Arundel Cotter, *The Authentic History of the United States Steel Corporation* (New York, 1916), Ida M. Tarbell, *The Life of Elbert H. Gary, the Story of Steel* (New York, 1925).

[27] This generalization is based on the annual reports of the several companies.

nents, and rarely sold such parts to outside companies. But Ford's insistence on having a completely integrated organization from mine to market, concentrated largely in one huge plant, proved to be one of the most costly mistakes in American business history.

Control of parts and accessory units led to a diversification of the types of products these manufacturing companies made and sold. Such diversification brought, over time, important changes in business organization. Even more significant for stimulating product diversification was the new "full line" strategy adopted by a number of these recently consolidated concerns. Such a policy, initiated largely to help assure the maximum use of the new departments, encouraged technological as well as organizational change.

Pioneers in developing "full lines" in the producers' goods industries were the two great electrical companies: General Electric and Westinghouse. Unlike almost any other of the leading American industrial companies in 1900, these two had begun as research and development rather than manufacturing organizations. Because of their origins, they had the skilled personnel and the necessary equipment to move, in the mid-1890's, from making lighting equipment alone to manufacturing many lines of electric traction and power machinery products.[28] Allis-Chalmers, International Steam Pump, and American Locomotive began, shortly after their formation and subsequent consolidations, to develop new lines using electric and gasoline engines.[29] International Harvester, building up a number of farm implement lines, also started to experiment with the use of the gasoline engine for machinery on the farm. In this same first decade of the twentieth century, rubber, explosive, and chemical companies began to turn to industrial chemistry in their search to develop broader lines of products.

Continuing diversification came, however, largely in industries where science, particularly chemistry and physics, could be most easily applied. And it was in these industries, and in those which were directly affected by the coming of two new sources of power, electricity and the internal combustion engine, that the major innovations in American industry came after 1900. The chemical, automotive, power machinery, rubber, and petroleum industries led the way to the development of new processes and products, new ways of internal organization and new techniques of external competition as the new century unfolded. The metals industries and those processing

[28] As is well described in Harold C. Passer, *The Electrical Manufacturers* (Cambridge, 1953).

[29] The development of new lines by Allis-Chalmers, International Steam Pump, and American Locomotive is mentioned in their annual reports in the first decade of the twentieth century. International Harvester's similar "full line" policies are described in Cyrus McCormick, *The Century of the Reaper* (New York, 1931), Chaps. 6–9, and United States Bureau of Corporations, *The International Harvester Co., March 3, 1913* (Washington, 1913), especially pp. 156–158.

agricultural goods have, on the other hand, changed relatively little since the beginning of the century. In these industries, the same firms make much the same products, use much the same processes, and compete in much the same manner in the 1950's as they did in the 1900's. For them the greatest period of change came in the last decade of the nineteenth century.

Conclusion: The Basic Innovations

The middle of the first decade of the new century might be said to mark the end of an era. By 1903, the great merger movement was almost over, and by then the metals industries and those processing agricultural products had developed patterns of internal organization and external competition which were to remain. In those years, too, leading chemical, electrical, rubber, power machinery and implement companies had initiated their "full line" policy, and had instituted the earliest formal research and development departments created in this country. In this decade also, electricity was becoming for the first time a significant source of industrial power, and the automobile was just beginning to revolutionize American transportation. From 1903 on, the new generators of power and the new technologies appear to have become the dominant stimuli to innovation in American industry, and such innovations were primarily those which created new products and processes. Changes in organizational methods and marketing techniques were largely responses to technological advances.

This seems much less true of the changes during the 20 to 25 years before 1903. In that period, the basic innovations were more in the creation of new forms of organization and new ways of marketing. The great modern corporation, carrying on the major industrial processes, namely, purchasing, and often production of materials and parts, manufacturing, marketing, and finance—all within the same organizational structure—had its beginnings in that period. Such organizations hardly existed, outside of the railroads, before the 1880's. By 1900 they had become the basic business unit in American industry.

Each of these major processes became managed by a corporate department, and all were coordinated and supervised from a central office. Of the departments, marketing was the most significant. The creation of nationwide distributing and selling organizations was the initial step in the growth of many large consumer goods companies. Mergers in both the consumer and producer goods industries were almost always followed by the formation of a centralized sales department.

The consolidation of plants under a single manufacturing department usually accompanied or followed the formation of a national marketing organization. The creation of such a manufacturing department normally meant the concentration of production in fewer and larger plants, and such consolidation probably lowered unit costs and increased output per worker. The creation of such a department in turn led to the setting up of central traffic, purchasing, and often engineering organizations. Large-scale buying, more rational routing of raw materials and finished products, more systematic plant lay-out, and plant location in relation to materials and markets probably lowered costs still further. Certainly the creators of these organizations believed that it did. In the extractive and machinery industries integration went one step further. Here the motives for controlling raw materials or parts and components were defensive as well as designed to cut costs through providing a more efficient flow of materials from mine to market.

These great national industrial organizations required a large market to provide the volume necessary to support the increased overhead costs. Also, to be profitable, they needed careful coordination between the different functional departments. This coordination required a steady flow of accurate data on costs, sales, and on all purchasing, manufacturing, and marketing activities. As a result, the comptroller's office became an increasingly important department. In fact, one of the first moves after a combination by merger or purchase was to institute more effective and detailed accounting procedures. Also, the leading entrepreneurs of the period, men like Rockefeller, Carnegie, Swift, Duke, Preston, Clark, and the DuPonts, had to become, as had the railroad executives of an earlier generation, experts in reading and interpreting business statistics.

Consolidation and departmentalization meant that the leading industrial corporations became operating rather than holding companies, in the sense that the officers and managers of the companies were directly concerned with operating activities. In fact, of the 50 companies with the largest assets in 1909, only United States Steel, Amalgamated Copper, and one or two other copper companies remained purely holding companies. In most others, the central office included the heads of the major functional departments, usually the president, vice presidents, and sometimes a chairman of the board and one or two representatives of financial interests. These men made major policy and administrative decisions and evaluated the performance of the departments and the corporation as a whole. In the extractive industries a few companies, like Standard Oil (N. J.) and some of the metals companies, were partly holding and partly operating companies. At Standard Oil nearly all important decisions were made in the central headquarters, at 26 Broadway, which housed not only the presidents of the subsidiaries but the powerful policy formulating and coordinating committees.[30] But in some of the metals companies, the subsidiaries producing and transporting raw materials retained a large degree of autonomy.

[30] Hidys, *Pioneering in Big Business*, Chap. 3 and pp. 323–388.

The coming of the large vertically integrated, centralized, functionally departmentalized industrial organization altered the internal and external situations in which and about which business decisions were made. Information about markets, supplies, and operating performance as well as suggestions for action often had to come up through the several levels of the departmental hierarchies, while decision and suggestions based on this data had to be transmitted down the same ladder for implementation. Executives on each level became increasingly specialists in one function—in sales, production, purchasing, or finance—and most remained in one department and so handled one function only for the major part of their business careers. Only he who climbed to the very top of the departmental ladder had a chance to see his own company as a single operating unit. Where a company's markets, sources of raw materials, and manufacturing processes remained relatively stable, as was true in the metals industries and in those processing agricultural goods, the nature of the business executive's work became increasingly routine and administrative.

When the internal situation had become bureaucratic, the external one tended to be oligopolistic. Vertical integration by one manufacturer forced others to follow. Thus, in a very short time, many American industries became dominated by a few large firms, with the smaller ones handling local and more specialized aspects of the business. Occasionally industries like oil, tobacco, and sugar, came to be controlled by one company, but in most cases legal action by the federal government in the years after 1900 turned monopolistic industries into oligopolistic ones.

Costs, rather than interfirm competition, began to determine prices. With better information on costs, supplies, and market conditions, the companies were able to determine price quite accurately on the basis of the desired return on investment. The managers of the different major companies had little to gain by cutting prices below an acceptable profit margin. On the other hand, if one firm set its prices excessively high, the other firms could increase their share of the market by selling at a lower price and still maintain a profit. They would, however, rarely cut to the point where this margin was eliminated. As a result, after 1900, price leadership, price umbrellas, and other evidences of oligopolistic competition became common in many American industries. To increase their share of the market and to improve their profit position, the large corporations therefore concerned themselves less with price and concentrated more on obtaining new customers by advertising, brand names, and product differentiations; on cutting costs through further improvement and integration of the manufacturing, marketing, and buying processes; and on developing more diversified lines of products.

The coming of the large vertically integrated corporation changed more than just the practices of American industrialists and their industries.

The effect on the merchant, particularly the wholesaler, and on the financier, especially the investment banker, has been suggested here. The relation between the growth of these great industrial units and the rise of labor unions has often been pointed out. Certainly the regulation of the large corporation became one of the major political issues of these years, and the devices created to carry out such a regulation were significant innovations in American constitutional, legal, and political institutions. But an examination of such effects is beyond the scope of this paper.

Reasons for the Basic Innovations

One question remains to be reviewed. Why did the vertically integrated corporation come when it did, and in the way it did? The creation by nearly all the large firms of nationwide selling and distributing organizations indicates the importance of the national market. It was necessary that the market be an increasingly urban one. The city took the largest share of the goods manufactured by the processors of agricultural products. The city, too, with its demands for construction materials, lighting, heating, and many other facilities, provided the major market for the metals and other producers' goods industries after railroad construction slowed. Without the rapidly growing urban market there would have been little need and little opportunity for the coming of big business in American industry. And such a market could hardly have existed before the completion of a nationwide railroad network.

What other reasons might there have been for the swift growth of the great industrial corporation? What about foreign markets? In some industries, particularly oil, the overseas trade may have been an important factor. However, in most businesses the domestic customers took the lion's share of the output, and in nearly all of them the move abroad appears to have come after the creation of the large corporation, and after such corporations had fashioned their domestic marketing organization.

What about the investor looking for profitable investments, and the promoter seeking new promotions? Financiers and promoters certainly had an impact on the changes after 1897, but again they seem primarily to have taken advantage of what had already proved successful. The industrialists themselves, rather than the financiers, initiated most of the major changes in business organization. Availability of capital and cooperation with the financier figured much less prominently in these industrial combinations and consolidations than had been the case with the earlier construction of the railroads and with the financing of the Civil War.

What about technological changes? Actually, except for electricity, the major innovations in the metals industries seem to have come before or after the years under study here. Most of the technological improvements in the agricultural processing industries appear to have been made to meet the demands of the new urban market. The great technological innovations that accompanied the development of electricity, the internal combustion engine, and industrial chemistry did have their beginning in these years, and were, indeed, to have a fundamental impact on the American business economy. Yet this impact was not to be really felt until after 1900.

What about entrepreneurial talent? Certainly the best-known entrepreneurs of this period were those who helped to create the large industrial

TABLE 1

THE FIFTY LARGEST INDUSTRIALS

(Numbers indicate relative size according to 1909 assets)

CONSUMERS' GOODS COMPANIES

Agricultural Processing	*Extractive*	*Manufacturing*
3. Am. Tobacco	**2.** Standard Oil	**4.** Int'l. Harvester
8. Armour & Co.	**26.** Va.-Carolina Chem.	**10.** U.S. Rubber
9. American Sugar	**35.** American Agri. Chem.	**12.** Singer Mfg. Co.
13. Swift & Co.		
30. Nat'l. Biscuit		
33. Distillers' Securities		
50. United Fruit		

PRODUCERS' GOODS COMPANIES

Agricultural Processing	*Extractive*	*Manufacturing*
6. Central Leather	**1.** U.S. Steel	**7.** Pullman
18. Corn Products Co.	**5.** Amalgamated	**15.** Gen. Elec.
21. Am. Woolens	(Anaconda) Copper	**16.** Am. Car & Foundry
	11. Am. Smelting &	**19.** Am. Can
	Refining	**22.** Westinghouse
	14. Pittsburgh Coal	**24.** DuPont
	17. Colo. Fuel & Iron	**29.** Am. Locomotive
	20. Lackawanna	**36.** Allis-Chalmers
	23. Consolidation Coal	**44.** Int. Steam Pump
	25. Republic Steel	**46.** Western Electric
	27. Int'l. Paper	
	28. Bethlehem Steel	
	31. Cambria Steel	
	33. Associated Oil	
	34. Calumet & Hecla	
	37. Crucible Steel	
	38. Lake Superior Corp.	
	39. U.S. Smelting & Ref.	
	40. United Copper	
	41. National Lead	
	42. Phelps Dodge	
	43. Lehigh Coal	
	45. Jones & Laughlin	
	48. Am. Writing Paper	
	49. Copper Range	

corporation. If, as Joseph A. Schumpeter suggests, "The defining charac-
teristic [of the entrepreneur and his function] is simply the doing of new
things, and doing things that are already done, in a new way (innovation),"
Rockefeller, Carnegie, Frick, Swift, Duke, McCormick, the DuPonts, the
Guggenheims, Coffin of General Electric, Preston of United Fruit, and
Clark of Singer Sewing Machine were all major innovators of their time.[31]
And their innovations were not in technology, but rather in organization and
in marketing. "Doing a new thing," is to Schumpeter a "creative response"
to a new situation, and the situation to which these innovators responded
appears to have been the rise of the national urban market.

There must be an emphasis here on the words "seem" and "appear."
The framework used is a preliminary one and the data itself, based on
readily available printed material rather than on business records are hardly
as detailed or accurate as could be desired. More data, more precise and
explicit questions, and other types and ranges of questions will modify the
generalizations suggested here. For the moment, however, I would like to
suggest, if only to encourage the raising of questions and the further compilation and analysis of data, that *the* major innovation in the American
economy between the 1880's and the turn of the century was the creation
of the great corporations in American industry. This innovation, as I have
tried to show, was a response to the growth of a national and increasingly
urban market that was created by the building of a national railroad network—the dynamic force in the economy in the quarter century before 1880.
After 1900 the newly modified methods of interfirm and intrafirm administration remained relatively unchanged (as did the location of major markets
and sources of raw materials) except in those industries directly affected
by new sources of power and the systematic application of science to industry.
In the twentieth century, electricity, the internal combustion engine, and
systematic, institutionalized research and development took the place of
the national urban market as the dynamic factor in the American industrial
economy.[32]

[31] Joseph A. Schumpeter, "The Creative Response in Economic History," *Journal of
Economic History*, Vol. VII (May, 1947), p. 151, and also his *Theory of Economic Development*,
trans. Redvers Opie (Cambridge, 1934), pp. 74–94.

[32] This point has only been considered briefly here, but has been developed at some
length in my "Development, Diversification and Decentralization," to be published in a
book of essays tentatively titled *The Postwar American Economy* under the sponsorship of the
Department of Economics, Massachusetts Institute of Technology.

Alfred D. Chandler, Jr.

2

The Railroads:
Pioneers in
Modern Corporate Management

The railroads had to be innovators in many of the ways of modern corporate management. A generation before John D. Rockefeller, Andrew Carnegie, or Gustavus F. Swift began to turn their attention to the needs of administering a big business, railroad managers were forced to work out the basic methods of communication and control essential to the operations of the modern business corporation. The railroaders were innovators not because they were necessarily more perceptive, energetic, or imaginative than other contemporary businessmen, but rather because they were the first to face the challenge of handling efficiently large amounts of men, money, and materials within a single business unit.

Moreover, the new challenges came suddenly, first appearing in the decade of the 1850's. With the possible exception of the Western Railroad in Massachusetts and the Reading in Pennsylvania, few railroads had the mileage or the volume to create administrative problems before that decade. Then as the nation's railroad system grew quickly, a number of large roads almost simultaneously came into being. If one assumes that administrative challenges are created by size and complexity of business activities, then one can deduce without even looking at historical data that the pioneers in modern corporate management must have been these new large railroads. And certainly historical reality endorses this hypothesis.

I

In the late 1840's the nation's first great railroad boom began. Between the start of the California Gold Rush and the opening of the Civil

Reprinted from *Business History Review*, Vol. XXXIX, Spring, 1965, pp. 16-40.

War, the basic railroad network east of the Mississippi was laid down. By 1841, some 3,500 miles of road had been finished. During the next four years of hard times, less than 1,000 miles were constructed, and most of this was in New England. Then from the end of 1848 until 1860, railroad mileage in the United States increased fivefold, rising from just under 6,000 miles to over 30,000 miles. Particularly significant was the completion of the great east-west trunk lines and the very rapid construction of railroads in the Old Northwest. The New York and Erie reached Dunkirk on Lake Erie in 1851. The Baltimore and Ohio arrived at Wheeling on the Ohio River in January, 1853. That next summer the twelve railroads connecting Albany and Buffalo were consolidated into the New York Central. A few months later, the Pennsylvania reached Pittsburgh on its own tracks. Further to the West, construction boomed. With only 600 miles of track in 1849, the Old Northwest had 11,000 by 1860. In 1849, Chicago had only one short line. By 1854, that city was already the leading railroad center in the United States with several alternate routes to the Atlantic seaboard and with direct rail connections to four places on the Mississippi River.

As the network grew, so did the size of individual roads. By 1855, at least thirteen roads were working more than 200 miles of road, while the four trunk lines were managing lines whose volume of activity was at least twice that of the largest railroad in the country in 1849.[1] Where only two American railroads were capitalized at over $10,000,000 in 1850, at least ten had a greater capitalization by the middle of the decade, and five had issued over $19,000,000 worth of stock and bonds. The same pattern of growth held for the number of employees and for the volume of freight and passengers carried. A very brief period, specifically from 1849 to 1855, can then be identified as the time when modern business administration first appeared in the United States.

No other business enterprises in the 1850's had as large initial costs, operating expenses, payrolls, and required so many, so varied, and so technically difficult decisions as did the new large railroads. In manufacturing, the textile companies were the biggest enterprises. Yet the total initial costs of the biggest mills rarely reached $500,000. As late as 1850, only forty-one mills in the country had been identified as having a capitalization of $250,000 or more.[2] In agriculture, only the very largest of the slave-manned cotton, sugar, and rice plantations in the South were of this size. In transportation, canals called for a larger initial investment, but still much less than the large railroads. The initial cost of the Erie and Champlain

---

[1] Henry V. Poor's "Railroad share list, including mileage, rolling stock, etc." in *American Railroad Journal*, Vol. 29, pp. 24–25 (January 14, 1856).

[2] Evelyn H. Knowlton, *Pepperell's Progress: History of a Cotton Textile Company, 1844–1945* (Cambridge, Mass., 1948), p. 132.

Canals came to a little under $7,500,000.[3] Steamboat lines, of course, required a much smaller initial investment than either canals or textile mills. As Louis C. Hunter has stressed: "The construction cost of a single mile of well-built railroad was enough to pay for a new and fully-equipped river steamboat of average size."[4] Even a medium-sized road like the Western, with its 156 miles connecting Worcester and Albany, cost about the same as the Erie Canal to construct, while during the 1850's the completion of a major trunk line such as the Pennsylvania or a large western road such as the Illinois Central came to well over $20,000,000.[5] By the time the Pennsylvania had completed the expansion of her system between 1869 and 1873, the total costs of building and equipment were close to $400,000,000.

Comparable with construction and equipment costs were the differences in operating ones. The expenses of operating one of the largest American textile enterprises, the three integrated mills of the Pepperell Manufacturing Company at Biddeford, Maine, during the 1850's went over $300,000 a year only once, and that was in 1859.[6] The Western Railroad's operating costs were $607,549 in 1850, but those of a trunk line were still much higher. The Erie listed its running expenses for 1855 at $2,861,875 (a drop of $544,000 from the previous year), and the Pennsylvania for the same year reported its at $2,049,918. By 1862, the Pennsylvania's operating expenses stood at $5,431,072, and in 1869, before its major expansion, at $12,203,268.[7] Even the largest canals had much lower running costs than the textile mills, since they, like the turnpikes, did not own and operate carriers which used their facilities. Steamboat lines cost little more to run. The annual expenses of the largest coastal and river lines remained well below that of a medium-sized textile corporation.[8]

---

[3] Nathan Miller, *The Enterprise of a Free People: Aspects of Economic Development in New York State during the Canal Period, 1792–1838* (Ithaca, 1962), pp. 85, 109; Henry V. Poor, *History of Railroads and Canals of the United States* (New York, 1860), pp. 359–362.

[4] Louis C. Hunter, *Steamboats on the Western Rivers: An Economic and Technological History* (Cambridge, Mass., 1949), p. 308.

[5] Poor, *History of Railroads and Canals*, pp. 163, 474, and his "Railroad share list" in the *American Railroad Journal*, and *Report of the Investigating Committee of the Pennsylvania Railroad Appointed by Resolution of the Stockholders at the Annual Meeting Held March 10, 1874* (Philadelphia, 1874), p. 115.

[6] Knowlton, *op. cit.*, p. 459.

[7] Poor, *History of Railroads and Canals*, pp. 163, 287; *Sixteenth Annual Report of the Board of Directors of the Pennsylvania Railroad Co. to the Shareholders, February 2, 1863* (Philadelphia, 1863), p. 20; and *Twenty-Third Annual Report of the Board of Directors of the Pennsylvania Railroad Co. to the Stockholders, February 17, 1870* (Philadelphia, 1870), p. 8.

[8] The largest steamboat line on the western rivers was one of six boats, and the expenses of an average western steamboat of 211 tons for a season of eight and a half months was $26,569. So that the total annual cost for the largest line would have rarely been over $175,000. Moreover, most lines were cooperative arrangements between different owners rather than centrally administered and financed corporations. Hunter, *op. cit.*, pp. 320–35, 361–63.

The difference in operating costs between a railroad and large factory came more in the expenses of maintaining roadbed, machinery, and other equipment than in the paying of workers. The Pepperell mills in the 1850's employed an average of about 800 workers, which was a larger number than the Western Railroad hired in the same decade.[9] On the other hand, a major trunk line like the Erie had more than 4,000 employees by the middle of the decade, and by the late 1880's the Pennsylvania Railroad had come to employ close to 50,000 men in its system. At that time, very few textile mills or any other manufacturing enterprises hired more than 2,000 workers.

Size was only one dimension of the unique challenges facing managers of the new, large railroads in the 1850's. Their day-to-day operations called for far many more and far more complex decisions than did the working of a mill, canal, or a steamship line. Unlike a textile company, whose group of mills could be viewed within half an hour, a railroad was spread over hundreds of miles and included a wide variety of activities and facilities such as shops, terminals, stations, warehouses, office buildings, bridges, telegraph lines, and so forth. Weeks would be required to view all its men and equipment. Unlike a canal which had the same geographical spread, the railroad ran, maintained, and repaired its own equipment used in the transporting of goods and passengers. So every day railroad managers had to make decisions controlling the activities of many men to whom they rarely talked or even ever saw.

Moreover, these operational decisions had to be made much more quickly and involved more critical responsibilities than did most decisions made in the management of a textile factory, canal, or river steamboat. The condition of freight and the safety and indeed, the very lives of passengers, depended on continuous effective decision-making. As important for efficient operations of the lines were the continuing decisions as to the number of cars to be sent on scheduled runs in order to meet the constantly changing demands for freight space at the different stations, which each day loaded different amounts and variety of traffic which had to be moved in quantity in both directions over several hundreds of miles of track. As complicated were the longer range decisions on the setting and adjustments

---

[9] Knowlton, *op. cit.*, pp. 425–27; Edward H. Mott, *Between the Ocean and the Lakes, the Story of the Erie* (New York, 1899), p. 483; *American Railroad Journal*, Vol. 29, p. 280 (May 3, 1856); George H. Burgess and Miles C. Kennedy, *Centennial History of the Pennsylvania Railroad Company* (Philadelphia, 1949), p. 807. This figure did not include those employed by the Pennsylvania Company, that is, on the lines west of Pittsburgh and Erie. The payrolls on the Western Railroad (of Massachusetts) stood at $175,000 in 1850. Those for the Pennsylvania in 1854, the year the road was completed, for the Transportation Department alone were $1,067,142.44. *Eighth Annual Report of the Directors of the Pennsylvania Rail Road Company to the Stockholders, February 5, 1855* (Philadelphia, 1855), p. 34.

of rates and the determination of costs, profits, and losses. Not only were administrative decisions of coordination and appraisal more complex and involved a larger amount of men, money, and materials than factories or other types of transportation enterprises, but so were the still longer range ones involving expansion by construction or purchase of the development of new terminal and other facilities, the purchasing of new equipment, and the methods used to finance such expansion.

By creating brand new business needs, size and complexity brought brand new answers. The need for many railroad companies to obtain almost simultaneously vast sums of capital to build and equip their roads stimulated new ways of financing. Not only did these railroad companies' demands bring the development of new financial instruments such as preferred stock and mortgage, income, and convertible bonds, but they also led to the centralizing and institutionalizing of the American investment market in New York City.[10] Heavy initial capital costs and high operating ones created intensive pressure to keep these costly facilities running at full capacity and so led to radically new patterns of competition and cooperation among business units, to entirely new ways of pricing or rate-making, and to new motives and methods for enlarging the individual enterprise. Because decisions on pricing and expansion so intimately affected the fortunes of so many farmers, merchants, and manufacturers, and the very life of so many American communities, voters demanded and obtained a new type of government regulation of private corporate enterprise. The employment of a large number of workers, many of them far more skilled than the laborers in textile, shoe, meat-packing, and other contemporary factories, led to the creation of some of the very first large, modern national craft unions. Finally, the fund of experience required to administer a large railroad brought the first technologically trained administrators to American business, men who completed engineering training and then rose up the managerial ladder, making a lifetime career of railroading.

One of the first and most significant challenges raised by the coming of the large railroad was its administration. There were few precedents to guide those groping to devise rational ways to supervise, coordinate, and plan for the use of far more men, money, and equipment than any other private enterprise had hitherto had to administer. Even the experiences of the earlier railroads were of little help. After all, the management of a road whose line could be traveled in two or three hours, whose annual gross earnings were under $250,000, and whose equipment included ten to a dozen locomotives and twenty to thirty cars, was a far simpler task than the administration of a railroad with 500 miles of track, with an annual revenue

---

[10] Alfred D. Chandler, Jr., *Henry Varnum Poor: Business Editor, Analyst, and Reformer* (Cambridge, Mass., 1956), Chap. 4, and pp. 129–44.

of $5,500,000, and equipped with more than 150 passenger and baggage cars and over 2,700 freight cars powered by more than 200 locomotives.[11] Daniel C. McCallum, General Superintendent of the Erie, and one of the most creative of the early railroad administrators, effectively pointed to the difference:[12]

> A Superintendent of a road fifty miles in length can give its business his personal attention and may be constantly on the line engaged in the direction of its details; each person is personally known to him, and all questions in relation to its business are at once presented and acted upon; and any system however imperfect may under such circumstances prove comparatively successful.
>
> In the government of a road five hundred miles in length a very different state exists. Any system which might be applicable to the business and extent of a short road would be found entirely inadequate to the wants of a long one; and I am fully convinced that in the want of a system perfect in its details, properly adapted and vigilantly enforced, lies the true secret of their [the large roads] failure; and that this disparity of cost per mile in operating long and short roads, is not produced by *a difference in length*, but is in proportion to the perfection of the system adopted.

The four great east-west trunk lines, completed between 1851 and 1854, were the first to meet this challenge and so were the first to create modern administrative systems for business enterprises. All four added singificant innovations to the development of modern corporate enterprise. The Baltimore and Ohio Rail-Road defined formally the lines of communication and authority and created large, formal administrative departments. McCallum of the Erie was the first to outline the principles of modern business administration and to indicate the type of data required to carry out such principles. J. Edgar Thomson and his associates on the Pennsylvania effectively applied McCallum's principles to the Baltimore and Ohio's structure and began to solve certain complexities of control through the development of the line-and-staff concept for the delegation of duties and of the "divisional" type of organization. So effective was their work that the Pennsylvania not only became the largest business enterprise in the nation (if not the world) but also was just as famous for being one of the most

[11] The comparison has been made between the Erie of 1855, as given in Mott, *op. cit.*, p. 483–84, and the descriptions of the earlier roads in J. Knight and Benjamin H. Latrobe, *Report Upon the Locomotives, and the Police and Management of Several of the Principal Rail Roads in the Northern and Middle States* (Baltimore, 1838), and especially the sections on the Boston and Worcester (pp. 19–25) and the Boston and Providence (pp. 7–13) and Poor, *op. cit.*, (pp. 102–106). The Pennsylvania, for the same year (1855) had 100 passenger and baggage cars, close to 1,700 freight cars, 100 locomotives, and received a gross income of over $4,500,000, according to the *Annual Report* made at the annual meeting of the stockholders on Feb. 4, 1856.

[12] *Reports of the President and the Superintendent of the New York and Erie Railroad to the Stockholders for the Year Ending September 30, 1855* (New York, n.d.), p. 34.

efficiently administered. Nevertheless, little of the work and imaginative ideas of men responsible for the destinies of these roads affected the financiers and politicians who put together and then administered the New York Central. Their intuitive, less carefully considered answers brought the "departmental" type of structure, and their answer suggests what might be considered the "natural" (or evolutionary), as differentiated from the "rational," growth of large-scale business organizations.

II

The oldest of the trunk lines was the first to systematize its operations. In 1847, when its President, Louis McLane and its Chief Engineer, Benjamin H. Latrobe, began to make plans to complete the construction of the Baltimore and Ohio across the mountains to Wheeling, they agreed that the road needed a "new system of management."[13] Up to this time, the road had been operated under plans drawn up in 1834, when the company had completed the eighty miles of road from Baltimore to Harper's Ferry.[14] That scheme briefly outlined the duties of the principal officers of the road, including the Chief Engineer, the Superintendent of Gradation, Masonry, and Construction, and the Architect and Superintendent of Depots, who were concerned primarily with construction, and the Superintendent of Transportation, the Superintendent of Machinery, the Auditor, and the Treasurer, who were largely concerned with operations. Their roles were, however, only briefly defined and the relationship of one position to another was not made clear.

Rapid growth of traffic (particularly from newly opened coal mines), "the great augmentation of power and machinery demanded by the increasing business," and the anticipated increasing volume of business as the Ohio Valley was reached, all created the need to develop more systematic organization. Assisted by a committee of the Board, Latrobe devised a revised plan "after diligent investigation, with aid of the experience of other roads in New England and elsewhere."[15] The objectives of the plan were clearly outlined:

[They] consisted in confining the general supervision and superintendence of all the departments nearer to their duties, and, by a judicious subdivi-

[13] *Organization of the Service of the Baltimore & Ohio R. Road, under the Proposed New System of Management* (Baltimore, 1847), p. 3. The new system was accepted by the Board on Feb. 10, 1847.

[14] *Laws and Ordinances Relating to the Baltimore and Ohio Rail-Road* (Baltimore, 1834).

[15] This and the following quotation are from the *Twentieth Annual Report of the President and the Directors to the Stockholders of the Baltimore and Ohio Rail-Road Company* (Baltimore, 1846), p. 13. Pages 11–14 of this report tell of the developments bringing the need for reorganization. Pages 15–23 describe the plans for building the line across the mountains.

sion of labour, to insure a proper adaptation and daily application of the supervisory power to the objects under its immediate charge; in the multiplication of checks, and to effecting a strict responsibility in the collection and disbursement of money; in confining the company's mechanical operations in their shops to the purposes of repairs, rather than of construction; in promoting the economical purchase and application of materials and other articles needed in every class of the service; and in effecting a strict and more perfect responsibility in the accounting department generally.

The resulting *Organization of the Service of the Baltimore & Ohio R. Road* was certainly one of the first lengthy organization manuals published by an American business enterprise. The Chief Engineer's department was little changed. Surveys were made by three different "parties" of engineers. Then once the route had been decided, the line was divided into several "divisions" each under the supervision of an Assistant Engineer, who administered the construction, aided by the "assistants of the several residences within their respective divisions."[16] This organization thus closely followed the pattern used for the construction of other large canals and railroads during the 1830's and 1840's.

The major innovation was the departmentalizing of the road's operations. The opening words of the 1847 manual were:[17]

> Under the System now to be detailed, the operation of the Road will be classed under two general headings, into which they are properly divisible, viz: those relating to
> *First*—THE WORKING OF THE ROAD
> *Second*—THE COLLECTION AND DISBURSEMENT OF THE REVENUE
> These two departments although equal as regards subordination, have their business so much blended that they are mutually dependent on each other in almost all their transactions.

Therefore, efficient operations required a careful definition of the internal organization of both departments.

The biggest task of the second of these departments was to make certain that the very large number of financial transactions was carried out efficiently and, even more important, honestly. The business of a railroad the size of the Baltimore and Ohio had not only come to involve many more daily financial transactions than did that of any other type of business of

---

[16] *The Twenty-First Annual Report of the President and the Directors to the Stockholders of the Baltimore and Ohio Rail-Road Company, Oct. 1, 1847* (Baltimore, 1847), pp. 60–61; *The Twenty-Third Annual Report of the President and Directors to the Stockholders of the Baltimore and Ohio Rail-Road Company* (Baltimore, 1849), p. 40; *The Twenty-Fourth Annual Report of the President and Directors to the Stockholders of the Baltimore and Ohio Rail-Road Company* (Baltimore, 1850), pp. 53–54; also Daniel C. Calhoun, *The American Civil Engineer: Origin and Conflict* (Cambridge, Mass., 1960), pp. 49–50; and *By-Laws of the Board of Directors [Adopted April and May, 1847] Together with the Charter of the Pennsylvania Railroad Company* (Philadelphia, 1847), p. 7.

[17] This and the four following quotations are from the *Organization . . . of the Baltimore and Ohio Rail-Road, 1847.*

the day (even that of a large bank) but it also had many more employees handling these transactions. Ticket agents, freight agents, conductors, station masters, purchasing officers, as well as the operating executives with their pay rolls, all handled and had to account for relatively large sums of money.

The new organization manual, therefore, outlined detailed procedures which were to assure the proper receipting of the funds and their forwarding to the company's main office on Hanover Street in Baltimore and to make certain that the monies to pay wages, bills, rents, and other charges reached the right persons at the right time. All these transactions had to be checked and double-checked. It is significant that the executives in this earliest of big businesses realized the value of such data for the administration of the road. The office of the Chief Clerk, which compiled and checked these receipts and reports, issued "daily comparisons of the work done by the road and its earnings with the monies received therefore." Daily figures would, in turn, be summarized into monthly reports and would provide the senior officers and the board with their information on the road's earnings. While the clerk's offices also supervised the funds the company paid out and reported expenses, they made little attempt to break down these operating expenses into their component parts or to allocate costs against the types of goods and passengers carried.

The Chief Clerk was subordinate to the Secretary who was, in turn, under the Treasurer, the road's senior financial officer. The Secretary became responsible for all internal transactions. Besides inspecting all passenger and freight accounts and exercising "due control and supervision" over his subordinates, he was to transmit all reports and documents concerning finances to the President and the Board and to "prepare statements of the affairs of the company whenever required by the Board, the President or the committee on finance." As these functions grew on the Baltimore and Ohio and most other roads, they were taken over by an executive who was given the title of Comptroller.

The Treasurer, besides reviewing the work of the Secretary or Comptroller, also handled external financing, including the routine arrangements for assigning shares of stock or bonds to merchants or bankers who had agreed to market them, for assuring the proper recording of the sale or other transfer of securities from one person to another, and for the sending out of dividends and interest payments. The decisions as to what type and how many securities were to be sold and by whom and the size of the dividends were of course those of the President and the Committee on Finance of the Board of Directors. But they usually made them after consulting with the Treasurer and the Secretary.

The 1847 organization manual of the Baltimore and Ohio devoted more pages to the organization of the operating department than to that of the financial offices. Here the planners had hoped to attain their objectives "by confiding the departments of transportation, of construction and repairs of the road, and of repairs of machinery to separate superintendency, each being subject to the immediate supervision of a professional engineer, under direction of the President."[18] The professional engineer, a new officer, was given the title of the General Superintendent with three officers reporting to him. One, the Master of the Road was now "specifically charged with the maintenance of the road, bridges, depot structures, and fixtures of every kind, water stations and all other appurtenances of the road of a fixed character as distinguished from the locomotive or car department."[19] Under him were several Local Supervisors of the Road, who directed the work done on the maintenance and repair of all fixed structures in their area and had full responsibility for personnel, including appointing foremen in workshops, as well as bridge watchmen and water station and switch keepers. The Master of Machinery had "the care of all Locomotives and Cars, and the shops and buildings in which they are sheltered." He obtained the necessary men and materials to run his shops and, with the approval of the General Superintendent, appointed the shop foremen. Like the Master of the Road, the head of the Machinery Department was to visit all different working units regularly and was to check over all payrolls before their presentation to the Chief Clerk.

The third operating department, that of the Master of Transportation, was rated the most important. His duties were to:

> embrace all such as belong specially to the forwarding of passengers and tonnage over the road. He will receive and deliver passengers, goods, and the mails at the several stations, and regulate (under the direction of the General Superintendent) all the movements of the trains. He will employ and appoint, with the concurrence of the General Superintendent and President, all officers and hands necessary to accomplish these results, not already otherwise provided for.

The latter included engineers, firemen, conductors, fuel and lumber agents, and depot agents. The depot agents in turn supervised six types of employees—clerks, weight masters, car regulators, laborers, watchmen, and porters. The manual carefully defined the duties of all these different sorts of employees. The Master of Transportation was to carry out his duties and supervise his subordinates in much the same way as did the other two department heads by making weekly trips over the line of the road, by checking carefully on records forwarded by his subordinates, and by making his weekly reports to the General Superintendent.

Over the three departments was, as the manual noted, "an officer of

[18] *Twentieth Annual Report of the Baltimore and Ohio Rail-Road, 1846*, p. 13.
[19] This and the four following quotations are from the *Organization . . . of the Baltimore and Ohio Rail-Road, 1847*.

general duty . . . who, besides the duties peculiar to himself, is charged with the supervision and control of the whole system, subject to the President and the Directors." Except for the handling of the revenues, the General Superintendent's office was the central focus of both authority and communication. Into his office flowed a series of reports. Each of the three department heads forwarded their weekly and monthly results. The Master of Machinery, for example, was to report on "the conditions and performance during the week of each locomotive and engine in service or under repair—and of the condition of the cars, as also of the stationary machinery and workshops—and will present a monthly estimate of the probable expense of their repair during the ensuing month." Besides reading reports, the senior operating executive was expected to be constantly talking with the department heads, taking trips over the road, as well as conferring with the President and the road's financial officers.

By the 1847 reorganization, Latrobe and McLane had set up one of the very first functionally departmentalized, administrative structures for an American business enterprise. Of the two great departments, the first, headed by the Treasurer, supervised finances. The second, run by the General Superintendent, administered operations and transportation, and was further subdivided along functional lines. A smaller, third department in the central office, headed by an Attorney, handled a wide variety of legal matters involved in the operations of the railroad ranging from the obtaining or revising of charters to the settling of claims for damages and losses. As the departments took over the day-to-day operating decisions, the President was able to concentrate more effectively on the long-range activities of raising and allocating funds.[20] While such a departmentalized structure would be expanded and become more complex and more refined as the railroads grew in size, it remained essentially the organization by which American railroads were to be administered.

III

The first refinements in this structure were carried out by the New York and Erie, which, on its completion in 1851, was the largest railroad in the United States. Because it was much longer than the Baltimore and Ohio and used more men and equipment, the Erie was required to set up new, specialized offices. These included the passenger and the freight departments (which supervised the setting of rates, the negotiating of contracts,

[20] Possibly one reason for the change was that President McLane had no time for day-to-day operations. For the two previous years, he had been in England raising money for his road and also acting as United States Minister, in which capacity he helped to negotiate the Oregon Treaty. *Dictionary of American Biography*, Vol. XII, p. 114.

and the obtaining of business) and the purchasing office, which was to buy goods for the road in quantity. Secondly, greater size meant that the immediate supervision of the movement of trains and traffic could no longer be administered by one man. Instead, the road was split into five different divisions, each about a hundred miles in length, and each under the charge of a Division Superintendent. The enlarged administrative structure raised new problems of overall coordination and control, and called for the development of more sophisticated types of information to assure the necessary control, and for the formulation of principles of administration to clarify the lines of communication and authority.

The first major reorganization of the Erie came in 1853 as a result of the Board of Directors' concern for high costs and for competition. The Directors had complained, and rightly, that the cost per mile on the Erie was higher than on shorter roads. Moreover, in the summer of 1853, the consolidation of the several lines connecting Albany and Buffalo into the New York Central, threatened to increase the competition for existing traffic. To meet these challenges, the Board recommended "the establishment of a system" to assure the better accountability of expenses and more effective appraisal of performance of men and managers. The Directors hoped to achieve this aim by making available "comparisons of the expenses of the various operations with those of other similar roads, with the several divisions of the road itself; and the expenses of different conductors, enginemen, etc. with each other."[21] By 1853, the Erie had appointed its new functional officers and set up the geographical operating divisions. Then the Directors gave the task of perfecting its administrative system to Daniel C. McCallum, who, after serving a brief time as Superintendent of one of the new divisions, in 1854 became General Superintendent.

McCallum, the inventor of an inflexible truss type of bridge, was an able civil engineer.[22] He approached the problem of the management of men much as he faced that of the building of a bridge or fashioning other material forms. First he sought "general principles of organization and administration."[23] Definition of such principles, he believed, was particularly important in that "we cannot avail ourselves to any great extent of the plan of organization of shorter lines in framing one for this, nor have we any precedent or experience on which we can fully rely in doing so." McCallum's six general principles of general administration were these:

[21] *Report of the Directors of the New York and Erie Railroad Company to the Stockholders, November, 1853* (2nd ed., New York, 1853), pp. 47–48.

[22] *Dictionary of American Biography*, Vol. XI, pp. 565–66. McCallum put his administrative talents to effective use during the Civil War, when he was commissioned "director and superintendent" of all the Union railroads necessary for the prosecution of the War.

[23] This and the following two quotations are from *Reports of the President and Superintendent of the New York and Erie Railroad, 1855*, p. 35.

1. A proper division of responsibilities.
2. Sufficient power conferred to enable the same to be fully carried out, that such responsibilities may be real in their character [i.e. authority to be commensurate with responsibility].
3. The means of knowing whether such responsibilities are faithfully executed.
4. Great promptness in the report of all derelictions of duty, that evils may be at once corrected.
5. Such information, to be obtained through a system of daily reports and checks that will not embarrass principal officers, nor lessen their influence with their subordinates.
6. The adoption of a system, as a whole, which will not only enable the General Superintendent to detect errors immediately, but will also point out the delinquent.

The carrying out of these principles called, first, for a careful definition of the duties of the different officers and of the lines of authority and communication between these offices. Secondly, came the development of effective data to flow through the lines of authority and communication. The tasks of the different executives concerned with functional activities, such as the handling of freight and passengers, the purchase of fuel, telegraphic operations, maintenance of motive power, and rolling stock, were easy enough to outline. It proved more difficult to clarify the relations between the functional officers and the regional division superintendents and the relations of both to the General Superintendent.

McCallum tried to give the Division Superintendents the power necessary to carry out their responsibilities for the day-to-day movement of trains and traffic by an express delegation of authority. These regional officers were to be:[24]

> . . . held responsible for the successful working of their respective Divisions, and for the maintenance of proper discipline and conduct of all persons employed thereon, except such as are in the employment of other officers acting under the directions from this office, as hereinafter stated. They possess all the powers delegated by the organization to the General Superintendent, except in matters pertaining to the duties of General Ticket Agent, General Freight Agent, General Wood Agent, Telegraph Management, and Engine and Car Repairs.

To further increase their control over their subordinates, McCallum gave each officer "the authority, with the approval of the President and General Superintendent, to appoint all persons for whose acts he is held responsible, and may dismiss any subordinate when, in his judgment, the interests of the company will be promoted thereby."[25]

[24] *Ibid.*, p. 27.
[25] This and the following quotation are from *ibid.*, p. 40.

Next, the Erie's General Superintendent stressed the importance of having well-understood lines of authority and communication. "All subordinates should be accountable to and be directed *by their immediate superiors only;* as obedience cannot be enforced where the foreman in immediate charge is interfered with by a superior officer giving orders directly to his subordinates." Some modifications to this general rule were necessary, however, because the men responsible for freight and passenger traffic had to work closely with the Division Superintendents in the movement of trains as well as with their own superiors in the central freight and traffic officers. As McCallum put it:[26]

> It will be seen that their subordinates cannot communicate with higher officers, but through them, and can only be communicated with by the same means. There are, however, some exceptions to this rule, conductors and station agents report, daily, their operations directly to the General Superintendent; and it is in great measure through these means that the business—so far as it is related to the movement of trains, amount of freight carried, and its prompt transaction—is controlled.

To illustrate still more clearly these lines of authority and communication, McCallum drew up a detailed chart—certainly one of the earliest organization charts of an American business enterprise.[27]

Finally McCallum turned to devising detailed and accurate information to flow constantly through these channels of communication and authority. "It is very important," he stressed, "that the principal officers should be in full possession of all information necessary to enable them to judge correctly as to the industry and efficiency of subordinates of every grade."[28] Only in this way could effective and impersonal control of many officers and men be assured.

Hourly, daily, and monthly reports, more detailed than those called for earlier on the Baltimore and Ohio, provided this essential information. The hourly reports were primarily operational and gave, by telegraph, the train's location and the reasons for any delays or mishaps. "The information being edited as fast as received, on convenient tabular forms, shows, at a glance, the position and progress of trains, in both directions on every Division of the Road."[29] Just as important, the tabular forms were filed away to provide an excellent source of operational information, which among other things proved especially useful in determining and eliminating "causes of delay." McCallum's use of the telegraph brought universal praise from the railroad world both in this country and abroad. What impressed

---

[26] *Ibid.*, p. 51.

[27] Chandler, *op. cit.*, pp. 147–48.

[28] *Reports of the President and Superintendent of New York and Erie Railroad, 1855,* p. 41. McCallum gives a full account of his reporting systems in this report, pp. 34–35, 51–54.

[29] This and the following quotation are from *ibid.*, p. 52.

other railroad managers was that McCallum saw at once that the telegraph was more than merely a means to make train movements safe, but also a device to improve better coordination and better administration through this extremely efficient new technique of communication.

Daily reports, the real basis of the system, were required from both conductors and station agents. They covered all important matters of train operation as well as the movement of freight and passenger traffic. Moreover, reports from two different sources on train movements, car loadings, damages, misdirected freight, and so forth acted as a reliable check on the efficiency and the honesty of both conductors and agents. Daily reports were also required from the engineers. These were compiled into a monthly statement giving for each engine the miles run, operating expenses, cost of repairs, and work done, and were submitted as part of the monthly report required of each Division Superintendent. The Division Superintendent's reports covered all operations of his division, including capital costs, running expenses, and work done on all types of equipment. Similar monthly reports were required from the heads of passenger, freight, telegraph, and motive power departments. As in the case of the hourly reports, "the information thus obtained is embodied in the statistical accounts kept in this office," wrote McCallum, to be used by himself and his assistants to assist in the administration of the road.[30] By such accounts, the General Superintendent was able to make the types of comparative appraisals between the different divisions and between them and other roads for which the Erie's Directors had earlier asked. On the other hand, McCallum paid much less attention to devising useful monthly estimates of anticipated expenditures which the Directors had also wanted.

Besides assisting in operations, these statistical data were essential to the rational setting of rates charged for transportation. For only an analysis of these operating reports could provide the information necessary to determine the costs of carrying an item and whether, therefore, the rate charged was profitable or not. McCallum also realized fully that rates depended on more than just costs. The Erie and other roads had recently lost money because they had raised rates they had found "unremunerative" only to discover that in so doing they had threatened to "destroy this business."[31] Higher rates by reducing traffic had cut net revenue. "To guard against such a result, and to establish the mean, between such rates as are unremunerative and such as are prohibitory, require an accurate knowledge of the cost of transport of the various products, both for long and short distances." Important too was knowing which way the item was moving along the line of the road, for prices should be "fixed with reference to securing, as far as possible, such a balance of traffic in both directions as to reduce

[30] *Ibid.*, p. 53.
[31] This and the following two quotations are from *ibid.*, p. 79.

the proportion of 'dead weight' carried." Unused or excess capacity on a return trip warranted lowering prices for goods going that way.

McCallum's concern, however, was almost wholly with operating expenses. He said little about what costs should be allocated to the construction or capital account, or whether the costs of repairs were to be considered as capital or running expenses. Nor did he consider ways to account for long-term depreciation of engines, rolling stock, rails, and other equipments. Other railroad men were already giving serious attention to these needs which were soon to create a revolution in accounting practices.[32] Yet these problems were more properly in the province of the financial and especially the comptroller's office, rather than the concern of the operating department.

In the systematizing of large-scale operations, McCallum was certainly an outstanding pioneer. Once faced with the challenge he immediately saw the importance of defining the functions of each office and the lines of authority and communication among them and of developing accurate data to flow through these channels.

McCallum's innovations received wide attention. Henry Varnum Poor, the editor of the *American Railroad Journal*, was particularly impressed by his achievements and devoted much space to them. For example, Poor noted in 1854 that McCallum had already increased the efficiency at the same time he reduced the working force. Moreover, he continued:[33]

> By an arrangement now perfected, the superintendent can tell at any hour in the day, the precise location of every car and engine on the line of the road, and the duty it is performing. Formerly, the utmost confusion prevailed in this department, so much so, that in the greatest press of business, cars in perfect order have stood for months upon switches without being put to the least service, and without its being known where they were. All these reforms are being steadily carried out as fast as the gound gained can be held.

Poor even had McCallum's organization chart lithographed and offered copies for sale at $1 a piece. Douglas Galton, one of Britain's leading railroad experts, described McCallum's work in a Parliamentary report printed in 1857. So too did the New York State Railroad Commissioners in their annual reports. Even such a popular magazine as the *Atlantic Monthly* carried an article in 1858 praising these ideas on railroad management.[34] Unquestionably McCallum's principles and procedures had a significant

---

[32] The revolution in accounting practices, procedures, and principles caused by the coming of the railroads with their heavy capital outlay and large constant costs is suggested in A. C. Littleton, *Accounting Evolution to 1900* (New York, 1933), Chap. 14, and Edward C. Kirkland, *Men, Cities, and Transportation* (2 vols., Cambridge, Mass., 1948), Vol. I, pp. 336–44.

[33] Quoted in Chandler, *op. cit.*, p. 147.

[34] *Ibid.*, pp. 148, 153, *American Railroad Journal*, Vol. 29, p. 280 (May 3, 1856).

impact on the development of the internal organization of the large business enterprise in America.

IV

It was, however, on the Pennsylvania rather than on the Erie that McCallum's concepts of large-scale administration were tested and built upon. Before the end of the decade, the Erie had fallen into the hands of unscrupulous financiers, who, like its notorious Treasurer, Daniel Drew, cared little about efficient administration. McCallum soon left the road to develop a profitable bridge building business. On the Pennsylvania, however, engineers rather than financiers continued to run the road. J. Edgar Thomson, the builder and first operator of the Georgia Railroad, had come to the Pennsylvania in 1849 to take charge of its construction. In 1852, he became its President and controlled its destinies until his death in 1874. Although the road's structure was given its initial form in 1852, the major reorganization did not come for five more years.[35] The need did not arise because the road was not fully constructed until 1854. Even then, it was much shorter than the Erie and only used half the number of engines, rolling stock, and other equipment.

Then increasing traffic plus the need to reduce costs, emphasized by the coming of a business depression, brought a new scheme of management to the Pennsylvania. The resulting departmentalization of the road's administration followed the lines first outlined on the Baltimore and Ohio, except that there were two financial departments: Accounting (headed by a Controller and Auditor) and the Treasurer's.[36] The growing number of financial transactions and importance of the data developed by checking on these transactions made the work of the first of these units increasingly significant. The Pennsylvania also had a larger legal office than the Baltimore and Ohio, for in 1857 it was very much involved in taking over the old state system of transportation and also in promoting and financing its feeder lines to the West.

In outlining the structure of the operating department, Thomson

[35] The 1852 organization plan more carefully defined financial and accounting procedures and placed internal accounts under the control of an "Auditor," who remained part of the Transportation Department, reporting to the General Superintendent. The operating side of the Transportation Department had a new and somewhat intricate organization outlined by Herman Haupt, who became Chief Engineer after Thomson became President. Haupt had visited the leading railroads in New York and New England "for the purpose of examining their systems of accounts, plans of organization, machinery and everything connected with the operation of a road." Frank A. Flower (ed.), *Reminiscenses of General Herman Haupt* (Milwaukee, 1901), p. xvii; *Dictionary of American Biography*, Vol. VIII, pp. 400–401. The coming of the more systematic organization along the lines of the Baltimore & Ohio and the Erie waited until 1857.

[36] *Pennsylvania Railroad Company: Organization for Conducting the Business of the Road, Adopted December 26, 1857* (Philadelphia, 1858).

built closely on McCallum's model. Authority was to be commensurate with responsibility; lines of authority and communication were to be clearly defined; and detailed data were to flow through these channels. The General Superintendent had full responsibility for traffic, trains, contracts, personnel, rules, and all else needed to run the railroad. He was also to be the communications point between the transportation and the financial offices. "Orders signed by the Accounting Departments to Officers and Agents of the Transportation Department (read the new organization manual) will be sent to the General Superintendent and distributed by him."[37]

The Division Superintendents had the responsibility for the movement of trains and traffic and were delegated the authority of the General Superintendent in order to carry out these duties. Thomson went further than McCallum in clarifying the relations of functional officers in the field to the Division Superintendent and to their own superiors in the central office. As on the Erie, the station masters and conductors carried out their day-to-day activities under orders from the Division Superintendent, while the Freight and the Passenger Agents set the rates and developed procedures for handling business. The Pennsylvania now applied the same principle to the members of the Motive Power Department working the line of the road. The Division Superintendent directed their daily work as well as hiring and firing of shop personnel, while the Master of Machinery set rules and standards for "the discipline and economy of conducting the business of their shops." The concept that executives on the line of authority handle people, and the other officers, the staff executives, handle things was first suggested in the Pennsylvania organization manual of December 26, 1857, in this way:[38]

> The Division Superintendents shall, on their respective divisions (subject to the direction and approval of the General Superintendent), exercise all the powers delegated by the organization to the General Superintendent for the control and use of the road, its branches and connections, for the transportation of Freight and Passengers, including the movement of Motive Power employed thereon, whether engaged in the transportation of Freight and Passengers, or in the construction and repairing of the road, or the supply of fuel and materials. They shall also have charge of all em-

---

[37] This and the three following quotations are from *Organization of the Pennsylvania Rail Road, 1857*. The quotations are from pp. 11, 7, 7, and 7–8, respectively. In 1857, there were only two Resident Engineers, each reporting to the General Superintendent. After 1863, there was a Resident Engineer for each of the three divisions. *By-Laws and Organization for Conducting the Business of "The Pennsylvania Rail-Road Company," as revised and approved by the Board of Directors, May 13, 1863* (Philadelphia, 1863), p. 14.

[38] A line and staff distinction came, of course, only in the definition of the relationship of regional and functional officers. Thus the major Pennsylvania shops in Altoona were not included in any operating division and so their executives therefore reported directly to the Superintendent of Motive Power.

ployees connected with Motive Power and Transportation on their respective Divisions, and see that they perform the duties assigned them, preserving discipline in the arrangement of the Locomotives to their particular service, securing the service of competent engine men, and other responsible persons for the Motive Power, as the General Superintendent and the best interests of all the company may require. They shall be furnished with copies of all rules and regulations, and orders to the foremen of shops, and others holding positions of responsibility and trust connected with the Motive Power, or Transportation of the company, and shall force their observance.

Although the local superintendent was delegated the power of the General Superintendent to control construction and repair work on his division, his authority over the maintenance and repair force was not as clearly defined as it was over the employees of the Motive Power Department. Resident Engineers were appointed who had charge of "the police and repairs of the road, its bridges and depots, telegraph poles, and the ordinary repairs of wires and fixtures outside of Telegraph Offices, wood and water stations, and their regular supply with fuel and water. They shall also have direction of such new work as shall be submitted to their charge by the President and Board." The Division Superintendent could apparently order the local civil engineers and their gangs to handle repairs and construction immediately needed to assure the continuing flow of traffic over the line, while the Resident Engineers were responsible for longer term upkeep.

For a short period after 1866, the Pennsylvania tried to give to the Superintendent of Motive Power more control over his subordinates on the lines of the road.[39] Apparently, the resulting ambiguities and confusions as to the location of authority and responsibility led the Pennsylvania's top executives to return to a full divisional structure. By 1873, even the men in charge of maintenance of way on the divisions, who had received the title of Assistant Engineer, were to "act under the direction of the Superintendent of the Division, and be responsible to him for the condition of the Road."[40] The Chief Engineer's task then became one of setting standards and procedures. While he was given line authority over new construction, he was specifically to be a staff officer and to "act as Consulting Engineer in all

[39] *By-Laws and Organization for Conducting the Business of the Pennsylvania Rail Road Company, as approved by the Board of Directors, May 13, 1863, and revised February 7, 1866* (Philadelphia, 1866), p. 13; *Organization of the Pennsylvania Rail Road, 1863*, p. 14; also Leland H. Jenks, "Early History of a Railway Organization," *Business History Review*, Vol. XXXV (Summer, 1961), p. 168. Oversight and distribution of rolling stock included "the numbering, weight and record thereof; also the numbers, marks of identification, weight and records, and the procuring of releases from certain risks required from the owners of cars not the property of the Company."

[40] This and the following quotation are from *By-Laws and Organization for Conducting the Business of the Pennsylvania Railroad Company, to take effect June 1, 1873* (Philadelphia, 1873), pp. 20, 25–26, respectively.

matters of Engineering pertaining to the Maintenance of Way of the Main Line and Branches, communicating with the President in regard to the same when necessary, and carrying out his views and instructions."

V

The structure originated on the Baltimore and Ohio and on the Erie and worked out on the Pennsylvania was adopted with some variations by two of the other three roads which operated 500 miles of track before 1860. The Illinois Central and the Michigan Southern, using the same functional departments, worked out a modified line and staff plan.[41] The Division Superintendents were delegated authority of the General Superintendent, but these roads began by placing the maintenance of way department under the Chief Engineer, who also had charge of new construction. Local engineers apparently reported directly to him, not to the division superintendent, although the existing evidence on this point is not clear. In the years following the Civil War, as more roads grew to a size of 500 miles or longer, they too adopted what had come to be called the "divisional" type of railroad organization by giving their division superintendents the responsibility and the authority for coordinating the flow of traffic across their lines, although line-and-staff distinctions were not defined as clearly as they were on the Pennsylvania.[42] Many large Western roads, for example, continued to have the maintenance of way department largely independent of the Division Superintendent's direct control.

The divisional form was distinctly an American innovation. It was created by American civil engineers, who turned to administering the great enterprises they themselves had constructed. Latrobe and Thomson were among the best known engineers of their day, as were John B. Jervis, the builder and the Chief Engineer of the Michigan Southern, and George B.

---

[41] *Reports and accompanying documents of the Illinois Central Railroad Company, made by order of the Stockholders at their Annual Meeting held at Chicago, March 19, 1856* (New York, 1856), p. 32, and the Illinois Central Railroad Company, *A Report to Stockholders at the Annual Meeting in Chicago, March 17, 1858* [n.p., n.d.], p. 2–3. John B. Jervis, the Chief Engineer of the Michigan Southern, suggests his organization experience in his *Railroad Property, a Treatise on the Construction and Management of Railways* (New York, 1861), especially Chs. 21 and 22. Jervis began by placing himself in charge of both the Maintenance of Way and Motive Power Departments. The Louisville and Nashville followed the same pattern when the engineer in charge of its construction, Albert Fink, became the head of both the road and machinery departments, *Testimony of Albert Fink before U. S. Committee on Education and Labor, Sept. 17, 1883* (Washington, 1883), p. 3. The annual reports of the Michigan Central, which was a smaller road in mileage than the Michigan Southern, suggest that a "departmental" type of operating structure initially evolved.

[42] The general acceptance of the divisional structure on American railroads by the end of the 1870's is indicated in Marshall M. Kirkman, *Railway Revenue: A Treatise on the Organization of Railroads and the Collection of Railway Receipts* (New York, 1879), pp. 78–81.

McClellan, the Chief Engineer of the Illinois Central, who helped fashion its early structure. Latrobe, Thomson, and Jervis had worked up the professional ladders from the late 1820's on, and were among the very first of this new type of professional engineer.[43] Significantly, only one, McClellan, had any connection at all with military life, and he was the least innovative of the lot.

These men did not borrow; they approached their brand new problems of building an administrative structure in much the same rational and analytical way as they approached that of building a railroad or a bridge. The resulting organization permitted a flexibility of control and a decentralization of decision-making that made possible more effective handling of traffic over tracks hundreds of miles long and as many miles away from the central administrative office. The local Division Superintendent was delegated the authority necessary to control and coordinate the flow of traffic and to remove quickly obstacles hindering or slowing the flow. On the majority of American railroads he could order train-men, conductors, station agents, machine shop heads, and often civil engineers concerned with maintenance and repairs to act immediately without checking in at their departmental headquarters.

Yet this type of organization was not necessarily a normal or "natural" form. The British railroads completed a decade earlier and many of the continental ones, too, had developed a centralized or "departmental" type of organization. Here the General Superintendent did not delegate his authority to the Division Superintendents. Instead, each functional officer on a regional division reported directly to and received his orders directly from his functional superior in the central office. The local office in charge

[43] Latrobe, the son of the architect of the Capitol in Washington, had training in mathematics and the law before joining the Baltimore & Ohio Railroad in 1831 at the age of 25 as a civil engineer, and by 1842, he had become Chief Engineer. Thomson began his career in 1827 at nineteen years of age on the surveying gang while laying down the line of the Philadelphia-Columbia Railroad in the Pennsylvania State System. In 1830, he had become an Assistant Engineer on the Eastern Division of the Camden and Amboy. After a brief visit to Europe, he took the post of the Chief Engineer of the Georgia Railroad, which, when completed, was the largest railroad in the United States. He remained on as General Superintendent until 1847, when he was asked to be Chief Engineer of the newly formed Pennsylvania Railroad, and he became its president in 1852. John B. Jervis had a comparable career. He began on the Erie Canal and then moved up the ladder by working on the Delaware and Hudson Canal, the Mohawk and Hudson Railway, the Schenectady and Saratoga Railroad, the Chemung Canal, the enlargement of the Erie Canal, the Croton Reservoir, the Hudson River Railroad, and the Michigan Southern. While acting as Chief Engineer, the latter helped build the Rock Island Railroad. As he pioneered in the development of the locomotive and other equipment, he might be considered to be a mechanical as well as civil engineer. McCallum was the self-taught son of a Scottish tailor, about whom little is known before his bridge-building and his work on the New York and Erie made him famous. For Jervis, Latrobe, McCallum, and McClellan, see *Dictionary of American Biography*, Vol. X, pp. 59–61, Vol. XI, pp. 25–26, 565, 581–82; for Thomson, see William B. Wilson, *History of the Pennsylvania Railroad Company* (2 vols., Philadelphia, 1899), Vol. II, pp. 238–39.

of transportation could not order the local master of machinery to make repairs on engines or local maintenance-of-way men to fix up some track. He reported the needs to his superior, who then notified the proper officer in the central office, who in turn sent the order to the proper subordinate in the area.

On the large early roads the departmental form of organization appeared only on the New York Central, and that road's history differed sharply from the rest. The Central was not the outcome of a grand engineering project, rather it was the product of an ambitious legal and financial move. It was one of the very first large consolidations of a number of different incorporated enterprises.[44] Coming as it did a decade after Buffalo and Albany were connected by railroad, it was the work of financiers and politicians, not engineers. Erastus Corning, Dean Richmond, John V. L. Pruyn, and Edwin D. Worcester, the Central's first senior executives, were among New York's richest men and among the most powerful leaders in her Democratic party. There was not a professional engineer among them. Even the new General Superintendent, Chauncy Vibbard, had no civil engineering training or apprenticeship comparable to the operating managers of the other large roads. He had been the Superintendent of one of the small constituent lines, the Utica and Schenectedy. Even after he became operating head of the consolidated road, he continued to carry on other activities besides his railroad work, including a profitable liquor business in New York City, and in 1861 he successfully ran for Congress.[45]

Neither Vibbard nor his senior executives paid serious attention to systematizing the organization of the new consolidated road, although one reason for bringing the many small roads together was to assure a more efficient and coordinated flow of traffic from the Hudson to the Lake. Fairly quickly the Central had a Financial Department headed by Worcester to administer both internal accounting and external financing. Vibbard's Transportation Department had five regional divisions, each headed by an assistant or "deputy" superintendent, while his functional assistants included only a "chief engineer" to supervise maintenance of way, and a wood agent.[46] Since there was little effort to work out a rational structure, Vibbard became a very busy man. Alvin Harlow, generalizing solely from this road's experience, has written:[47]

Chauncey Vibbard, the general superintendent, was trying to do the work of ten men. There was as yet no general manager, and the American

[44] The carrying out of the consolidation is described in detail in Frank W. Stevens, *The Beginnings of the New York Central Railroad* (New York, 1926), Chap. 17.

[45] *Dictionary of American Biography*, Vol. XIX, p. 263.

[46] *Annual Report of the New York Central Railroad for Year Ending September 30, 1857* (Albany, 1857), p. 34.

[47] Alvin F. Harlow, *The Road of the Century* (New York, 1947), p. 89.

railroad had not even heard of such officials as the freight and traffic managers, the general passenger agent, general freight agent, purchasing agent or several others now considered indispensable. Vibbard was them all.

The resulting lack of organization was further suggested by the fact that, in the late 1850's, Vibbard was still making verbal arrangements to buy wood for fuel. The resulting lawsuit led one amused pamphleteer to point out that pen and ink had not yet found their way into the Central's management.[48]

Because Vibbard had so much to do, it is hardly surprising that the different functional operating departments of the Central became and remained autonomous. As traffic expanded, the Transportation Department grew accordingly and the officers, which Harlow found wanting, began to appear. Yet the road's senior managers did little to bring these units into an integrated whole. So the men responsible for maintenance of way and bridges continued to report to the Chief Engineer, the shops to a Master of Machinery, or a Master of Car Repairs, and the station and freight agents to the General Passenger or the Freight Agent. The Division Superintendents had direct jurisdiction only over the movement of trains. Later when Cornelius Vanderbilt and his son, William, took over the New York Central and began to rationalize the structure, the existing organization became more explicitly the departmental type, comparable to that on the British railroads. Thus it seems safe to say that the departmental form of structure evolved, while the divisional type with its line-and-staff distinctions and its careful delegation of authority was explicitly created or invented.

VI

Intensified competition and increasing traffic brought two further significant structural developments in the organization of the large railroad during the years following the Civil War. One was the building of a separate Traffic Department to administer the getting and processing of freight and passengers. The other was the creation of a central office manned by general executives. These, including the President, Vice-Presidents, and a General Manager, concentrated less on day-to-day operation and more on long-term problems of cost determination, competitive rate setting, and strategic expansion. In both these developments the Pennsylvania made the largest contribution.[49]

While these two structural developments were of vital importance to the creation of the modern railroad corporation and were significant in

[48] *Ibid.*, p. 96.
[49] Jenks, "Early History of a Railway Organization," pp. 163–79.

the more general growth of the large corporate enterprise in the United States, they may be considered as less basic than those fashioned before the Civil War. The initial creation of the functional departments, the first definition of the lines of authority, responsibility, and communication, the concomitant development of data to flow through these lines, the earliest definition of the delegation of authority, and with it distinction between line and staff duties were the fundamental innovations on which later ones rested. The innovators who created these forms in the 1850's were those who first effectively met the new administrative challenges. And the most creative of those men who laid the groundwork for modern American corporate administration were three professionally trained engineers—Benjamin H. Latrobe, Daniel C. McCallum, and J. Edgar Thomson. Of the many contenders for the title of the founders of modern business administration, these three have the strongest claims.

Joseph A. Litterer

3

Systematic Management: Design for Organizational Recoupling in American Manufacturing Firms

During the latter decades of the nineteenth century, the American manufacturing industries went through a rather dramatic expansion. New products and new manufacturing processes were rapidly developed. Many firms grew in size and new ones were established. American products were not only widely distributed within the United States, but also in an ever-growing overseas market.

The growth of a European market for American industrial products dramatized the effectiveness of American firms in being able to compete on a price basis in Europe, even though they were using relatively high-priced American labor and incurring the cost of trans-Atlantic shipment. Comparison of managerial practices on both sides of the Atlantic reveals a number of ways in which American firms differed in their handling of internal manufacturing operations, apparently, with some advantage.[1]

The performance of American manufacturing firms and also the management of firms in these industries received growing attention by authors of journal articles and books. The discussion of the apparent success

[1] Edward Atkinson, *The Distribution of Products* (New York, 1885), p. 62; H. F. L. Orcutt, "Machine-Shop Management in Europe and America," *Engineering Magazine*, Vol. XVI (January, 1899), p. 549 (February, 1899), p. 706, Vol. XVII (June, 1899), p. 384; "A French Engineer on American Shop Management," *American Machinist*, Vol. XXI (January 20, 1898), p. 45; A. E. Outerbridge, Jr., "The Future of American Industries," *Journal of the Franklin Institute*, Vol. CXLIII (1897), p. 110.

Reprinted from *Business History Review*, Vol. XXXVII, Winter, 1963, pp. 369-391.   53

of American firms contained in this literature provides a somewhat incongruous background for the claims frequently, dramatically, and cogently made in the same literature during these decades that all was not well with the internal management of many firms. J. Slater Lewis at the close of one of his articles reflected the sentiments of many when he wrote,[2]

> A perfect organization I consider an essential and vital element in securing success, in whatever form of institution we may wish to carry on, whether political or religious, mechanical or social. I contend that it is not possible to found lasting a power upon a management in which systematic action is eliminated or ignored, a ramshackle condition of things is the ultimatum; and in many cases establishments have closed simply through a breakup from within of its [sic] managing machinery.

The general line of argument was that as a result of their very success and growth American firms had reached a point at which internal operations had become increasingly chaotic, confused, and wasteful. As this condition was both undesirable and in need of prompt correction, spokesmen for this point of view such as Lewis,[3] Henry Metcalf,[4] Alexander Hamilton Church,[5] H. M. Norris,[6] and John Tregoing,[7] insisted that some way was needed to put "method" into the management of firms to avoid confusion and waste, to promote coordination and to reestablish effective control by top management. The literature conveying this message contains not only the accusation of internal disorder, but many specific suggestions as to what could be done to improve internal management of the firm. This objective and these methods consititute the literature of Systematic Management.[8]

This particular paper examines some of the major developments in the literature concerned with American manufacturing industries of the period between 1875 and 1900, especially proposals which were intended to promote internal order and integration. The purpose of this examination is both to better understand the historical development of this particular management movement and to extend our understanding of the managerial function itself.

[2] J. Slater Lewis, "Works Management for Maximum Production," *Engineering Magazine*, Vol. XIX (May, 1900), p. 220.

[3] J. Slater Lewis, "Works Management for the Maximum of Production: Organization as a Factor of Output," *Engineering Magazine*, Vol. XVIII (October, 1899), p. 59.

[4] Henry Metcalf, "The Shop-Order System of Accounts," *Transactions of the American Society of Mechanical Engineers*, Vol. VII (New York, 1886), p. 441.

[5] A. Hamilton Church, "The Meaning of Commercial Organisation," *Engineering Magazine*, Vol. XX (December, 1900), pp. 391–98.

[6] H. M. Norris, "Shop System," *Iron Age*, Vol. LIV (November 1, 1894), p. 746.

[7] John Tregoing, *A Treatise on Factory Management* (Lynn, Mass., 1891), p. iii.

[8] For more detailed examination of the conditions facing firms at this time and what the authors of the period thought to be wrong with management, see Joseph A. Litterer, "Systematic Management: The Search for Order and Integration," *Business History Review*, Vol. XXXV (Winter, 1961), pp. 461–76.

THE BREAKDOWN OF COORDINATION

Focus on the Execution of Tasks and Operations

To no small degree the success of American manufacturing firms rested upon their diligent and successful use of division of labor. The general concept described and discussed by Jean Rudolphe Perronet, Adam Smith, and Charles Babbage,[9] was used, refined and extended by American manufacturers.[10] Briefly, these applications of division of labor took three different forms:

1. Specialization by product, which usually meant that the company adopted a restricted product line making, for example, just machine tools or perhaps just one type of machine tool. In contrast, at an earlier period firms in this industry would have been more likely to produce a complete array of mechanical products which might have ranged from locomotives to machine tools.

2. Specialization by technical operation, in which the steps or operations in making a product were divided and further subdivided to a level in which operations became quite limited in scope making them easy to specify and to learn.

3. Specialization by operation of the production process. This could take several directions, for example: (a) the most skilled employees would be put to work making production equipment which in turn was used by the less skilled employees of the firm; (b) once sophisticated production equipment was available skilled employees would be used to set up and adjust the machinery which would then be turned over to less skilled employees for operation.

[9] See for example, Jean Rudolphe Perronet, "Art de l'epinglier par M. de Resumuir, avec des remarques de M. Duhame du Monceau et des remarques et traités des Memoires de M. Perronet, Inspecteur General des ponts et chaussées," in *Descriptions des arts et des metiers, Faites et approuvés par Messieurs de l'Academie Royal des Sciences* (Vol. I, Paris, 1861); Adam Smith, *Wealth of Nations* (London, 1776); and Charles Babbage, *On the Economy of Machinery and Manufacturers* (London, 1832).

[10] With so much of current managerial practice and techniques having been developed and/or studied in manufacturing industries (e.g., the work of Taylor and the Scientific-Management movement, the Hawthorne studies by Mayo and Roethlisberger) the student of management history has reason to look for the roots of current practice in these industries. Actually, examining the company contacts of the authors writing the literature referred to in this paper, identifying the firms referred to, and the illustrations used in this literature, it should perhaps be more specifically described as dealing with the manufacturing industries most concerned with the design and manufacture of metal products; i.e., machine-tool manufacturers, metal-household-appliance manufacturers, such as sewing machines, hardware manufacturers, armament manufacturers, and the like. It should also be noted (as will be established in later portions of this paper) that the practices and techniques described as Systematic Management arose in response to conditions which could occur in almost any industry and are not the unique properties of the manufacturing industries, let alone unique to metal-working industries.

These practices are so prevalent today in the United States that we seldom think of them as unusual, but during the latter decades of the nineteenth century those in a position to compare American and European production techniques found the alternate uses of division of labor to be a differentiating pattern.[11] With this there tended to be a more intensive use of machinery, which took several forms. First, machinery was specialized as to product and operations to support the parallel high degree of specialization of workers' jobs. Secondly, there was the general effort by American manufacturers to use machinery whenever possible to supplement or replace manual labor.[12]

This is an all too brief synopsis of developments in handling some of the aspects of the internal administration of American manufacturing companies during this period. It is sufficient, however, to identify a major trend in these developments. Executives directing these companies, in attempting to find ways to make products more cheaply, sought to have individual operations or tasks more efficiently performed through specialization. Machines were designed to do a limited number of things well. That this attempt to make each operation faster and each job more efficient was successful is amply supported by the success of these companies. However, this direction of improvement contained in it seeds of serious problems which grew more significant as the degree of specialization was carried further. These problems were manifest in the internal inefficiencies noted by such authors of this period as Horace L. Arnold,[13] Church,[14] Lewis,[15] Metcalf,[16] Norris,[17] Oberlin Smith,[18] and Tregoing.[19]

Insufficient Facilitation of Integration

The growth of internal disorder, confusion, and waste which paralleled the more extensive use of specialized labor fell into two major categories:
  1. A breakdown of coordination among subordinates. In manu-

---

[11] Litterer, "Systematic Management: The Search for Order and Integration," pp. 462–68.

[12] H. F. L. Orcutt, "Machine-Shop Management in Europe and America, VI: Comparison as to Efficiency of Machinery and Methods," *Engineering Magazine*, Vol. XVII (June, 1899), p. 384.

[13] Horace L. Arnold, *The Complete Cost-Keeper* (New York, 1899), esp. p. 10 and Henry Roland [Horace L. Arnold] "An Effective System of Finding and Keeping Shop-Costs," *Engineering Magazine*, Vol. XV (April, 1898), pp. 77–78.

[14] *Op. cit.*

[15] *Op. cit.* and "The Mechanical and Commercial Limits of Specialisation," *Engineering Magazine*, Vol. XX (January, 1901), p. 709.

[16] *Op. cit.*

[17] *Op. cit.*

[18] Oberlin Smith, "System in Machine Shops," *American Machinist*, Vol. VIII (October 31, 1885), p. 1.

[19] *Op. cit.*

facturing firms there is a horizontal movement which begins with the receipt of an order from a customer and then continues through the company as work is advanced to complete the order. Typical of the late nineteenth-century period would be a flow which began with the receipt of an order by the sales department, followed sequentially by work in the engineering department, central-plant office, foundry, machining department, assembly department, and finally the shipping department. Yet during this period many firms found it increasingly difficult to get the necessary coordination among departments and positions in this horizontal flow. The result, as Metcalf,[20] among others, pointed out, was that orders were lost or delayed, necessary parts or operations were forgotten or performed incorrectly—all of which culminated in a frustrating, wasteful, and somewhat confusing business situation.

2. A breakdown in relationships between top and lower levels of management. Accompanying the breakdown in horizontal coordination, as Arnold[21] noted, was a deterioration of the top or central manager's ability to maintain effective control over subordinate managerial positions. Central to this difficulty was the inadequate information the top managers had about the conduct of affairs in departments under subordinate managers. This in part seems to have come about as a result of: (1) the increased number of lower-level managers; (2) the fact that the amount of information necessary to centrally control operations had grown too large for one person, or small group of people, to absorb and use; (3) the fact that the vertical channels of communication within the plant were either too long or inefficient to carry the necessary information to top authorities; and (4) the subordinate levels of managers not possessing sufficient ability satisfactorily to handle their jobs.[22]

To put this simply, the problem was a gradual breakdown of the integration of work flow at the lower levels of the company and a concordant deterioration in the ability of top executives to control work lower in the company hierarchy. In short, positions throughout the company were becoming less integrated, or we might say, the executive elements in the company organization were coming uncoupled.

What was apparently missing at this time was the realization that as work is progressively subdivided, producing some very distinct advantages, there is at the same time a progressively greater need for some way to put

---

[20] See for example Metcalf, "The Shop-Order System of Accounts," p. 441.

[21] Roland [Arnold], "An Effective System of Finding and Keeping Shop-Costs," p. 77.

[22] Some of this is stated directly and clearly in the literature. Other aspects of this vertical breakdown are inferred from statements made as to what should be improved or created in business firms. See for example, Litterer, *op. cit.*, pp. 469–71; Austin Robinson, "The Problem of Management and the Size of Firms," *Economic Journal*, Vol. XLIV (June, 1934), p. 242; N. F. Rolf, "Management and the Size of the Firm," *Review of Economic Studies*, Vols. XVIII-XIX (1949–1953), p. 148.

the subdivided elements of work back together in order to accomplish organizational objectives. To put this a little more succinctly, as work is subdivided the activities in the subdivided positions become interdependent on the execution of all other duties or jobs which have resulted from the same division of labor. For the system of work to be successful, the subdivided work must be integrated.

A Theoretical Examination of Organizational Uncoupling

Understanding the connection between the practice of intensive specialization of labor and machinery and the difficulties experienced by American manufacturing firms in the nineteenth century depends upon recognizing important organizational requirements which develop from a division of labor. Since familiarity with these requirements is central to understanding the significance of specific practices to be discussed later, it is necessary to digress briefly from the events of this historical period to consider some of the properties of a division of labor at any time.

Let us go back to Adam Smith's well-known description of manufacturing pins. To subdivide work to the point where one person is just cutting wires to length, has actually no usefulness unless there is someone else making pin heads and a third party fastening these two together. We recognize easily that in dividing work we will not have a finished product, in this one case a pin, until all parts are provided. Hence, there is little difficulty in recognizing this aspect of the interdependency of a subdivided system of work.

There is another aspect of interdependency which is often not so readily recognized. Let us envision that in the manufacture of pins the first worker cuts from a length of wire a piece the proper length for a pin and lays it at the side of his work place. Upon seeing the piece laid down the worker in the next position picks it up and performs his task on it and when finished lays it down. In laying it down he signals the next worker to begin his work and so on through the production system. Looked at this way we see that the manufacturing work consists of a series of actions performed by job holders and further that these actions are linked in a particular way.[23] One action leads to a particular other action.[24]

The interdependency resulting from a division of labor thus has two aspects: (1) a dependency on all parts being present, a more or less static component; and (2) a dependency on a particular set of linked actions, a

[23] Admittedly, this linking is not always as direct as in the illustration. However, even when much more indirect or roundabout it always exists.

[24] Although using different terms this general point is made by George Homans in *The Human Group* (New York, 1950), esp. pp. 101–103.

more dynamic property which might well be called the kinematic aspect of a division of labor. In these terms, the difficulties of the late nineteenth century were not in dividing the technical work of a productive system into jobs, for this was apparently done well, but rather in failing adequately to facilitate the linked actions which were thus required.

Facilitation of linked actions is no great problem when the scale of operations is small enough for all the people with specialized jobs to see or at least to know what each is doing, thereby permitting them to have a good idea of where their particular task fits into the overall system and its goal. That is, the integration can be provided by the people involved in a division of labor when they share an understanding of the objective of the work.

As organizations become larger, however, and work is subdivided further, employees are spread out into several departments, perhaps even into several buildings. This makes it more difficult for individuals to see the overall flow of work and understand exactly where their particular job fits. In addition to this spatial separation, there develops a perceptual separation. As work is increasingly subdivided, it becomes more difficult for job holders to see clearly or easily the end result or product to which their particular work output contributes.

Integration can also be facilitated when work is on such a scale that one person can effectively supervise all of the interrelated tasks, such as the owner-manager of a small business. As organizations grow, however, supervisors also become more specialized, having under their control progressively smaller portions of the work of the organization. This may mean that only at the second or third level of management above the workers will there be an executive who will control all of the work on a particular order or product. Hence, while lower-level management might control and co-ordinate work over a portion of the horizontal flow, only at the higher, or perhaps the highest, level can overall integration be provided through the exercise of authority.

To exercise authority so as to provide coordination requires information and time to use it. But, as already noted, the numerous levels in management hierarchy make it increasingly difficult to get needed information promptly and accurately. Hence the twin difficulties of breakdown of horizontal flow and disruption of vertical control combine to lead to the problems of internal confusion and waste.

In summary then, the problem which developed during the late nineteenth century came about because the managerial decisions made focused on refining performance of jobs or activities within manufacturing firms, but at the same time largely ignored facilitation of the integration required in this division of labor. As a result, the organization of many firms became uncoupled. None of the authors concerned with this situation described the problem in these terms. They did, however, repeatedly describe symptoms which were evidence of this problem and their proposed solutions were specific devices to facilitate the required integration which was missing. In this sense their proposals were attempts to recouple the organization of the manufacturing firms which occupied their attention.

Development of Techniques to Facilitate Integration of Organizational Activities

Thus far two points have been examined, the symptoms of some managerial problems described in the business-management literature of the late nineteenth century and a clarification of the basic problem underlying these symptoms. The literature of Systematic Management was concerned not only, or even primarily, with these points, but rather with administrative solutions to these symptoms and problems. It is these administrative techniques designed to facilitate integration to which we now turn. Before examining them, however, it is first necessary to consider some of the possible approaches which could have been taken to correct the conditions noted above.

The requisite coordination could have been achieved in a number of ways, not all of which were really applicable or desirable in practice. For example, many of the problems could have been eliminated by reducing the size of the firm; however, this suggestion does not appear in the literature, nor would we expect it. Among more acceptable approaches are:

1. Use procedures which would direct personnel in what to do, when to begin, and when to have completed work. In this way all necessary work would be accomplished and if the instructions were supplied at the right times, duties would be synchronized with work movement. This was essentially what was involved in production control, inventory control, and some other administrative techniques developed during this period.

2. Have higher management supervise organizational activities more directly. To do this higher management, however, would need more reliable information about the performance of lower administrative units with which they could analyze performance and give accurate directions.

3. Conformity of the actions of lower-level managers to standards and directions of higher management could be increased if measures were taken to perform or predetermine the decisions which lower-level managers would make. To put this a little differently, top management could attempt to ensure coordinated actions by making all significant decisions itself, as (2) above suggests, leaving the lower levels of management to execute the decisions. The same general results could be accomplished, however, if some decisions were left in the hands of subordinate managers but steps

taken to ensure that the decisions would be the same, similar, or at least compatible with those which higher management would have made.

These were perhaps the principal approaches toward which specific administrative procedures or techniques mentioned in the Systematic Management literature of this period were directed. Many, perhaps most, of the techniques described by 1900 had been initially suggested in the literature sometime within the preceding twenty years.[25] Those techniques mentioned earlier for the most part were in such an undeveloped state as to be of little if any usefulness. By the turn of the century, however, many techniques had been developed to the point where they were of reasonable utility in facilitating the integration of organizational activities along the directions indicated above. In short, during a period of approximately twenty years a number of administrative techniques reached a state of development where they could function to help correct the problem of organizational uncoupling.

It is hardly possible to consider all the administrative techniques discussed in this literature of Systematic Management in the short scope of this paper. Attention will be directed, however, to a few of the major techniques discussed and their general pattern of development until the turn of the century.

Promotion of Horizontal Coordination

There were a number of developments which were involved with promoting the horizontal movement of materials, orders, and so forth through the company. Perhaps the most interesting was what we would today recognize as production control. The basic concern with production-control systems, then as now, was to record an order for the plant, plan when work should begin on each of the sub-orders, ensure their being finished on time, and to have the customer's order assembled and shipped when requested.

One of the first production-control systems to be presented in any detail was the one used by the Yale Lock Manufacturing Company. It was developed by Henry R. Towne, at that time president of the company, and was first publicly described in 1882.[26] It operated in the following fashion: Upon receipt of an order from a customer the office would prepare an order, today we would call it a shop order, for the factory. For this a specialized two-part form had been developed. Each order would be identified by its own number. The shop order would then be sent to the

---

[25] The journals surveyed in this study were examined back to their inception or at least until 1820 if that occurred earlier.

[26] "Shop Systems of the Yale Lock Mf'g. Co.," *American Machinist*, Vol. V (February 18, 1882), p. 6.

production superintendent who would in turn forward it to the department foreman who he thought should be responsible for the order. Upon receipt of the shop order the foreman would determine the date the order would be completed, put this date on the form, and send half the form back to the production superintendent.[27]

Crude and simple though this system was it contained a number of important elements from which a fairly consistent development can be traced to the elaborate and sophisticated production-control systems of today. This simple system contained the following elements: (1) it identified and recorded an incoming order; (2) it routed work on the order to an appropriate department; and (3) it provided a minimal amount of feedback in the form of an estimated completion date.

But this particular production-control system had two major weaknesses. First, it did nothing to prescribe how the flow of work should be coordinated by the department foreman who received the production order. It was up to him directly to coordinate not only the work his department performed on the order but also to make arrangements to get parts and materials from other departments. This condition was improved in a number of subsequent developments. The first of these was described by Henry Metcalf in a paper before the American Society of Mechanical Engineers in 1885.[28] Metcalf was a professional army officer, in ordnance, who had developed a production-control system while in charge of the shops at the Frankfort Arsenal. Metcalf introduced the use of what would today be called routing slips, which were prepared in the plant office and indicated which departments the order should pass through to have work performed or parts made or assembled. These routing slips accompanied the materials on their passage through the plant. In short, centrally prepared instructions for the flow of the order accompanied the order at all times. R. F. Van Doorn later described a system developed at Struthers, Wells & Company of Warren, Pennsylvania, which went one step further in that it had centrally prepared orders for parts which might go simultaneously to a number of departments which would work concurrently on parts. When completed, work would then begin on assembling the products for the customer's orders.[29] In short, coordination was provided by close control of production orders by the production-control system.

A second major weakness of Towne's production-control system was the very limited amount of feedback on the order. There was no direct way of telling the progress of work at any time after the order was sent to a department except when the order was finally completed and the order

[27] *Ibid.*, p. 7.

[28] Metcalf, "The Shop-Order System of Accounts," p. 446.

[29] R. F. Van Doorn, "A Complete System for a General Iron Works," in Arnold, *The Complete Cost-Keeper*, p. 143.

blank returned to the central-plant office. Through a series of managerial refinements this condition was gradually corrected. Tregoing described an improved system in which a record was sent back to the central office every time the material on an order moved from one department to another.[30] The next step in the development of production control, described by Hugo Diemer in 1900,[31] had the central office control the physical movement of all parts and materials.

In a period of less than fifteen years during the late nineteenth century we can thus find described in the literature of Systematic Management production-control systems which became progressively more detailed in specifying the work to be performed. The development advanced from the preparation of an order for a quantity of one of the company's products, through specifying the parts to be made to complete an order, to the point (as we shall see later) where the operations necessary to make parts were specified. Each of these orders was prepared in written form and consequently the volume of paper work grew enormously from a single piece for each customer order, to a piece of paper for each part of a product on a customer order, to finally, a separate written order for each operation performed in making each part of a product.

Development of Means to Facilitate Vertical Coordination

In addition to administrative devices to promote horizontal coordination, there were also a number of developments concerned with improving higher management's control over affairs throughout the company. Some of these were attached to the devices involved with promoting horizontal coordination. For example, production-control systems not only informed people along a horizontal movement of materials of what to do and when to do it, but they also provided, as has been noted above, information on the status of production to higher levels of management. Information about the status of production, however, was not the only data desired or needed by higher management to permit them to integrate more effectively the work of the company.

One of the developments of interest during this period was that of cost accounting. Although elements existed long before this time, until the late 1870's cost acounting largely consisted of prime-cost accounting. That is, cost accounting was primarily a matter of the collection and display of data relevant to the cost of materials and labor used in the company operations. These data were gathered in a way which did not permit any detailed analysis of products or operations. Completely missing was any real con-

---

[30] Tregoing, *Treatise on Factory Management*, p. 1.
[31] Hugo Diemer, "The Commercial Organization of the Machine Shop, II: The Production Department—Bills of Material," *Engineering Magazine*, Vol. XIX (July, 1900), p. 511.

sideration of overhead costs. Refinements in cost accounting late in the century, however, provided a valuable tool for keeping higher management informed on company activities and also for the analysis of problems and difficulties.

During the last two decades in the nineteenth century cost accounting advanced rapidly from a crude, fairly limited tool of management to a well-rounded flexible instrument for various types of analysis. There were many technical improvements such as valuation of inventories, machines, and other physical facilities which will not be discussed here. Instead, attention will be given to those directions of development which in one way or another throw the most light on the conduct of management during this period.

At the beginning of our period cost data were usually collected on the basis of the department, process, or product. Information with this much detail provided some general understanding of how affairs were progressing within a plant, but did not provide enough detail for a thorough diagnosis of internal problems. Van Doorn pointed out,[32]

> In general terms, a cost-keeping system is valuable exactly in proportion to the minuteness of detailed information which it affords. The manager is concerned, finally, with gross results, but he can change those gross results only by modifying the details of his practice, and before he intelligently can change practice details he must know his costs in detail.

In an effort to gather more detailed data, Metcalf developed procedures for collecting information on the shop order, parts, tools, or machines on which worker-time and materials were used.[33] This was soon extended by Henry Leon Binsse of the Newark Machine & Tool Works, in a paper before the American Society of Mechanical Engineers in 1887,[34] so that information was gathered not only on the machine being used to make a product or part but also on the operation performed on the machine.

These efforts to gather data in more detailed form were paralleled by an effort to obtain the information more promptly. The tradition in financial accounting of having records summarized yearly or quarterly influenced early practice in cost accounting. It became increasingly obvious to authors such as Diemer, however, that for cost accounting to be a really useful management tool, data would have to be gathered more promptly.[35] This effort to transform cost accounting from primarily a historical record

---

[32] *Op. cit.*, p. 83.

[33] Henry Metcalf, *Cost of Manufacture and the Administration of Workshops, Public and Private* (New York, 1885), Chap. 12, esp. pp. 152–56.

[34] Henry Leon Binsse, "A Short Way to Keep Time and Cost," *Transactions of the American Society of Mechanical Engineers,*" Vol. IX (New York, 1888), p. 380.

[35] Hugo Diemer, "The Commercial Organization of the Machine-Shop, VI: The Figuring of Total Costs," *Engineering Magazine*, Vol. XX (November, 1900), p. 229.

to a record of current cost markedly changed the nature of cost accounting and greatly increased its usefulness. Before cost data could be gathered in great detail, however, and promptly used, implementing mechanisms had to be provided.

Numerous procedures for gathering cost data were discussed in the literature. Cost-accounting systems did not have the same advantage as financial accounting in being able to gather considerable portions of the necessary data from documents and records prepared for other purposes, such as bills of lading, invoices, and the like. At the same time, some of the newer systems, such as production control and inventory control, did provide records which were to a degree useful in operation of cost-accounting systems. In fact, the relationship between these three is frequently so close that many articles in the literature, such as those by Metcalf, Diemer, Binsse, and Van Doorn mentioned above in addition to others by Lewis[36] and Church,[37] to name but a few, describe all three control systems as an integrated administrative procedure.

Some of the more advanced and detailed production-control systems were able to provide a fairly clear picture of material costs. They could not help much, however, in determining the other side of prime cost, labor costs. Labor costs had to be gathered through procedures specifically designed for that purpose. In an effort to keep the collection of these data as simple as possible, many of the earlier writers suggested ways in which current employees could, as part of their job, provide this information. For example, some writers such as Horace L. Arnold,[38] reporting on practices at the Strieby and Foote Company of Newark, N. J., and A. J. Shaw,[39] reporting on systems he had seen, discussed labor-cost-collection systems where the foreman played a central role. Others, however, especially those with plant experience, recognized that the foreman had too many other things to distract him and therefore another approach was advisable. Metcalf devised a system in which time data would be provided by employees by having them fill in a card or slip giving the hours they worked on a particular part or operation. The same card was used to report the machines and other things used.[40]

Binsse and others were quick to point out, however, that the chance of getting the employees to provide these data was very likely doomed to failure or at least serious disappointment in that they might either provide no information or that the information they did provide would turn out to be inaccurate. Recognizing that the foreman did not have the time and

[36] J. Slater Lewis, *The Commercial Organization of Factories* (London and New York, 1896).

[37] Church, "The Meaning of Commercial Organisation," p. 391.

[38] Arnold, *The Complete Cost-Keeper*, p. 16.

[39] A. J. Shaw, "Machine-Shop Time and Cost Accounts," *American Machinist*, Vol. IX (April 3, 1886), p. 3.

[40] *Op. cit.*, Chap. 12, pp. 151–67.

that the employees did not have the interest or ability the suggestion was made that the only reasonable way to do this was to use time keepers.[41]

Let us summarize development thus far. There was a trend for cost-accounting data to be gathered in more detail and more promptly through the use of the specific procedure of an accounting system. Operation of much of the data-gathering end of this system was at first to be in the hands of the first-line supervisor. This was soon found to be impractical. This was followed by an attempt to have the employees perform this activity which also met with disappointment. Finally, the data-gathering activities were made the responsibility of an employee who had this as his sole, or at least a major, duty. These can be seen as efforts to provide detailed, accurate, and prompt information to higher management which could be used to evaluate lower-level performance and analyze problems—in short to reestablish higher management control.

Both horizontal and vertical coordination of effort, as noted earlier, can also be promoted by taking steps to enhance the likelihood that decisions of subordinates are identical or at least congruent. As a result, the general strategy followed at this time was to preform or premold managerial decisions. One of the more general ways of premolding decisions by subordinates is to use standing guides to action or decisions: that is, policies.[42] With such guides every new situation requiring a decision does not have to be considered as a completely independent event. Once the decision-requiring situation is classified, the general nature of the decision is indicated by the policy, producing a much higher degree of homogeneity among decisions and related, perhaps interdependent, matters. Although hardly developed to the point at which we will find policies discussed today, there were, nonetheless, discussions in the management literature of the late nineteenth century of a wide range of policies, as for example, policies of promotion from within,[43] on personnel matters such as accidents and sicknesses, advocated by E. P. Allis, owner of the Reliance Machine Works of Milwaukee,[44] and on company parties,[45] to name but a few.

A more precise way than policies of predetermining decisions, however, is to use decision rules. Decision rules tell the individual manager or supervisor that in a particular type of situation he is to act or make a decision in a specified way. This may, and frequently does, involve the use of certain types of procedures or computations and some such rules are

---

[41] Binsse, *op. cit.*, p. 380.

[42] It should be noted here that we are examining the use rather than the formulation of policies.

[43] "Promoting the Training of Workmen," *American Machinist*, Vol. VIII (February 14, 1885), p. 3.

[44] "Shop Benefit Associations," *American Machinist*, Vol. VI (December 1, 1883), p. 8.

[45] "Promoting the Training of Workmen," p. 3.

found in the management literature of the last century. For example, Fred Macey[46] proposed managers be made responsible for purchases and complete purchasing transactions in accordance with a rather lengthy checklist covering such things as handling salesmen, getting price information, and the nature of the sales agreement. Diemer also set forth guides for purchasing on such things as cash discounts on purchases under a certain size.[47] More common, however, were discussions of predetermined wage rates.

While concern over wage plans certainly did not begin during this period, this topic received the largest amount of attention in the Systematic Management literature of these decades. Prior to roughly 1880 most discussions of wage compensation centered around two plans: payment by time, that is day wages, and payment by pieces produced, the standard piece-rate incentive scheme. During the last two decades of the nineteenth century, however, many new plans were introduced in the literature and tried in practice. Most of these new proposals were based upon an analysis of the limitations or flaws of the two earlier plans.[48]

The Premium Plan, developed by F. A. Halsey, attempted to reduce the necessity for precise determination of work standards.[49] The Contract System, or Gain-Sharing, as the particular system introduced by Towne into the Yale Lock Manufacturing Company was called, attempted to give the workers anything they could save on the labor cost of doing a job.[50] Probably the most thoroughly discussed wage plan, however, was profit sharing.[51]

Regardless of the details of a particular plan, any wage plan sets forth certain specific ways in which employees will be paid. Hence, managers at the lower levels of the company have little individual decision-making to do relevant to wages. Plans of this and later periods were designed so the lower-level manager took some objective data, processed them according to the instructions of the wage plan, and determined an employee's pay. The principal area of discretion was the choice of the wage plan, which

[46] Fred Macey, "Successful Buying," *Iron Age*, Vol. LIV (September 13, 1894), p. 455.

[47] Hugo Diemer, "Functions and Organization of the Purchasing Department," *Engineering Magazine*, Vol. XVIII (March, 1900), p. 833.

[48] For some discussion of these limitations, see David F. Schloss, "The Basis of Industrial Remuneration," *Economic Journal*, Vol. II (December, 1892), p. 608; J. Slater Lewis, "Work Management for the Maximum of Production, II: The Labour Factor in the Intensification of Output," *Engineering Magazine*, Vol. XVIII (November, 1899), p. 201; Nicholas P. Gilman, *Profit Sharing Between Employer and Employee* (New York, 1891), p. 44–45.

[49] By F. A. Halsey, "The Premium Plan of Paying for Labor," *Transactions of the American Society of Mechanical Engineers*, Vol. XII (New York, 1891), p. 755.

[50] Henry R. Towne, "Gain-Sharing," *Transactions of the American Society of Mechanical Engineers*, Vol. X (New York, 1889), p. 600.

[51] For an interesting early history, the reader is directed to Sedley Taylor, *Profit Sharing* (London, 1884).

was a decision made by higher management. In effect then, top management was again reestablishing its control over one area of concern through the use of this type of decision rule.

Although the effort to promote order and integration in the conduct of organizational affairs took a number of different forms, without doubt the principal one during this period was the establishment of what shall be called administrative systems,[52] such as production-control systems, inventory-control systems, accounting systems, and the like. Although covering different areas and existing in different levels of development all of these had some common features:

1. Establishment of procedures which specified how a person in a position is to perform a task. Needless to say, many of these systems contained a number of procedures.

2. Links which connected different procedures. These in effect specified what the position occupant was to do after he had completed his procedure, which was usually to send the result of his work to another position or positions. These were clearly spelled out, leaving no doubt as to who should receive these items. These two elements of the systems provided the administrative machinery to automatically carry out certain elements of the managerial function. For example, once set up, a production-control system could ensure that the receipt of, and work on, an order would be taken without the order, or the direction of work on it, ever having been brought to the attention of higher management. In doing this, of course, we have the automatic coordination of one horizontal flow of work. This automatic aspect of Systematic Management will be discussed further in a later portion of this paper.

3. The existence of information-flows. In addition to this automatic coordination of horizontal flows, however, every system provided to some degree, frequently in conjunction with another administrative system, for an automatic flow of information to higher management which permitted it to know the status of work and frequently provided the data for the analysis of problems and the proposal for corrective action.

Centralized Planning and Operation of Administrative Systems: The Emergence of Staff

One thing characteristic of administrative systems was that they were centrally established by top or at least higher levels of management, then disseminated throughout the firm where lower levels of management were expected to execute or operate them. In this respect they were a digres-

[52] This more cumbersome term, "Administrative Systems," is used rather than just "systems" to avoid confusion with many other uses of this word, such as social "systems."

sion by which top management made a centralized plan for control and coordination which was to have decentralized operation.

We have earlier noticed that systems tended to follow a general pattern in which they were first established as fairly general, loose, administrative devices which through revision became progressively more detailed and specific. In each case, as the central planning of an administrative system became more detailed, it left a smaller area of discretion in the hands of lower members of the organization. Let us consider several examples.

In the earlier discussion on production-control systems it was noted that they became increasingly detailed in their operations. These refinements would have had a profound effect on the job of the individual worker. At first he was told what part to make. How the part was to be made was usually left up to his discretion. In the next step, he was told what operations to perform, removing a considerable element of decision-making on his part and also implying a considerably higher degree of specialization. There was still considerable looseness or latitude in his job, for among other things the worker was frequently and usually allowed to go and obtain the material he was to work upon and bring it to his work position. The next development advanced by Lewis changed this, however; when all the material to be worked upon was first assembled and only then were jobs assigned to individual workers.[53]

These decisions, reducing the worker's range of contact and restricting his autonomy, were made not as a result of an individual manager's preference about leadership or for that matter the style of leadership to be followed in an entire management group, but as a necessary adjunct to installing a formal control system.

Reduction in worker autonomy had a parallel development in the reduction of the decision-making prerogatives of the lower levels of management. In the early order-control system the foreman was told what units to produce. As we have seen, it was up to him to write orders for parts to his worker or to other departments. Before long, however, Arnold reported techniques used in the Struby and Foote Company where orders to make parts were being prepared by the office and issued to the foreman, and in some cases even the orders as to what operations were to be performed were being centrally prepared for the foreman.[54] Similarly, the assembly of raw materials and parts, once considered the province of the individual employee, then made the responsibility of the foreman, was eventually placed in the hands of others. In a plan reported by Van Doorn, materials were gathered by special stock clerks and released to the foreman only when

---

[53] J. Slater Lewis, *The Commercial Organization of Factories* (New York, 1896), p. 209.
[54] Arnold, *The Complete Cost-Keeper*, Chap. 4, esp. pp. 24–26.

all necessary materials were available and only at the time the production was to commence.[55]

Hence, in a two-fold progression, the foreman was told how to do certain aspects of his job and when, and secondly some of his activities were taken from his control and placed in the hands of a central-office employee. There was, in short, a general trend in which the responsibility for providing the requirements for production shifted from the hands of the lower levels of management, to a central position or department. The system presented by Diemer at the turn of the century clearly separated this responsibility from the lower-line managers, such as foremen, and placed it at a higher level.[56]

A second pattern to be noted in the development of central systems centered around the operation of a system and the assignment of responsibility for this activity. Once a system was devised it was frequently the practice to assign its operation as a duty of the regular members of the line organization.[57] This is understandable, since on one hand the systems were frequently intended to standardize something the foreman and/or the executive was already doing, and on the other because it appeared to be the least expensive step. But after a period of time, operation of a system was frequently shifted to special personnel. Hence, time keepers and cost clerks were added to provide information for cost systems, production-control clerks were added to keep track of orders and any information on them, and still other specialists were added to assemble any information on stocks of materials for production,[58] or eventually to assume control over all material and production facilities.[59]

Although not recognized as such, these new employees were the first step in creating staff positions, indicating that staff existed in fact before it was urged on industry on a theoretical basis by Harrington Emerson.[60]

The hope expressed in many articles during this period, that in some way higher management would be able to regain control of their expanding, more specialized operation, was realized in part through administrative systems operated by such new staff positions. These administrative systems and staffs, once established, conducted many of the routine coordinating functions in a semi-automatic fashion leaving top management free, presumably, to concern itself with things more properly its concern.

---

[55] Van Doorn, "A Complete System for a General Iron Works," p. 143.

[56] Diemer, "The Commercial Organization of the Machine-Shop, II: The Production Department—Bills of Material," p. 511.

[57] See for example C. A. Burton, "Machine Shop Cost and Time Accounts," *American Machinist*, Vol. IX (May 8, 1886), p. 6 or "Shop Accounts and Management," *American Engineer*, Vol. XII (December 22, 1886), p. 236.

[58] See for example Van Doorn, *ibid.*

[59] Diemer, *op. cit.*

[60] Harrington Emerson, *Efficiency as a Basis for Operations and Wages* (New York, 1900).

Discussion

An Emerging Technology of Management for Steady-State Conditions

Systematic Management in contrast to some literatures which preceded or followed was primarily concerned with developing techniques and guides for individual managers to do their work and for the management function as a whole to be executed. In particular, the literature was concerned with finding ways to carry out the regular or routine activities of management. Attention was primarily on operations rather than on planning and developing. In brief, it was concerned with the development of administrative systems to guide the steady-state portion of managerial activities. For the most part, many of the concepts and techniques presented and arguments developed were concerned with what today would be called satisficing, rather than optimizing, solutions.

There was in this early literature a large number of managerial devices which could be used in the conduct of the managerial function. These were adopted as standard practice in many firms and we find many of these techniques in use today. In fact, it is systems such as those we have been discussing and many others like them which constitute the great bulk of managerial activities. The particular administrative systems developed during this period represent what can be called the beginnings of a management technology.

The Basic Elements of an Administrative System

Although specific points of the various systems in the literature varied, they did have a number of common characteristics and it may be well to review them in order to gain a better understanding of what was involved in the systematic-management movement. Let us say that Systematic Management was that approach to management which attempted to build into the management structure certain operating processes which would assure coordinated effort in the achievement of organizational goals to previously established plans. As a result: (1) certain repetitive management activities were carried out through standardized managerial steps by special-manager personnel, thereby relieving line executives of this task; (2) the integration of perhaps widely scattered activities was brought about through formally designated interlocking responsibilities and the assured flow of precise information; (3) many repetitively occurring problems received pre-established solutions which simplified the range of the decision-making efforts lower-level managers had to carry out.

In examining the various systems discussed two factors seem common to all. One is a careful definition of duties and responsibilities coupled with standardized ways of performing these duties. The second is a specific way of gathering, handling, analyzing, and transmitting information. The first of these factors is self-explanatory. The second may require further elaboration.

The treatment of information in Systematic Management had three basic elements:

1. A selective data-gathering cycle. This usually consisted of some managerial apparatus to receive information keeping what was needed, rejecting the rest, and arranging the retained material in a designated format.

2. Specific methods of handling information. This may have included transmitting the information along specified paths, such as with production-control information, or treating the information in a special fashion, as for example making a specific series of calculations such as the wage-incentive plan.

3. The presentation of specialized results to designated recipients. That is, the processed information was presented in a special manner for purposes of control or analysis in order that it could readily be used by the individual for whom it was prepared.

Bureaucratization of the Managerial Function

Looking at the overall development of Systematic Management one cannot help but be struck with its similarity to descriptions of governmental bureaucracies. The reasons given for emergence of bureaucracy in government are strikingly similar to those we have found leading to development of Systematic Management. Bureaucracy is supposed to develop when top members of an organization make demands on the rest of the organization for greater control. Basically these demands take the form of greater reliability of performance within the organization.[61] These demands for greater control are thought to arise because of increased size of the organization or the emergence of special administrative problems.[62] The result is that rules and duties are established that guide the activity of the organization members, departments are created for special functions, and steps are taken to increase accountability—"paperwork" records are developed and maintained.[63]

The internal confusion and waste, and the desire to promote order

[61] Robert K. Martin, "Bureaucratic Structure and Personality," *Social Forces*, Vol. XIX (May, 1940), pp. 560–68.

[62] Peter Blau, *Bureaucracy in Modern Society* (New York, 1956), p. 37.

[63] Max Weber, from *Max Weber: Essays in Sociology* (trans. by Gerth and Mills, New York, 1958), esp. pp. 196–98, 215.

and to establish greater control of operations by top management, cited so frequently during the period during which Systematic Management emerged,[64] and the common reference to the size of individual firms as the factor causing these conditions are identical to the conditions cited as giving rise to bureaucracy, which meet the following standards:[65]

1:—A clear definition of the departments of business, that similar work and similar functions shall be grouped in one department.
2:—A positive definition of duties of each department and its relation to the general business.
3:—A clear fixing of the responsibility and a willingness to have responsibility rest with the heads of the various departments. . . .

In short, the similarity of the conditions leading to and the characteristics of both bureaucracy and Systematic Management suggest that Systematic Management may be looked upon as the beginning of bureaucratization of the managerial function.

SUMMARY

The literature of Systematic Management which appeared in the later decades of the nineteenth century identified some serious internal problems of business firms in the manufacturing industries. The problems were usually identified as internal disorder, confusion, and waste in the production areas of the firm described as arising from the organization becoming uncoupled with a resultant breakdown in coordination. The literature contained many proposed solutions for this general problem. Examination of the three most prominent types, production-control systems, cost-accounting, and wage systems, supports the contention that these solutions were intended to promote the coordination of horizontal flows and to facilitate greater control by higher management (vertical coordination) through improved upward flows of information and by the establishment of means (decision rules and policies) through which top management could preform or predetermine decisions of lower management.

This literature, containing many techniques and procedures for carrying out portions of the managerial function, represents the beginning of managerial technology. Many of the administrative systems discussed, when installed would have resulted in a centralization of decision-making in firms in this industry. The execution of these administrative systems was frequently assigned to positions which would today be recognized as

---

[64] In addition to earlier portions of this paper, see Litterer, *op. cit.*

[65] James N. Gunn, "Cost Keeping: A Subject of Fundamental Importance," *Engineering Magazine*, Vol. XX (January, 1901), pp. 703–704.

specialized staff. The literature, therefore, enables us to determine the time and method of origin of some specialized staffs in production operations. The expressed intent for establishing these systems and their properties were found to be characteristic of bureaucracy; thus this literature also identifies the time and some reasons for the origin of bureaucracy in manufacturing industries.

This study has examined the rise of Systematic Management primarily in the area of production. While the area and the techniques have been specific the problems and strategies for solutions are general. Systematic Management has been described as a general phenomenon illustrated in a particular setting. It is not a body of specific techniques such as production control or a wage plan, nor is it only of concern in production activities. Similar breakdowns in coordination resulting from the same general causes could develop in other areas of manufacturing firms such as the distributing activities of modern firms or in other industries such as airlines. Further, although specific techniques might not be transferable, the general solution strategies of scheduling interdependent work, improving upward flow of more detailed information, and installing preformed decisions would seem usable in any organizational setting. Systematic Management then would seem more accurately viewed as a mode of management likely to occur in any organization under certain conditions of size and labor specialization.

Ernest Dale
Charles Meloy

4

Hamilton MacFarland Barksdale
and the
DuPont Contributions
to Systematic Management*

To be admitted to the small group of the Olympians who have
contributed to the advancement of management requires both path-breaking

* Inspiration for and continuous support of this paper have been provided by John
Lee Pratt, for many years one of the principal executives of General Motors. For about ten
years he was one of Barksdale's "young men" and gave greatly of his time and memories
to this paper. In fact, without his help this article could not have been written, for there are
few who like Mr. Pratt still remember in detail the events of days more than fifty years ago.

The authors also are deeply grateful for the recollections of some of those associated
with Mr. Barksdale like Donaldson Brown at Du Pont, Ethel du Pont Barksdale Brown,
Irénée du Pont, L. E. Beardslee, W. F. Harrington, and E. F. Johnson.

The basic source material for this article was the "Barksdale papers" originally found
by the author through the kind help of Lammot du Pont Copeland. These papers recount
the transactions of the meetings of the High Explosives Operating Department of Du Pont
from 1909 to 1914. Unfortunately the papers of the previous years' meetings were not found,
even though we made extensive searches and obtained the cooperation of Amory Haskell
in searching for the Barksdale papers as well as those of his father, J. A. Haskell.

In addition, material was obtained from the large correspondence of H. M. Barksdale
(amounting to some 50,000 letters); company correspondence and papers made available
from the Hagley Museum and Longwood Library through the courtesy of Emile du Pont,
president, and P. J. Kimball, executive vice president of the Hagley Foundation, Eleutherian
Mills, Dr. Walter J. Heacock, Dr. Norman B. Wilkinson, and the Pierre S. du Pont collection
at Longwood (through the kindness of Frank L. Battan).

A great deal of the tremendous work of searching the papers and documents and
arranging them was undertaken by Charles Meloy, and George Long, who for many years
was associated with E. I. du Pont de Nemours. Without their assistance and winnowing,
the documentation would have been much less complete. Editorial assistance was provided
by Alice Smith and secretarial work by Della Jaffee. The authors alone are responsible for
errors and omissions of this paper.

Reprinted from *Business History Review*, Vol. XXXVI, Summer, 1962, pp. 127-152.
    75

ideas and the successful testing of those ideas in the market-place. For ideas by themselves, however elegant and intellectually challenging they may be, must be evaluated by experience so that the chaff may be separated from the wheat, and the subjective clearly distinguished from the objective. The only real test in business management is the test of experience. Such a test of the validity of an idea or a good theory has been well put by the economist Milton Friedman of the University of Chicago:[1]

> A theory is "simpler" the less initial knowledge is needed to make a prediction within a given field of phenomena; it is more "fruitful" the more precise the resulting prediction, the wider the area within which the theory yields predictions, and the more additional lines for further research it suggests. . . . The only relevant test of the validity of a hypothesis is comparison of prediction with experience.

To qualify as a contributor to the body of management knowledge, therefore, a man should have added significantly to what may be considered to be "good theory" in the light of the above criteria. This kind of theory includes contributions to such areas as these (the following list is by no means comprehensive):

1. The theory of *administration*, which is the framework for the exercise of administrative functions.

2. The theory of *scientific management*, which is really that body of knowledge which makes up the "sciences" or techniques of management.

3. The theory of *human relations*, which contributes to our knowledge of why men in business behave the way they do.

When the requisites for recognition as a pioneer are stated in this fashion, relatively few men qualify. The purpose of this paper is to advance for consideration as a management pioneer a man whose contribution is best known through the companies whose success symbolizes a fortunate combination of good ideas tested in the market-place, namely, Du Pont and General Motors.

This man is Hamilton MacFarland Barksdale, who probably was the single most original thinker on management among a number of outstanding thinkers in these two companies. He was, perhaps, the brightest of their rather remarkable stars. Yet because of his modesty and his belief that one's own happiness and success come through that achieved for others, he is hardly known to the outside world. It is over a century since Barksdale was born, and it seems appropriate to reexamine his qualifications to recognition as a pioneer thinker and contributor to management.

[1] Milton Friedman, "The Methodology of Positive Economics," in *Essays in Positive Economics* (Chicago, 1953), Vol. 3, pp. 10 ff.

Life of Hamilton MacFarland Barksdale

Born on June 30, 1861, of a distinguished Virginia family in Richmond, Barksdale graduated from the University of Virginia as a civil engineer. His first jobs taking him to underdeveloped areas in the state of Mississippi and later Colombia, South America—in "growth" industries like river development and railroads—laid the foundation of his life's career which was a continuous exploration into uncharted territories. While engaged in railroad building near Wilmington, Delaware, in 1887 Barksdale became acquainted with members of the Du Pont family who, under Lammot du Pont, Sr., had broken away from the main company. They were working on the development of the new explosive dynamite, which the then conventional attitude of the parent company had been obstructing. Barksdale joined their company, the Repauno Chemical Company, and rose rapidly in rank, first as secretary and then treasurer in 1893. When Repauno became part of Eastern Dynamite and was taken over by the Du Pont Company interests in 1893, Barksdale was made its general manager. His promotions were due largely to the fact that Barksdale was mainly responsible for development of the systematic approach to management started by Lammot du Pont.

Barksdale instituted regular meetings of the various department heads at Repauno, and participants were asked to prepare detailed papers on various management subjects—especially those requiring immediate and studied attention. In the discussions following these papers, "resolutions" were formulated and these sometimes constituted or were developed into working generalizations. The papers themselves covered a wide area of administration, scientific management, and human relations. The generalizations flowing from these presentations were tested by actual experience and were altered and refined thereby. The great success of these meetings was due in large part to the fact that they were conducted on an unusually high academic plane and that presentations were in the form of problems rather than complaints. Thus Barksdale worked out his "system of management" largely from 1887 until he joined the Du Pont Company in 1902 to help save it when it was faced with either atrophy or competitive absorption.

Repauno and Eastern Dynamite had been the only hold-outs against the rigidity of one-man control epitomized by General Henry du Pont until his death in 1889 and continued thereafter by his successors. General Henry had caused the withdrawal of his nephew, Lammot, from the company by refusing to consider the much-needed addition of dynamite to the company's product line. However, the more fundamental reason for the split was Lammot's realization that one-man control was bound to mean slow growth and, worse, failure to provide adequate succession. Lammot's fears were amply borne out: Henry's successors—Eugene du Pont and his relatives—all passed away within a few years, killed mainly by overwork, and the company lost ground during their tenure.

Thus, by 1902, there was no one available to succeed to the presidency of Du Pont except General Henry's son, Colonel Henry. However, Colonel Henry felt he did not have the necessary experience and was mindful of what the job had done to Eugene and his successors. He became a United States Senator instead, and lived to be 88!

The Du Ponts actually decided to sell the company to their principal competitor. If it had not been for the youngest of the partners—Alfred Irénée du Pont—who protested vehemently and got together with his two cousins, Pierre and Coleman, the company would undoubtedly have been sold. As it turned out, the three cousins managed to buy it for $2,400 cash (and $12 million in bonds)! But these young cousins (all in their thirties) were aware they did not possess the necessary management experience. Hence they turned to Barksdale and asked him to become president. They knew that he had developed a system of management at Eastern Dynamite and had trained a group of men who could competently exercise management skills.

Barksdale, however, was modest to the extreme. He refused the title, asserting that only someone bearing the name of Du Pont should head the company. It was thus that Coleman, the eldest of the three cousins, became president, while Barksdale was elected a director, vice president, and member of the Executive and Finance Committees. He became, in fact, general manager of Du Pont, though he did not have the title until 1911. (Prior to that time there was none, each department reporting directly to the Executive Committee). In 1913 he was appointed acting president. His principal years of activity at Du Pont spanned a twelve-year period from 1902 to 1914. While Coleman kept the industry in a constant state of flux and activity, buying up almost all of it within a few years, Barksdale coordinated and made a success of the newly acquired variety of enterprises.

The principal step taken by Barksdale and his "young men" was the efficient integration of the many different concerns that had been acquired separately. Each had been run as an independent operating unit. Each had its own sales organization and branch offices. There had been no attempt to improve products, to introduce new ones, or to promote serious research (which, it was said, "could always be bought in Europe"). But all this changed under Barksdale.

The business-as-usual stereotype gave way to the formula of "low prices, large volume." Sales activities were coordinated through the appointment of a sales manager. Trade reports were instituted. These included an appraisal by the salesmen of both customers and prospects. Scientists and trained men were brought in and given freedom to pursue their specializations. Some were even given time off to continue their formal studies. An experimental laboratory was set up for product and methods research.

Coordination

As a member of the Du Pont Executive Committee—one of the earliest general management committees in industry, and one of Barksdale's own innovations—Barksdale formulated objectives and policies, and initiated controls over the diverse operations. Other members of the committee were four Du Ponts: Coleman (chairman), Pierre, Alfred, and Francis (still under thirty and a brilliant chemist); J. A. Haskell; and A. J. Moxham (described as "an old-fashioned, homely type of capitalist, who carried an umbrella on sunny days and put his money to one hundred uses").[2] Members of the Executive Committee were vice presidents and served on the Board of Directors. Barksdale, with Coleman's aid, formed the Executive Committee to encourage executive participation and coordination. With Coleman's change of interest and illness a few years later, the power of the Executive Committee rose, and slowly it made an increasing number of operational decisions, while the president merely recommended changes in policies. From the very beginning of its existence, the Executive Committee ended sole control by one member of the Du Pont family. This had been Barksdale's intention in forming it.

The Executive Committee began by making general the policies, practices, and procedures developed at Repauno and established later by Barksdale and his associates through the H.E.O.D. (High Explosives Operating Department). Essentially these were put into effect by establishing central staffs, which developed the policies and controls that were enforced through the president and the Executive Committee.

Much of its work during these years was codified in the Du Pont "Bible" or "how-to" manual. For example, a central sales board was established which set up price schedules and rigidly enforced them. This ended price-cutting, rebates, secret agreements, and other price variants. Industrial explosives were now sold for different specific needs. Agents were replaced by the company's own salesmen, and assistance was given by technical experts, who helped customers in installations and by the promotion of multiple usage, safety, and economy. A Trade Record Bureau was set up centrally, and each cartridge of dynamite or pound of powder sold

[2] John K. Winkler, *The Du Pont Dynasty* (New York, 1935), p. 158.

anywhere had to be reported in duplicate to this bureau, which carried on a continuous analysis of actual and potential sales to each customer. Data supplied from the field were important in planning, estimating, and forecasting output.

Another staff department of growing importance was research; Repauno's Eastern Laboratory (1902) and the Experimental Station (1903) hired outstanding chemists and pioneered important contributions to more effective powder.

Location of plants, production efficiency, standardization, simplification, safety, and cost reductions were promoted toward a high degree of uniformity by Alred I. du Pont and his staff in black powder, by J. A. Haskell in smokeless powder, and by Barksdale in high explosives.

Development

The second major Barksdale innovation was the establishment of the Development Dpartment. Its first head was W. B. Dwinnell, who was followed by Irénée du Pont, R. R. M. Carpenter, and W. S. Carpenter, Jr. Its task was to find new outlets for the products of Du Pont factories and to make the company independent of, or at least less dependent on, outside sources of supply. (Du Pont was among the first to initiate purchase analysis, and it observed the rule that if someone else could manufacture more cheaply than Du Pont, in the long run it was more economical to buy than to make.) The Development Department was also to explore beyond explosives into fields that the company could logically enter with currently available technology and manpower. One of the guiding rules at that time was that the company would buy a going concern when it could rather than start from the beginning.[3]

The acquisition of the International Smokeless Powder and Chemical Company in 1903 provided Du Pont with its first nonexplosives business through International's diversification into lacquers. But this aspect of the acquisition was an accident. Actually it was in 1908, when Du Pont had excess nitrocellulose capacity, that Coleman appointed a committee to investigate ways and means of disposing of larger amounts of nitrocellulose for nonexplosive use. It was on this committee's recommendation that the firm in 1910 purchased the Fabrikoid Company, the country's largest artificial leather concern, to absorb the surplus nitrocellulose.

When Du Pont lost an antitrust suit, which was begun in 1907 and which culminated in a dissolution order in 1912, the parent firm was dissolved into three companies (Du Pont, Hercules, and Atlas), and its growth

---

[3] A "going concern" would have the advantage of providing Du Pont with "a company whose trade and reputation would already be established and which had an intimate knowledge of manufacture." 1914 Progress Report of the Development Department.

in explosives was curtailed. As Lammot du Pont explained: "The dissolution was notice to the Du Pont Company that it could not expand in the explosives field, having already been dissolved for being too large, and that was a very powerful influence for branching out into other lines."[4] As it began to branch out, Du Pont's basic policies were: (1) the entry into new fields or old ones with a prospect of improvement; (2) the accompaniment of Du Pont dollars with Du Pont trained men; and (3) investment aimed frequently at ownership or control.

World War I added greatly to the pressures for diversification. The company acquired huge surplus funds for investment because of its great sales expansion, and the Executive Committee felt it would "be able to invest [those funds] for greater benefits to our stockholders than by handing them out as a dividend and having these stockholders try and invest [the money] for themselves." The company also was looking for utilization of likely excess capacity. As early as 1915, Barksdale foresaw the problem of excess capacity that was the aftermath of a wartime economy: "When the war is over our difficulty, in common with many American manufacturers, is going to consist in making a creditable showing in earnings against the keen competition which will exist because of the huge increases in manufacturing facilities, and any increases in fixed charges, which do not increase earnings, will increase this difficulty."[5] As John J. Raskob put it, "After the war it will be absolutely impossible for us to drop back to being a little company again; and to prevent it, we must look for opportunities, know them when we see them, and act with courage."[6]

The company was also anxious to utilize its expanded staffs. According to Irénée du Pont, "We had trained personnel, and we were in a position with the know-how we had . . . to find industries to which we could contribute something and utilize the personnel which we had trained, especially the upper brackets of the company."[7] There were many other advantages for Du Pont in diversification, such as economies of buying, acquisition of new markets, and so on. Finally, an economist was added to the staff during World War I in recognition of the growing interdependence of the firm with the national economy.

The quick growth of the Du Pont company in the early twentieth century was not, by any means, due to Barksdale alone. The three cousins, Alfred, Coleman, and Pierre du Pont were the prime movers who set the company on the path to growth and managed the difficult job of financing. Alfred was responsible for the idea and got the other two to join him. In particular, Coleman was responsible for the many acquisitions that gave

---

[4] W. S. Haynes, *American Chemical Industry* (New York, 1945), Vol. 3, p. 189 n.
[5] Barksdale letter dated July 26, 1915, to J. J. Raskob.
[6] Ernest Dale, *The Great Organizers* (New York, 1960), p. 54.
[7] *Ibid.*

the company the lion's share of the powder and explosives market (70 per cent in 1906[8]), and Pierre "chained to the desk" made it work from a financial point of view.

But in the administrative field they borrowed largely from and built upon the management system that Barksdale had developed for Repauno through the H.E.O.D. meetings. His staff was used extensively by the other two product departments for aid and improvement in their work. Not all the techniques used were Barksdale's personal creation, but many he had inspired as a catalyst and others were the creation of one or more of the young engineers whom he had trained at Eastern Dynamite—or in the High Explosives Dpartment. Among these were Irénée and Lammot du Pont (sons of Lammot du Pont, Sr.), Donaldson Brown (who later married Barksdale's daughter), John Lee Pratt, E. F. Johnson, W. F. Harrington, and others. It was this group that enabled the company to digest Coleman's many acquisitions while simultaneously increasing its efficiency.

Many other companies, Carnegie Steel, General Electric, McCormick Harvester, and others, were pioneering new management techniques similar to those developed by Barksdale and the men he had trained. His contributions, however, have perhaps had a wider influence since their conceptualization and their applicability, as well as the dynamism of the Du Pont company, ensured their spread throughout a number of companies and to other industries. The achievements which stemmed at least in part from his work included:

First, the growth of the Repauno Chemical Company and Eastern Dynamite (an amalgamation of three companies).

Second, the rescue and full success of Du Pont explosives, 1902–1905.

Third, when Du Pont was split into three entities (which in addition to itself included Hercules and Atlas) in 1912 as a result of antitrust action, it was able to supply all the personnel for the three organization, and each of the three was eminently successful. "Mr. Barksdale played an important role in this reorganization. Evidence of his highly constructive service to the company is the fact that during the great expansion which took place shortly after the reorganization, many top managerial positions in the two separated companies, as well as in du Pont Company itself, were filled by highly competent men who had been trained under Mr. Barksdale."[9]

Fourth, the latter growth of Du Pont itself. Since Barksdale died in 1918, and was in ill health and comparatively inactive for some time before that (although until close to the end, he was consulted on important matters relating to company policy), it would be absurd to think of the present company as his creation. But much of the management know-how that

[8] John K. Winkler, *op. cit.*, p. 164.
[9] Donaldson Brown, *Some Reminiscences of an Industrialist* (privately printed, 1957), p. 29.

enabled Du Pont to become the largest and by far the major supplier of explosives to the Allies in World War I evolved from the systems originally established by Barksdale and his group.

Fifth, the reorganization and growth of General Motors. However much was added later, by the Du Ponts and men who grew up in General Motors itself (notably Alfred P. Sloan, Jr.), Barksdale's work undoubtedly contributed to the systems instituted at General Motors during P. S. du Pont's presidency, 1920 to 1923, and later under Sloan. The approach to management problems—the development of an attitude and a philosophy, the concept of rational systems and techniques and a group management system that employed the complementary skills of many (through the devices of the executive and finance committees) stemmed from Du Pont, and the Du Pont system itself had evolved from the systems Barksdale introduced at Repauno and Eastern Dynamite. Also many of the men who assisted Pierre du Pont and Sloan in the rehabilitation of GM when it was near disaster in 1920 were originally Barksdale men.

The GM participation also proved to be Barksdale's last—he was elected a director of the corporation and of the Chevrolet Motor Company. He became an early shareholder, probably before Raskob became involved in General Motors. Barksdale used to discuss management problems with W. C. Durant, the president of Chevrolet and later the promoter-financier of GM. After his loss of the GM presidency, Durant used to say that it might not have happened had he listened to Barksdale's counsel on good management.

Barksdale had given virtually all his life to the cause of developing a system of management that could be and was successfully applied in practical business. After he reached the age of 50, his health began to fail. This led to a decline in his participation at Du Pont until the influenza epidemic carried him away almost imperceptibly (October 18, 1918).

But until the end his inquiring nature persisted. He was continually searching for new truths, developing and discarding, testing and formulating. Possessing an analytical and practical mind, he recognized the essential problems of business and was able to use the tools of scientific analysis to develop workable solutions. Most important of all, he was able to arouse and develop the curiosity of others in the management of business and human affairs.

He had an almost uncanny ability to spot young talent, to attract it toward him, to develop it as lovingly as a gardener his flowers, as carefully and conscientiously as a surgeon trains his assistants. He was painstaking and persistent in his development of his young men (as in Milner's "nursery" of the subsequent administrators of British colonies there was a Barksdale "nursery" to develop the administrators of large American enterprise), not only technically and managerially, but also in the fine details of language and expression, precision and conciseness. He had an exceptional gift of inspiring and stimulating those with whom he was associated. Yet he was not an easy teacher: he insisted on thoroughness and perfection of technical knowledge, on probity and honesty, and on the fact that the best was never good enough. He was therefore the kind of leader who is always remembered in after years—gratefully and warmly. And he retained the loyalty and friendship of both the highest executives and the lowliest employees.

John Lee Pratt's first-person experience with Barksdale is a good illustration of the latter's interest in young men. Pratt put himself through the University of Virginia and after some teaching experience, looked for a job. He received three offers: one from General Electric, which required a postgraduate technical course; a second from the American Bridge Company, of a job that paid $75 a month; and the third from Du Pont for $60. Pratt consulted his professor and was told that he should take the Du Pont job, even though the American Bridge position would have paid 25 per cent more, because the privilege of working with Barksdale would make it worth his while. He accepted the Du Pont offer, and, within the first month, Barksdale invited him to dinner—an honor and an opportunity which general managers did not usually offer a young recruit. From then on, Barksdale was Pratt's principal guide in his career, which ultimately led to a position as second-in-command at General Motors where he made major contributions to its management.

The Barksdale Contributions to Management

Barksdale's influence, like that of many great teachers, was thus largely personal and frequently evident in the contributions of others. Many of his ideas were developed orally and hence there grew up a real oral tradition at Du Pont. Contributions to management not committed to paper became common property of the managers, who passed them on to their subordinates and successors. Hence it is not always possible to cite chapter and verse for a specific contribution.

And because Barksdale was a modest man whose happiness in life came from the happiness and success of others, the ideas that he originated were often presented by others. He believed profoundly that to allow another man to present an idea was one of the best ways of getting that man to carry it out, much more effective than merely lecturing upon it at an H.E.O.D. meeting. He acted more as an originator and a catalyst than as a detailer. He saw his job as one of stimulating others to think about and work out new ideas in management. And also, being a good chief executive, he was glad to get others to work out ideas. He insisted, however, that the approach be one of looking forward, not backward: ". . . it is useless to speculate upon what might have been, and the important point is to determine the wisest course for the future under the circumstances now existing."[10] But unlike many present-day executives who insist that "management is getting things done through other people" he did not shirk personal involvement or ultimate responsibility. On the contrary, Barksdale acted as a guide and stimulator every step of the way, making his subordinates rewrite, rethink and reappraise their papers. And he was a stickler even to the point of improving style, grammar, and punctuation. For he was an early believer in the practice that an idea, however good, is stillborn if others cannot understand and appreciate it.

Hence when we speak in the following pages of Barksdale's contributions, it must be borne in mind that while at times he clearly was the sole author, at other times the ideas bore the names of his subordinates, though in most instances it is likely that Barksdale was at least a co-author, if not the principal one. As we refer to "Barksdale" we mean, rather, Barksdale and his young men, with Barksdale usually the principal contributor or at least "*primus inter pares.*" So many years separate the contributions from their authors and almost all of them have passed away, hence the historian cannot unravel precisely who said and did what. But this is not really important in comparison to the importance of the ideas themselves.

And here Barksdale's principal contribution to management was his emphasis on the need for *systematization* in the solution of business problems. He wrote: "The history of innovations and inventions has been practically the same. The steam engine was scoffed at, the telegraph was laughed at and the telephone at first was hardly considered worthy of either derision or laughter, and System has been no exception to the rule. But System cannot be either thrown or laughed out of Court. A decision has been handed down in its favor in the Supreme Court of Business. It is alike the foundation upon which to build and the keystone in the arch of success."[11]

By "systematization," Barksdale meant the use of guidelines or criteria to govern business decisions and planned adaptation of them to specific problems. Criteria served as a series of rules or generalizations which would aid in the solution of specific problems, toward which a planned approach was required.

The generalizations were always made with reference to a basic goal or objective. This was principally the best possible long-run utilization of the capital invested by the owners in the business, i.e., the optimum rate of return on investments. As Barksdale put it: "The objects to be sought in any earnest effort at organization are EFFICIENCY (including thoroughness combined with promptness), ECONOMY (measured by ultimate results achieved), and PERMANENCY (the last being secured by the development of competent 'understudies' in every important position)."

[10] Barksdale letter dated April 29, 1901, to Eugene du Pont.
[11] High Explosives Operating Department [hereafter H.E.O.D.] meeting minutes, 1906.

These were perfectly proper objectives in the light of the philosophy and mores prevailing in the business society of that day. Hence Barksdale put major emphasis on making his enterprises "second to none" in product quality and price. Starting from that basis, most other requirements of the business would be met.

The costing and pricing "credo" expressed by the Accounting Department at this 1905 meeting reflected the principles of Barksdale's thinking:[12]

> Our Company's aim is to make the powder business a model that all others may follow, and one of the points it emphasizes and is now paying particular attention to, is that it is satisfied all of the saving due to reduced cost of manufacture, reduced cost of selling and from other sources does not belong to the Company, but that the Company should be satisfied with a fair return on the capital and brains invested and that the balance belongs to the consumer of the goods. Now, it did not reach this decision because of its sympathy with the consumer, but on the other hand believes it is a business principle that in the end will work the most good for our Company. What better weapon do you want for fighting competition than to be able to offer your goods at a price below which your competitors can afford to sell and at the same time make a profit for your Company? This plan fully carried out, I believe, would practically do away with the fighting competition, because there would be no competition to fight. It is not the aim of the company to force the very highest price possible, simply because it might be able to do so in some particular locality because of no competition or for other reasons, but it is most desirable to establish a fair and just price all over the country, but before we can do this, it is of the greatest importance to know exactly what it costs us to manufacture and deliver these goods to the customer.[13]

Hence we find Barksdale in his writings, speeches, and letters principally occupied in giving his enterprise a "competitive edge" over others by the superiority of technology—which is interesting to note in the light of so many current executive pronouncements that technology is a minor matter not worthy of the attention of a real administrator. Barksdale always insisted that an administrator had to know thoroughly what he was administering.

CONTRIBUTIONS TO MANAGEMENT TECHNIQUES

It was thus in the attempt to "get out" the goods that Barksdale developed contributions to "scientific management" or rather, as we have pointed out, sciences for management or management techniques. It is interesting to note today that the most basic technique for Barksdale was the quest for the discovery of new products or the improvement of existing

---

[12] Barksdale letter dated Jan. 12, 1911, to A. J. Moxham on the subject of committee principle.

[13] Report from Acctg. Dept. at H.E.O.D. meeting in Nov., 1905, presided over by Barksdale.

ones. In that endeavor he hired Ph.D.'s in the sciences (his company was one of the first to do so in America) and established research laboratories. As Dr. Chambers, one of the last survivors of the Barksdale researchers put it: "There was plenty of scope and funds to make a fundamental contribution to the Company's product line—even though the research might take some years and the actual return on the investment years more." And the researchers were kept free from administrative details. They were not, like so many good researchers today, promoted to administrative posts—a move that often affects both research and administration adversely.

The development of products so discovered was undertaken most carefully through the use of "negative criticism." Barksdale would ask for all the reasons why the particular product should *not* be commercialized and then if all the negative reasons were still outweighed by those favoring go-ahead, the next stage would be pilot operations. And not only were pilot plants constructed; the product was also carefully tested in the field. Only then did Barksdale give the all-out signal for large production and sales.

On the *production* side, Barksdale stressed technical and engineering competence in the construction of the powder mills. His writings on this subject are still minor classics in the explosives industry. A newspaper article of the day, announcing a promotion of Barksdale, included the observation that he is considered "the greatest dynamite expert in the world." In matters relating to design, layout, and construction, he anticipated many modern ideas. Even on the fringes of "scientific management" there were many contributions—too detailed and too technical to describe here—such as the flow of work, improvements in the scheduling of materials, inventory management, and the introduction of purchase analysis.

Barksdale often stressed that "there is nothing worth more to the concern in the long run than goodwill and the reputation of its goods. . . . We cannot expect to become thoroughly acquainted with (our goods) in a few days or months, or years; it is the study of a lifetime, but each day should add something to our store of knowledge."[14] He had summed up that daily practice in an assuring letter written some years earlier to Messrs. T. W. & C. Bidwell (March 9, 1894): "We will make at once a careful investigation (of your complaint) . . . and if the fault is ours, we think we can locate it. We are at all times anxious to rectify any mistake or error on our part. We might add, however, that we expend more money than other high explosives manufacturers in the country in the way of able superintendents and chemists in order to insure that our product shall be the best that can be made and that its quality shall at all times be uniform."

In the matter of *sales techniques* his two principal contributions were the establishment of market analysis and technical services in the marketing departments. A statistical division carried out a function that today is known

[14] H.E.O.D. meeting minutes, 1906.

as comparison shopping and testing. Samples of competitive material were obtained for analytical and comparative purposes and the findings of the tests provided talking points for sales meetings and conferences.

The Trade Analysis Bureau kept a complete inventory of all customers—actual and potential. It stated in each case the record of actual purchases and the company's share in each of them, making it possible to lay out a program for reducing the difference between the two. Joined with this was a program of extending the use of the product by discovering and promoting as many new applications as possible. This was accomplished principally by adding technical experts to the sales department to demonstrate product uses and applications to the customer. This also made it possible for salesmen to sell different products to the same customers rather than have several differently specialized salesmen call on them.

In 1905, one of the members of the H.E.O.D. was able to tell the meeting:

> It may be a matter of some pride for you to know that we have one of the best sales department record systems in the country. I visited a number of the largest and most highly systematized concerns in the world and spent several days in each place, with the result that I discovered that not only had we very little to learn from them, but they had a great deal to learn from us. In fact, the largest concern of all, after a thorough investigation of our methods, decided to introduce them in their entirety into their home and branch offices. All the systems I investigated were fatally defective in one particular; that is, they do not supply their district managers with any paraphernalia or methods to watch trade, notwithstanding they are so highly systematized in the home office.
>
> In addition to this, one of the largest manufacturers of system outfits has for years used the Wilmington Trade Record Division as the best illustration of what may be accomplished in that line in sales departments, with the result that numerous large concerns throughout the country have inspected and adopted our Trade Record methods.

In developing the management techniques, Barksdale was concerned that always the most economical results be achieved. Hence he was forever emphasizing the need for standardization, reducing variety to the absolute practical minimum, and having the customer pay the additional amount where, for special orders, cost varied from standard. And in setting up the standards, Barksdale was deeply concerned with obtaining the best; hence his recurring emphasis on "the one best way"—made so familiar later by the writings of the Gilbreths.

Contributions to Human Relations

But with all his concern for what was best and most modern technically, Barksdale was supremely mindful of the ethical and human framework within which the economic efforts were carried on. In setting a high *ethical conduct*, Barksdale laid strong emphasis on absolute truthfulness and complete honesty in all dealings. Even in the case of minor moral lapses he would engage in lengthy correspondence and discussions to point up the failings and would not rest until the disturbances were rectified.

The following letter written to a company agent in 1896 is a model of the great respect Barksdale held for the dignity of an individual:

> I think a careful and dispassionate consideration of the situation will make clear to you that your troubles are largely imaginary and that you will also see that from our standpoint, and the data at hand, there were grounds for our recent criticisms. Nothing but freindly feelings are entertained towards you at this end and there is a total absence of any cause whatever for discouragement on your part. An energetic discharge of your duties, interest in your work and a broad-minded view of the situation is all that anyone can expect of you, while without these attributes, success in this, or any other business, would be impossible.
>
> I hope that you will accept this letter in the spirit in which it is written, which is one of neither faultfinding nor complaint, the principal object having been to endeavor to make clear to you the apparent difference of circumstances when viewed from two entirely different standpoints, and I hope that it may be of assistance to you in the future.

Again, in the matter of *safety*, he put the welfare of even the lowliest workman ahead of any economic consideration, even though, in fact, proficiency in the latter made the former possible. Thus he insisted on absolute safety in the building of the powder mills, devoting many papers on the subject and culminating in his famous "Theory of Barricades" (truly "revolutionary" implications here!). And his concern spread to individual workmen to the extent of several lengthy papers on match searches (matches were forbidden because of explosion dangers), from which developed a code of safety, discipline, and safety training.

In 1910, Barksdale chairmanned a committee which drew up a table of safe distances for the location of buildings storing explosives. The study represented an exhaustive compilation of worldwide data on the effect of explosions and was translated into graphs and charts. Safe distances were thus determined according to the poundage of the explosives stored and whether or not the buildings were barricaded.

Also, in the matter of safety the story is related by Donaldson Brown of the occasion when Barksdale questioned a foreman on proper operating precautions. Having received the correct responses, he then asked the man what he would do if the thermometer reading for a certain mixing vat rose to an unmanageable level. The man then proceeded to detail the steps he thought necessary. Barksdale shook his head and interrupted: "No, no— you run just as fast as you can and get behind that barricade over there. We can rebuild the nitro-glycerine plant. We cannot rebuild you."

In the 1908 H.E.O.D. program he noted how important it was for the Superintendent himself or his representative to look after the people who are injured—after the first aid has been rendered, that is—by calling on them to see what could be done in cases of distress and showing them that interest was being taken in them. At such a time, he pointed out, it is very important that the employee feel that the company is his friend.

To maintain good safety, Barksdale said that there were three points to be kept constantly in mind: careful inspection of apparatus and prompt repairs to apparatus which needs repairs; careful selection of men and swift discharge of any man who proves himself careless or negligent or in any other way undesirable; and prompt and efficient exhibition of sympathy or kindness to the injured employee.

From here it was only a short and natural step to considering the *relation of the worker to productivity*, the effect of his living conditions on his work, the reasons for good work and good results his productivity. Ultimately this led to the establishment of a Labor Efficiency Division, which concerned itself with the four "principles" of "Scientific Management in Powder Making":

(1) Find the best way to do a thing.
(2) Make this way standard as to both method and time.
(3) Teach employees how to reach a standard.
(4) Give them the right incentive to do it.

These principles were translated into a measured workload system. Some of the operations were linked to piece rates (with due account being taken of differences in the difficulty of operation and surrounding conditions as well as the volume of work, etc.) or to time payment where the speed of the machines in effect determined the speed of work.

Also Barksdale realized then, as management sociologists do today, that it is usually difficult for an executive of the company to "get close" to the men and to obtain from them a comprehensive and accurate knowledge of their attitude toward their work and the company. An ideal way to determine true sentiments, he ventured, was to have someone mingle with the employees both during and outside of working hours, perhaps on the basis of comradeship.

In mentioning the company's need for knowledge of its workers' attitudes, Barksdale spoke of his hope that the day would come when outside men (doing similar work for other corporations) could be hired by the company to perform as "motivational researchers." Perhaps Barksdale was looking ahead to their coming when he wrote: "I believe such men could get the information . . . more accurately and in less time than could one of our own important employees."[15]

---

[15] Barksdale letter dated Jan. 4, 1912, to Employee's Committee.

Contributions to the Theory of Administration (Management Skills)

Now the method that Barksdale principally pursued in making his contributions to theory of àny kind was *comparative analysis*. When he anticipated or was made aware of a problem, he first looked around to see whether there was an experience or a series of experiences on which he could draw for a solution (he frequently compared the experiences of the different plants). Usually this would be an historical experience or the experiences of one or more executives. Barksdale would study these experiences, examine them for relevance, cull from them what appeared to him to be comparable, and then make the necessary adaptation for the solution of the current problem. From a number of such experiences and adaptations he, or one of his subordinates, would then prepare a paper with conclusions that would serve as guideposts or criteria in solving other similar problems in the future. These papers would be written and read in advance of the bi-annual meetings of H.E.O.D., and would then be discussed and questioned at the meetings. From the papers and discussions Barksdale would often draw generalizations or "policies" (guidelines) representing the sense of the meetings, and they would become precisely that in the conduct of the business. Usually they were developed by integrating experience with what appeared to be best in theory for the business. Barksdale was forever testing his policies to see how they worked out and was forever ready to modify his conclusions in the light of valid experience. In stating a policy, he always emphasized the need to leave room for individual effort, initiative, and thought.[16]

And the test for him was in rate of return on investment, which it was his aim to maximize within that framework of ethical, human, and legal bounds which had been set up for him by society and which he was constantly trying to widen. In this respect he was always working on what he considered to be the dimensions of leadership.

Innovation: through original and applied research, underpinning of technology wherever possible, and a development department devoted to discovering new uses for old products as well as new acquisitions. Barksdale liked to quote Governor Bates' observation that "in any field of endeavor the man who considers his education finished, or who thinks he has learned all there is to know in his trade, profession or business, will soon see the rearmost light of the procession pass by."[17]

Representation: principal stress on the relation of the company to its owners, with appropriate relations to employees and the local community. Thus, in regard to salary increases of employees, Barksdale took a position that might well redirect the thinking of some company managers today

[16] H.E.O.D. meeting minutes, 1905.
[17] *Ibid.*

who often consider the stockholder the lowest entity on the corporate totem pole: "You must consider the plain business side of such propositions. It is all right and proper for you to be anxious to see your men get along, but you should not allow this feeling to blind you to the fact that we have, all of us, got to show at the end of the year a reasonable interest upon the money invested in these businesses or be compelled to acknowledge that we have made a failure."[18]

Interpretation: Continuous emphasis on teaching and understanding as well as on correction to facilitate understanding of managerial goals.

Administration: Most important of all—continuous development of administrative skills.

In this development, Barksdale always proceeded within the framework of forecasted possibilities (toward that end an economist was appointed) and related this to possible economic objectives. And then there had to be the appropriate organization to reach these goals. Initially Barksdale worked this out on the production level with the individual powder mill as a unit of organization. He sketched out the various stages of growth of a powder mill, setting out the additional functions necessitated by larger size and the coordinate positions, thereby setting up assistant superintendents as well as assistants to superintendents. He took delegation of operating responsibilities as a matter of course, partly in order to make growth possible, largely also to train younger men and to offer them better opportunities. But as the size of the enterprises grew, especially by acquisitions, Barksdale's thinking turned increasingly to group management as the only practical means to ensure long-run continuity. His thoughts pro and con regarding such an organizational instrument are well set out in the following excerpts from his memorandum on group management dated January 12, 1912, addressed to A. J. Moxham:

1. To relieve as far as seemed practicable the individual members of the Executive Committee of the immediate direction of the Company's routine daily operations, thus enabling them to devote more time to the larger problems arising in connection with the Company's welfare.

2. To relieve the Executive Committee as a whole of the detailed consideration of the very numerous and voluminous reports which had grown out of our method of administration and which, in spite of efforts to that end, it had not been found feasible to materially reduce.

3. To develop and broaden the younger men in the organization to a greater and more positive extent than had been achieved as a result of the Operative Committee.

I might add the observation that in most matters of importance I think the old proverb applies—"Two heads are better than one"—and while I recognize that committee authority as compared with individual authority makes for greater consumption of time, I believe this disadvantage to be more than offset by the broader point of view and the greater conservation secured through committee action.

[18] Barksdale letter dated Aug. 17, 1894, to E. C. McCune.

Barksdale had earlier observed that:

> ... we do not act enough as individuals, do not give the different things brought up for consideration that kind of individual analysis, which results in formation of definite and clear opinions; or in those cases where comparisons of costs are made, we do not go carefully enough into the individual cases to be able to explain on the floor why conditions at our individual plants are as they are. . . .
>
> We cannot come to these meetings without previous thought upon the subjects to be considered and derive any particular benefit from them, or, modifying that statement,—we do not get the amount of benefit we should get from a number of minds working upon the same problems, or the amount of benefit we should get from a previous mental consideration of the subjects presented with a consequent forming of definite individual opinions and the reasoning out of clearcut explanations, of why things are as they are.[19]

Barksdale urged that this situation be changed.

To these observations of Barksdale on Committee Management might be added those of Irénée du Pont, under Barksdale's direction.

"I offer you the following thoughts and arguments relative to the advisability of the modification of the 'committee rule'":[20]

Advantages

1. Too hasty decisions and errors occasioned thereby must be to a large extent eliminated, not only because more minds consider the matter, but because it is necessary to take more time.

2. The opportunity of a man making a decision without knowledge of another branch is materially decreased.

3. Where a decision is by a committee, the matter is more likely to be weighed in a non-personal manner and the decision arrived at more along the lines of a solution of the problem, whereas one man is often swayed by a personal feeling or preconceived ideas.

4. Greater weight would be given the decision, should it result in a serious accident. For instance, if we decide to barricade B blasting magazines, on four sides, that being the consensus of opinion of our most competent men, and it later were to transpire that magazines so barricaded instead of being less dangerous became greatly more so, it is hardly within the bounds of likelihood that a court could find us grossly negligent, whereas if the matter were decided on by one individual and it were shown that other people had expressed ideas diametrically reverse, it is possible that the Company might be considered grossly negligent.

5. Of necessity a greater number of men are familiar with the affairs of each particular branch, and consequently the death or sickness of one man cannot seriously cripple any branch of the organization.

6. It is much easier and causes less friction to make changes advancing men, because their places do not have to be filled with such thoroughly tried understudies.

[19] H.E.O.D. meeting minutes, June 21, 1907, Program 15A.
[20] Irénée du Pont letter dated Jan. 14, 1911, to William G. Ramsay.

Disadvantages.

1. There is a strong tendency toward procrastination and it is inevitable that decisions on the average are made much more slowly than where one man is responsible for the decisions.

2. Divided responsibility may tend to a decision on insufficient grounds, because should failure result each has the moral support of the others that the mistake was not foreseeable.

3. A great deal of time is used up in calling meetings together and transacting the business and in writing up and approving the minutes of the meeting.

4. Additional time is lost because the time of a number of men is taken in the place of one.

Considering the pros and cons it seems to me that the middle course would be the most desirable one. It uses the personal responsibility for most decisions but settles more important matters by a committee of the most competent men we have. I think that if each committee will observe parliamentary rules and if they analyze each proposition promptly on presentation and refer it to the man with power to act, except in the most important cases, we will not lose a great amount of time and still obtain the advantages of committee work.

And from group management as an organization, Barksdale was led to consider its operating bases through the formulation of criteria, which he tested by experience at Du Pont, such as:

1. Unity of leadership—the absolute clarity of command at each level of management rather than the usual diffusion and confusion. "The problem is to subdivide and yet to maintain unity—necessary elasticity, yet requisite cohesion."[21]

2. Homogeneity of outlook, heterogeneity of ability was the foundation of successful policy-making by a committee—that is, members of the top company committee were to have reasonably similar goals for the company but should differ in the experiences brought to bear upon the deliberations.

3. The division of activity below the top committee into the major profit-building blocks—principally on a product basis (or departmental basis—as soon as a product volume was large enough to justify the administrative expense). Delegation of authority and responsibility were emphasized increasingly with growth.

Barksdale had this to say about business growth and departmentation: ". . . the most *efficient organization* is not obtainable by segregation in accordance with the names or title that may have, through carelessness or otherwise, come into use—but by segregation in accordance with the thing to be accomplished.

When a business is large enough to make segregation into departments or divisions desirable, the segregation should be determined by the essential

[21] Barksdale letter dated Jan. 2, 1912, to A. J. Moxham.

elements into which the problem is divisible, not by the character of education, or the experience or the work of the man employed."[22]

Occasionally, Barksdale would have to redefine areas of responsibility
for the agents and representatives in the field. Often, these members would
forward picayune matters to the home office for disposition. In one such
instance, Barksdale wrote back to the agent:

> It seems to us here entirely unnecessary for you to refer these small
> matters to us; there is a certain portion of the business of each office which
> we must leave to the judgment of the agent in charge. In fact, we expect
> them to assume such responsibility and thus relieve us. For instance, in the
> present case you are well aware of the minimum prices at which you sell . . .
> while you are much better posted than we are as to the importance of this
> particular small sale and can, therefore, judge better as to whether the mini-
> mum prices should be applied or not. In the future, please bear in mind
> that we have an enormous number of important matters constantly before
> us here, and that it is frequently very trying to be called off from these to
> consider a case like the one in point. Try and handle these matters without
> calling upon us for assistance.

*   *   *

4. Clear definition of the mission of each unit of organization so that
it would be fully accountable for its actions and clearly established lines of
authority and communication. As Barksdale wrote to a Du Pont executive:
"I am exceedingly sorry that you should have communicated with Mr. . . .
direct in a matter of this sort. It is important that no office but this one should
write to any of the works changing methods or instructions.[23]

5. Outstanding support of all operating activities from central staff
services. An illustration is Barksdale's memo to P.S. du Pont where he cites
the advantages of a "centralized" pooling of research efforts of Du Pont,
Hercules and Atlas; rather than a separate research facility at each plant.
[Note: This arrangement would only be for the 5-year period of Du Pont
"guardianship" of the new companies.]

Better results are secured through coordinated rather than disjointed
efforts, Barksdale believed, because:

(a) The detailed experience of a larger number of operating units
would always be available;

(b) The ideas and suggestions of a larger number of practical,
experienced men would be brought together;

(c) Economy (would be achieved) in capital expenditure and in
administration, also in experimentation and research, since one experiment would serve for all, and fruitless ground would be covered only once;

(d) Cooperation (among committee members) along such important
lines would, of necessity, engender a better feeling between, and a clearer
understanding of, each other than if there were no such contact;

[22] Barksdale letter dated Feb. 10, 1911, to W. G. Ramsay.
[23] Barksdale letter dated Jan. 29, 1896, to M. M. Pratt.

(e) There would be no need to cut down the existing organization, and existing facilities (laboratories, etc.) could be employed at practically full capacity.

6. Control (could be exercised) through financial measurement based on the rate of return on investment and independent of operations.

7. Coordination (could be achieved) through the instrument of a budget and continuous examination at regular intervals of promise and fulfillment.

8. Rewards for fulfillment would be possible through highly attractive compensation, bonuses and stock options and penalties for non-fulfillment ("by their fruits ye shall know them").

9. Continuous linkage of ownership to management would be provided, and those who have a stake in the business are likely to make better decisions than those who do not.

10. Organizational balance would be easier to achieve. Changing problems could be continuously reviewed, and the solution of these delegated to those best qualified to handle them.

Now these and other organizational skills were continuously held together by the skill of communication on which Barksdale laid first stress, as can be seen from one of the few lengthy reflections on this subject :[24]

Before we part I want to talk to you a little while upon a side of our work which affects me personally. It isn't possible in so large an undertaking as we are carrying on for the individual upon whom rests the responsibility for directing the work to do anything more than direct in a general way. To go into details is impossible. He performs his duty best when he succeeds in working out an organization—a scheme of organization—and then placing in each position to be filled the best available man and then endeavoring to see that in a general way the objects sought for by the organization and by the personnel are achieved. . . . I know of no point at which there is failure, except to appreciate the full importance of cooperation, and unless that cooperation is achieved—the organization as a whole can't reach a full measure of success, and I, consequently, as an individual (will) fail. . . . To appreciate that importance (of cooperation) it is necessary for us to appreciate the magnitude of the operation ($1^1/$_4 to $1^1/$_2 mill. per month cash expenditure). That expenditure takes place at a large number of points scattered from the Atlantic to the Pacific and from the Great Lakes practically to the Gulf. . . . I readily understand that men placed as superintendents must of necessity find it more difficult to get the broad point of view. I have been similarly placed.—I have been in charge of important works far distant from headquarters. I have gone through all the sensations you gentlemen have. I have dubbed many things as red tape which I would not have considered as such if I had taken the broad view. I was performing my duties as well as I knew how. I was at them every working hour my strength would permit. I was being called upon for information and data that seemed to me quite unnecessary. . . .

[24] H.E.O.D. meeting minutes, Oct. 11, 1909.

Now it may be that these reports are unnecessary. A year ago we felt this might be the case and a committee was appointed to go into this and everything was eliminated that could be. I can readily understand that these reports cannot always be gotten off as the Main office wants them to, but I don't understand why, when a man finds that he cannot do that, he doesn't come forward and say so and give the reasons, and not let the man who is 1,000 or 2,000 miles away, and trying his best to help in the work of successful operation of the plants, remain in total ignorance.

Personally, I am entirely satisfied that each superintendent who so departed from standard practice had a good reason for doing so. The mere fact that he had a good reason for doing it made it important from the standpoint of the welfare of all of us that this reason be stated. We have accomplished what we have only by a combination of all our brains . . . combined experience and combined observations. It isn't possible to continue an organization as large as ours if the individuals are going to, without advice, without any explanation, depart from standard methods adopted. The whole object of the organization is to get cooperation, to get for each individual the benefit of all the knowledge and all the experience of all individuals. If it isn't accomplished, the organization is a failure, and that is where this thing hurts me. . . . I am going to make a personal plea to you gentlemen to make it a point to take the broad view, not to look upon your own plant as the only thing to which you can render assistance, but to place yourself more in the position of one of several who are working for a common end. If you will bear those points in mind . . . I certainly would appreciate it because I certainly don't want to make a failure.

Such, then, were Barksdale's contributions to the theory of management techniques, human relations, and administration as we have been able to obtain them from the documents and interviews. Whether his contributions entitle him to enter the haven of the "immortals of management" (he is not listed in Urwick's *The Golden Book of Management*)[25] is for the reader to judge.

However, it may be pointed out that Barksdale, unlike the other pioneers of management, made substantial contributions to the theory of administration, i.e., to the conduct of top management, a subject which they largely ignored.

Barksdale also made important contributions to the techniques of management, though not in the detailed, continuous, and sometimes massive fashion of Taylor, Gantt, and Gilbreth. And much more than these three, he was ever aware of the impact of the administrative and managerial activities of top management on the worker. This Barksdale amply demonstrated by his great humanity and concern for human beings. Rather than the two major industrial empires he helped to build, and more than his system of general management thought, the actual practice of those ideas in day-to-day relationships is probably what he would want most to be remembered for.

[25] Lyndall Urwick, *The Golden Book of Management* (London, 1956).

Those of us who have gone through the many records and evidentiary documents showing the Barksdale touch are strongly convinced of the managerial genius of this man. In keeping with his humility and complete devotion to his job, he made no great speeches, nor did he submit his principles and concepts in writing for publication. Had he done so, his name would undoubtedly be etched much deeper and clearer in the annals of management history.

Perhaps the greatest significance of Barksdale was that he had the courage to strike out along paths that no one else had dared to explore and in the process make a deeply significant contribution to systematic management. Also, he was able to pass this knowledge on to others and stimulate them to similar efforts. His work is an example to all those who seek to improve management science of what can be done intellectually as well as economically.

David F. Hawkins

5

The Development
of Modern Financial Reporting
Practices among American
Manufacturing Corporations

As late at 1900, the amount of financial information presented to stockholders by the managers of most publicly owned American manufacturing corporations was meager. The little information actually revealed was "invariably colored by the point of view of the corporation, and frequently unreliable because of 'sins of omission.' "[1] In fact, so secretive were some manufacturing companies that even into the twentieth century they failed to make available to investors any financial information other than the company's capitalization and dividend record. Included among this group was the American Sugar Refining Company, which had some 10,000 stockholders and was one of the most actively traded stocks on the New York Stock Exchange.

This lack of financial information pertaining to manufacturing concerns was in contrast to the reporting practices of public utilities, insurance companies, banks, and railroads whose activities (being more in the public service) were more closely regulated and more fully reported. Even here, however, practice varied in accordance with state requirements, and there were some notable nonreporters. For instance, in 1866, the treasurer of the Delaware, Lackawanna, and Western Railroad Company, in response to a request for information from the New York Stock Exchange replied simply: "The Delaware Lackawanna R.R. Co., make no reports and publish no statements and have done nothing of the sort for the last five

[1] Arthur S. Dewing, *Corporate Promotions and Reorganizations* (Cambridge, 1914), p. 12.

years."[2] Another railroad company, the New York Central and Hudson River Railroad, failed even to render an annual report to its stockholders during the 1870's and 1880's.[3] Later, in 1900, one financial chronicle complained that the Pacific Mail Steamship Company's report each year was "largely what C. P. Huntington and his associates desire it to be, they own a heavy majority interest."[4]

After 1900, the level and frequency of corporate financial disclosure by industrial management began to rise slowly and the credibility of its representations began to improve—a process which is still going on today. These changes in the quality of the financial reporting practices of American manufacturing concerns have stemmed from four principal sources. First, gradual recognition by some managers of their public responsibility. Second, increasing criticism of management accounting and reporting practices by a number of influential groups and individuals outside of the management class. Third, direct federal government regulation, such as the so-called Securities Acts of 1933–1934. Fourth, the recognition by the American accounting profession, and acceptance by the business community, of some common accounting and reporting standards. Underlying and contributing to these forces for change have been a number of social, political, and economic factors such as the emergence of a large number of small investors, the evolution of big business, and the increasing willingness of the public to seek government action to reform undesirable commercial practices.

Corporate Publicity before 1900

During much of the nineteenth century the amount of financial data revealed by business corporations to the American public, including stockholders, depended upon the whim of managers.[5] State laws were vague, and corporate charters were often silent on the question of management's financial reporting responsibility. Also, up until at least 1880, public sentiment, except in the case of public-service corporations and financial institutions, expressed no opposition to management's predilection toward corporate secrecy. Consequently, because managers rarely made public any more financial information than was absolutely necessary, businessmen generally did not keep stockholders fully informed of the results of their companies' operations.[6] There were few pressures upon them to do otherwise; corporate secrecy was customary—a carryover from the days when

[2] Birl E. Shultz, *Stock Exchange Procedure* (New York, 1936), p. 12.
[3] Norman L. McLaren, *Annual Reports to Stockholders* (New York, 1947), p. 5.
[4] *United States Investor*, Vol. XI (January 20, 1900).
[5] McLaren, *op. cit.*, p. 4.
[6] Marian V. Sears, "The American Businessman at the Turn of the Century," *Business History Review*, Vol. XXX (December, 1956), p. 418.

individual proprietors and partners had no reason to report to anyone outside the firm.[7]

The Level of Disclosure

The modern reviewer of management financial reporting practices during the nineteenth century is immediately struck by the limited amount of information made public by manufacturing firms—even the larger ones with widespread public ownership. Not only was there inadequate financial disclosure, but some companies were irregular in the frequency with which they issued reports. For example, between 1897 and 1905, the Westinghouse Electric and Manufacturing Company neither published an annual financial report to its stockholders, nor held an annual meeting.[8]

Before 1900, for the few publicly held manufacturing corporations in existence, it was possible for investors to obtain some information pertaining to the companies' capitalization, if not from management, from the standard financial sources such as *Hunt's Merchant's Magazine*, and later, the *Commercial and Financial Chronicle*.[9] Less frequently was a simple balance sheet available and seldom were sales and profit figures released—an income statement showing sales less the major expense items was indeed rare. In addition, few of these published financial facts were accompanied by either a company or independent auditor's certificate, since neither the theory

[7] In contrast, beginning in 1844, the British Parliament passed a series of comprehensive statutes, called Companies Acts, which were designed to regulate the formation, management, and winding-up of public companies. Several of these acts prescribed minimum standards for financial disclosure to investors and called for an independent audit of these financial reports. The Directors Liability Act of 1890, which was construed as one of the Companies Acts, made directors under certain conditions liable to compensate persons damaged by false statements in prospectuses or other documents soliciting application for securities. Thus, by 1900, in Britain, the disclosure to investors of certain reliable financial information was mandatory under the threat of legal liability.

[8] McLaren, *Annual Reports*, p. 5. On February 20, 1901, the board of directors of Westinghouse Electric and Manufacturing Company, issued a two-page report to a special meeting of the stockholders. The report contained no financial statements but did give the company's sales and total dividends, interest, and sinking-fund payments for 1898–1900.

[9] In 1914, Arthur S. Dewing published a historical study of a number of the corporate reorganizations which had occurred between 1891 and 1913. One of his sources of information was the financial journals. Speaking of the reliability of the financial press in general, and the *Commercial and Financial Chronicle* in particular, Dewing said: "As a general rule, . . . the statements of the press comprise merely the facts made public through the publicity department of the corporation, or unreliable quotations and hearsays,—the 'news' upon which the stockmarket trader feeds. In some cases, there are covert attempts to influence the investing public by the insidious 'write-up,' with which many financial papers prostitute their pages. Distinctly the most useful publication that we have is the *Commercial and Financial Chronicle*. Its accuracy is striking. Over and over again, the present writer has compared original reorganization plans and corporation reports with the *Chronicle* digests, and almost without exception no important error has been discovered. The files of the *Chronicle* too, are accessible to most people. . . ." Dewing, *Corporate Promotions*, p. 12.

nor practice of these procedures was common in America. The public had to rely upon managements' integrity in determining if published financial information was reliable. These disclosure practices grew out of the fact that in the formative years of most manufacturing companies all or almost all shares were owned and controlled by the original owner-manager family and there was consequently little need to communicate internal affairs outside the firm.

About 1900, the textile industry's record of financial disclosure stood halfway between that of the nonreporters, such as the American Sugar Refining Company, and the better companies with respect to financial publicity, such as the American Tobacco Company. The textile industry can therefore be used as a convenient standard.

A typical annual financial statement for a textile firm issued about 1900 would be that of the Davol Mills, a small textile company quoted on the Fall River securities market. Few industrial firms provided more financial information; many provided less.

In May, 1899, the Davol Mills management rendered to its stockholders the elementary balance sheet shown in Table 2. No profit and loss statement was provided.[10] Stockholders had to estimate the firm's profitability by taking the net year-to-year changes in the balance-sheet item labeled "Balance profit and loss" and adding any dividend payments.

The Davol Mills type of balance sheet, although issued in 1899, is comparable to the better industrial financial reports issued prior to about

TABLE 2

BALANCE SHEET, DAVOL MILIS, MAY, 1899[a]

Assets	
Land and water power	$ 25,800.00
Buildings	96,900.00
Machinery	377,300.00
Cash and debts receivable	98,892.00
Manufacturing, merchandise, material, and stock in process	171,963.00
	$770,855.00
Liabilities	
Capital stock	$400,000.00
Debts	329,100.00
Balance profit and loss	41,755.00
	$770,855.00

[a] *Moody's Manual of Industrial and Miscellaneous Securities* (New York, 1900), p. 517.

[10] Strangely, the American textile industry's performance with respect to financial disclosure during the nineteenth century appears to have grown worse as the century progressed. In 1850, the stockholder reports of textile firms in New England generally provided far more financial information than the Davol Mills report of 1899.

1880. These were usually those of the textile firms. Later, after 1890, a few of the newly created industrial combinations sometimes published more detailed financial statements. By modern standards, even in these cases, the amount of data released was sketchy but was adequate to the social and economic environment of the late nineteenth century. The financial information relating to the American Tobacco Company dated December 31, 1899, and shown in Table 3 may be considered representative of the better financial statements published by some of the emerging combinations after 1890.

TABLE 3

FINANCIAL STATEMENT, THE AMERICAN TOBACCO COMPANY, DECEMBER 31, 1899[a]

Assets			
Real Estate, Machinery, Fixtures, etc.		$ 4,636,838.17	
Leaf Tobacco, Manufactured Stock,			
Operating Supplies, etc.		10,286,750.31	
Stocks in Foreign Companies		4,363,755.00	
Stocks in Other Companies		17,929,986.86	
Cash		4,445,592.02	
Bills and Accounts Receivable		3,525,453.49	
Patents, Trade Marks, Good Will, etc.		31,887,166.98	
Total Assets			$77,075,542.83
Liabilities			
Capital Stock—Common		$54,500,000.00	
Preferred		14,000,000.00	
		$68,500,000.00	
Scrip Issue May 1st, 1896		3,024,490.00	
Provision for Regular			
Quarterly Dividend on			
Preferred Stock, payable			
February 1st, 1900	$ 280,000.00		
Provision for Dividend			
of $1\frac{1}{2}\%$ on Common			
Stock, payable February			
1st, 1900	817,500.00		
	$1,097,500.00		
Accrued Interest on Scrip	30,135.70		
Acc'ts. and Bills Payable	1,729,481.59		
Accrued Commissions	50,245.97		
Advertising Fund	68,259.98	2,975,623.24	
Total Liabilities			74,500,113.24
Surplus			$ 2,575,429.59
As per Statement Dec. 31st, 1898		$22,557,688.87	
Deduct 100% Stock Dividend on			
Common Stock, May 1st, 1899		21,000,000.00	
		$ 1,557,688.87	
Added in 1899 from Income Account		1,017,740.72	
			$ 2,575,429.59

[a] American Tobacco Company, *Annual Report, Fiscal Year Ending December 31st, 1899* [Newark, 1900], p. 3.

Companies such as American Tobacco which issued the more detailed financial reports usually did so because of enlightened managers or because of their heavy dependence on outside sources for capital. Other well-known contemporaries that issued financial statements similar to, or more detailed than, the American Tobacco report included: Continental Tobacco Company, American Hide and Leather Company, General Electric Company, National Biscuit Company, and Federal Steel Company—in 1899 the company issued one of the most complete financial reports published to the date.

Reluctance to publish financial information was common among both large and small companies. Generally, as might be expected, the small and the closely held manufacturing corporations were the more secretive; that is, they issued either no financial information, or they published less than that set forth in Table 2. Yet, as late as 1900, there were some notoriously secretive managements among the large publicly traded corporations. This group included such companies as International Silver Company, which represented about 75 per cent of the nation's total silver products, and Virginia-Carolina Company, which controlled practically all of the southern phosphate rock and fertilizer manufacturing facilities. Another large publicly owned company, the American Tin Plate Company, which controlled 95 per cent of the tin-plate production in the United States and whose stock was traded on the New York and Chicago stock exchanges, published in 1900 a balance sheet containing only four asset and five liability accounts. In other words, the public's knowledge of the financial affairs of these giant manufacturing companies, such as American Tin Plate, was about the same as for little Davol Mills—little or none.

Factors Contributing to Financial Secrecy

During most of the nineteenth century, American industrial managers had good reason to be inclined toward corporate financial secrecy. The heritage of owner-manager attitudes was probably most important. In addition, state law, public apathy, the accepted method of distributing securities, and the absence of accounting standards contributed to this lack of financial information.

The principal reasons why corporate managers were so secretive with regard to their companies' financial affairs were four in number: there was no tradition of publicity, for no one would have thought of asking individual proprietors, partners, or early family owners to divulge such information; management believed the public had no right to information on these matters; managers feared that by revealing financial information they would unwittingly assist their competitors; and, to many, the doctrine of *caveat emptor* seemed as applicable to buyers of securities as to purchasers of horses. For instance, during the testimony heard before the Industrial Commission in 1899, Henry O. Havemeyer, the president of American Sugar Refining

Company, and commission member Thomas Phillips had the following exchange:

> Phillips: You think, then, that when a corporation is chartered by the State, offers stock to the public, and is one in which the public is interested, that the public has no right to know what its earning power is or to subject them to any inspection whatever, that the people may not buy stock blindly?

> Havemeyer: Yes; that is my theory. Let the buyer beware; that covers the whole business. You cannot wet-nurse people from the time they are born until the day they die. They have got to wade in and get stuck and that is the way men are educated and cultivated.[11]

The testimony of another witness before the Commission, Charles W. King, secretary and general manager of the New Jersey Corporation Agency,[12] illustrates another of the reasons for secrecy:

> Livingston (Commission Member): Now, then, when the people ask for information, why not just give it? You say because it would be giving away your private business. Well, you did not think of that when you went to the public for your franchise, did you?

> King: The public may not be your competitors; but you may have competitors, and in giving it to the public you would have to give it to your competitors.[13]

These comments of Havemeyer and King represented in part an inheritance by late nineteenth-century management of a number of the attitudes of the owner-managers of the century's earlier industrial ventures. During much of the nineteenth century, the typical manufacturing company had been a small, closely held enterprise serving local markets. It was often an extension of an individual proprietorship or a partnership. Ownership and management, if not the same persons, were closely related and the owners were in continual personal touch with the affairs of the enterprise. Because there were few or no outside investors, there was consequently little need for management to think about the problems of financial disclosure.[14] Under these conditions a company's financial statement was considered private, just as were the financial affairs of any private citizen.

State corporation laws reflected this anti-publicity sentiment of managers and their agents. In general, the requirements of nineteenth-century

---

[11] *Preliminary Report of the Industrial Commission on Trusts and Industrial Combinations* (Washington, 1900), p. 122.

[12] The New Jersey Corporations Agency was formed in 1895 for the purpose of furnishing corporations chartered in New Jersey, but operating out of state, with the necessary facilities for complying with the state's liberal incorporation laws. Mr. King's office represented several hundred such corporations including the Amalgamated Copper Company, the American Car and Foundry Company, the American Thread Company, the Pressed Steel Car Company, and the American Soda Fountain Company.

[13] *Preliminary Report of the Industrial Commission*, pp. 1109–1110.

[14] B. Bernard Greidinger, *Preparation and Certification of Financial Statements* (New York, 1950), p. 3.

state corporation laws can be broken down into two major groups: reports submitted to public authorities and reports submitted to stockholders.[15] The reports required by state authorities were generally considered as confidential statements between the state and the corporation and as such were not available for public inspection. These reports or statements which corporations were required to make to state officers can be further divided into three subclasses: detailed reports, those requiring financial statements in some detail as to assests and liabilities; general statements as to the condition of the company; and simple reports, those requiring the names and residences of directors and the agent or person upon whom processes might be served. By 1900, detailed reports were required in 16 states, general statements in five states, and simple reports in six states. The remainder of the states required no report whatsoever.

About half the states provided for the second major class of reports—reports to stockholders. This category may also be arranged into three subcategories: periodic reports to the stockholders; reports at the demand of the minority stockholders; and reports which combined the two prior categories. Nine states fell within the first division, seven under the second, and three under the third. In general, these statutes merely specified that an "annual report" be provided the stockholders. Seldom were the contents of the report specified or a provision included to require the mailing of annual reports to those stockholders who were unable to attend the stockholders' meeting.[16] To have imposed the burden of detailed public reports upon management would not have improved a state's chances of attracting incorporations—a lucrative business few states wished to discourage.

It would seem, as long as manufacturing firms were relatively small, closely held, and served local markets, public sentiment was in accords with management's belief that financial secrecy was appropriate. In general, until the 1880's, when large industrial combinations began to be formed for the first time in the United States, the vast majority of the American public subscribed to the simple principles of laissez-faire economics related to marketing. In particular, the public recognized, as did common law, the tenet of *caveat emptor* as governing commercial transactions. Of course, the one major exception was public-service corporations. In the case of manufacturing concerns, if investors bought securities, if consumers purchased goods, and if employees sold their services without full knowledge of the issuer, manufacturer, or employer's financial condition, that was not the

---

[15] Frank E. Horack, *The Organization and Control of Industrial Corporations* (Philadelphia, 1903), pp. 79–122.

[16] For instance, Horack commented on the provision of a Michigan corporation law of 1899 relating to periodic statements to stockholders thus: "In the chapter on manufacturing corporations in the Statutes of Michigan, section 15 reads, '. . . as often as once in each year a true statement of the accounts of said corporations shall be made and exhibited to the stockholders.' How and when the statement is to be made is not mentioned; nor is any penalty attached for failure or refusal." *Ibid.*, p. 116.

concern of the public. It was a private matter between two parties directly involved. Few buyers and apparently fewer sellers were disturbed by the absence of financial statements.

The accepted method of marketing new industrial securities also placed little pressure upon management for greater financial disclosure. During the nineteenth century investors bought securities primarily on the basis of their confidence in the promoter or the investment banker offering the issue. In particular, investment bankers, it was widely believed, undertook searching investigations of all securities before they were offered to the public, only offered securities of "investment quality," and "practically guaranteed the security."[17] Consequently, prospectuses offering new industrial securities seldom ran more than two pages and contained sketchy financial data. The first test of a security was the reliability of the investment bankers involved, not the financial conditions of the issuing company. Since such bankers usually sold securities in large blocs to a few selected, well-known buyers, reputable, strong firms like J. P. Morgan & Co. continually strove to merit their reputation. Under these conditions, as long as companies paid their dividends, investors rarely needed, or demanded, financial statements.

Finally, the absence of a strong accounting profession and an established body of accounting theory in America contributed to the inadequacy of management's financial reports. Not only was there nondisclosure, but when information was released it was of dubious value since different companies used different accounting concepts to measure and report similar transactions. For instance, the concept of depreciation was little understood. A number of firms never made provisions for depreciation. Some related depreciation expense to changes in appraised asset values.[18] There were also several other areas where accounting practice was far from standardized and the use of alternative accounting practices created confusion—including the treatment of unusual charges and credits, the valuation of assets, and the consolidation of subsidiaries.

These accounting vagaries existed partly because little attention had been given in the United States to the logic of accounting.[19] Prior to 1900,

[17] See, for example, Edward S. Meade, "Lecture III—Initial Stages of Organization," *Corporation Finance* ("*Business 25*"): *Official Report of the Lectures in Full in 1908–09, Graduate School of Business Administration, Harvard University* (Mimeographed, Boston, 1908), pp. 46 ff. Later, in the same lecture series, George O. May, a prominent public accountant, cast some doubt on the thoroughness of these investigations. He said: "I have had personal familiarity with [securities] which were accepted by bankers and by them offered to the public without adequate investigation and on a basis which was essentially unsound. . . ." "Lecture VIII—Flotation," *ibid.*, p. 118. These lectures are deposited in the Archives of the Harvard Graduate School of Business Administration, Boston, Mass.

[18] George O. May, *Financial Accounting* (New York, 1943), pp. 118 ff.

[19] See, for example, Roy J. Sampson, "American Accounting Education, Textbooks, and Public Practice Prior to 1900," *Business History Review*, Vol. XXXIV (Winter, 1960), pp. 446 ff.

nearly all of the American textbooks pertaining to the subject were concerned principally with the rules of bookkeeping. Since colonial times, accounting education had been the preserve of those who taught such elementary subjects as commercial arithmetic, penmanship, and business letter writing. This condition existed principally because accounting generally was not considered a fit subject for university curricula; there was no strong professional body of accountants to improve the level of training (or to keep out the many charlatans who posed as public accountants); and businessmen neglected the subject.

In addition, the function of public accountants and their reports was misunderstood. For a company to call in independent auditors to examine its books was often taken by the public as an indication of suspected fraud, irregularity, losses, and doubt regarding the reporting company's financial strength. Some managers regarded such action as a reflection on their integrity. Even as late as 1900, many businessmen were still "reluctant to call in an accountant and many investigations by public accountants were made secretly, often at night and on Sundays."[20] Consequently, it is not surprising that an English chartered accountant wrote of American practice before 1905: "the profession of accounting has hitherto been little understood in America."[21] The accountant in the United States was "little known, little recognized, little wanted,"[22] most accountants neither could nor desired to modify management's desire for corporate secrecy.

TOWARD THE SECURITIES ACTS AND IMPROVED DISCLOSURE, 1900–1933

The emergence of big business and the sudden expansion of the number of investors in manufacturing concerns led to a demand for fuller and more reliable corporate financial disclosure. In response, management improved somewhat its financial reporting practices, but not enough to satisfy the proposed standards articulated by both its friends and its critics.

After 1900, the industrial sector of the American economy no longer approximated the laissez-faire economic model of the earlier period. Out of the combination and merger movement of the late nineteenth century had come a number of large publicly owned manufacturing companies. Management and ownership of firms gradually ceased to be identical. As the years passed, particularly during the 1920's, this process of transforming previously closely held private companies into publicly owned corporations continued. The number of stockholders in the United States increased from

[20] Robert H. Montgomery, "What Have We Done and How?," *The American Institute of Accountants [1887–1937] Fiftieth Anniversary Celebration, 1937* (New York, 1938), p. 80.
[21] Richard Brown (ed.), *A History of Accounting and Accountants* (Edinburgh, 1905), p. 278.
[22] Montgomery, *op. cit.*, p. 80.

some 500,000 in 1900, to about 2,000,000 in 1920, and then to an estimated 10,000,000 by 1930. Big business kept getting bigger. The affairs of these publicly owned corporations, unlike their single-owner predecessors, it was increasingly said, should be carried on without detriment to the public interest:[23] manufacturing corporations were becoming even more vested with a "public interest" than yet spelled out in nascent antitrust legislation.

The Critics of Big Business

Almost as soon as businesses became big, a number of people became disturbed by their growth in power and critical of their practices. It was argued by many, for instance, that the large combinations should be dissolved since the very existence of these new and powerful industrial groups threatened the fundamental civil liberties and morality of American society.[24] Also, it was believed, the rise of big business rendered the rule of *caveat emptor*, which was based on the assumption that both the seller and buyer were of equal strength and capable of knowing all the facts surrounding any transaction, incongruous with the times. The fact of the matter was that the giant corporations and their puny individual employees, customers, small businessmen, and investors were not of equal strength. Since businessmen had abused their great power, it was argued by many outside the management class, the commercial doctrine of *caveat emptor* was no longer acceptable.[25] Therefore, by implication, the doctrine's corollary of corporate secrecy was no longer appropriate.

One of the most popular remedies suggested to rectify this imbalance of power and to end the predatory methods of large corporations was improved corporate financial publicity. For example, in 1900, the Industrial Commission recommended to Congress:[26]

> The larger corporations—the so-called trusts—should be required to publish annually a properly audited report, showing in reasonable detail their assets and liabilities, with profit or loss; such report and audit under oath to be subject to Government inspection. The purpose of such publicity

[23] *Preliminary Report of the Industrial Commission*, p. 5.

[24] J. D. Glover, *The Attack on Big Business* (Boston, 1954), pp. 103 ff.

[25] Louis D. Brandeis, *Other People's Money and How the Bankers Use It* (New York, 1914), p. 103.

[26] *Preliminary Report of the Industrial Commission*, p. 6. The *Final Report of the Industrial Commission* issued in 1902 repeats the above recommendations. In addition, it also contains a "supplementary statement" by Thomas W. Phillips, a Commission member. Mr. Phillips wanted the Commission to amplify its recommendations in the area of corporate publicity to provide for a government official to whom all corporations would submit audited annual reports containing a specified list of points on which data were to be provided. In addition, Phillips proposed this official be given a staff of examiners who would at irregular periods and without notice appear at the offices of each corporation to examine, verify, and report upon its books. The reports of the examiners were to be made public. *Final Report of the Industrial Commission* (Washington, 1902), pp. 669–73.

is to encourage competition when profits become excessive, thus protecting consumers against too high prices and to guard the interests of employees by a knowledge of the financial condition of the business in which they are employed.

The increasing number of investors, it was thought, would also be protected by improved corporate publicity. While "little correlation between the issuance of informative reports and willingness on the part of investors to buy stock" was noted,[27] public opinion nevertheless was appalled by the stock market manipulations of many managements and promoters who sought to enrich themselves at the expense of their stockholders. According to one contemporary observer:[28]

> The suppression and misstatement of facts by corporations have in recent years misled investors as well as speculators to buy shares in concerns financially unsound and on the verge of bankruptcy. To prevent the "watering" of stock or to find some method of furnishing investors a basis of judging the condition of companies has absorbed the attention of the "public mind" for some time. "Secrecy" was said to be the evil; nor is it to be wondered at that "publicity" was the remedy suggested. No one word has been more frequently upon the lips of the American public in the last three years [1900–1903] than "publicity."

These pre-World War I demands for fuller financial disclosure, both by the critics of big business and the public, were generally ignored by management. Few companies, for instance, followed United States Steel Corporation's declared policy of presenting full and definite financial information,[29] which first found expression in the thirty-five pages of financial data contained in the company's annual report of 1902. In contrast, most managements did not seem to care about public opinion. They disregarded it.[30] In fact, some companies which had previously published

[27] Sears, op. cit., p. 421.

[28] Horack, Organization and Control of Industrial Corporations, p. 80.

[29] Preliminary Report to Stockholders of United States Steel Corporation to be Submitted at the First Annual Meeting . . . January 10, 1902 [Hoboken, N. J., 1902]. Commenting on this report, the Commercial and Financial Chronicle stated: ". . . we wish to call attention . . . to a single feature that ought to be an example for every industrial company in the land . . . What we wish to emphasize is the impression a reading of the report will, we believe, have upon every unprejudiced mind; which is that the United States Steel Corporation has nothing to conceal. Each stockholder obviously is told everything the management knows about the investor's property. . . . This open, honest way of treating the public . . . must tend to put [this company's] . . . securities . . . in a far safer class for investment than those of so many other industrial companies which adopt a more secretive policy." (February 1, 1902), p. 230. A modern review of this balance sheet expresses a somewhat different view: "When United States Steel Corporation was organzied in 1902 it showed no goodwill or other intangibles in its balance sheet. Thus all its capitialzation was ostensibly covered by its property account and working capital. Many years later, it was revealed that no less than $769 million of the plant account was a written-up item, popularly known as 'water.'" Benjamin Graham, David L. Dodd, and Sideney Cottle, Security Analysis (4th ed., New York, 1962), p. 213.

[30] Preliminary Report of the Industrial Commission, p. 296.

financial statements quit issuing financial reports altogether. For instance, in 1901, George Westinghouse, president of Westinghouse Electric and Manufacturing, said:[31]

> ... if some should be surprised that more complete statements have not been previously submitted to them, it can only be said that the Directors as well as the stockholders who own the largest amounts of stock, have believed that in view of the existing keen competition and the general attitude toward industrial enterprises, the interests of all would be served by avoiding, to as great an extent as possible, giving undue publicity to the affairs of the Company.

While the pioneer critics of big business had little direct impact on management, they greatly influenced, nevertheless, those who later played important roles in increasing the federal government's control over business affairs. For instance, before World War I, among early advocates of greater publicity of corporate affairs, few became more widely read and respected than the future Associate Justice of the Supreme Court, Louis D. Brandeis. In 1913, Brandeis who has been described "as the man who left the greatest mark on the philosophy of federal securities regulation in this country," said, "Publicity is justly commended as a remedy for social and industrial diseases. Sunlight is said to be the best of disinfectants; electric light the most efficient policemen."[32] Later in 1933, "it was Mr. Frankfurther—surrogate for Justice Brandeis—in his visits [with Franklin Delano Roosevelt] who argued . . . for this approach to business regulation."[33]

Following World War I, and until the economic and stock market disasters of 1929, there was a shift in the American political, social, economic, and ethical climate. The nation became more prosperous and the public grew weary and disillusioned with the crusades of the preceding progressive era. Businessmen were regarded with a new respect. The public, instead of disapproving, now looked upon the large-scale efforts to rig the securities market by such market operators as Harry F. Sinclair, Percy A. Rockefeller, and Bernard E. Smith with "breathless admiration,"[34] according to that master of the striking phrase, J. K. Galbraith.

Consequently, during the period 1918–1929, the public appeal of the critics of business waned but did not disappear. The critics of big business themselves, however, spurred on by their concern for the protection of the ownership rights of the rapidly increasing number of investors,[35] continued

[31] *Report of the Board of Directors of the Westinghouse Electric and Manufacturing Co. to the Stockholders, Special Meeting, February 20th,* 1901 [Pittsburgh, 1901], p. 1.
[32] Louis Loss, *Securities Regulation* (Boston, 1951), p. 123; Brandeis, *Other People's Money*, p. 93.
[33] Rexford G. Tugwell, "The Progressive Orthodoxy of Franklin D. Roosevelt," *Ethics*, Vol. LXIV (Oct., 1953), p. 16.
[34] John K. Galbraith, *The Great Crash, 1929* (Boston, 1955), p. 161.
[35] William Z. Ripley, *Main Street and Wall Street* (Boston, 1925), pp. vi-vii.

to put forth their pleas for improved corporate publicity. In 1926, for instance, Professor William Z. Ripley of Harvard University created "quite a flutter in financial centers,"[36] when he proclaimed: "let the word go forth that the Federal Trade Commission is henceforth to address itself vigorously to the matter of adequate and intelligent corporate publicity, and taken in conjunction with the helpful agencies at work the thing is as good as done."[37] Ripley was particularly disturbed by the "enigmatic" accounting practices which made possible financial "obfuscation" and "malfeasance." Another who spoke in the same vein was the young Adolph Berle, Jr., who, as part of his notion of the "social corporation," demanded as an expression of the public responsibility of management fuller disclosure of corporate affairs, particularly to investors.[38]

As with that of their predecessors, the immediate impact of such critics as Ripley was "almost nil,"[39] but, after 1930, when the nation lay in economic disorder, businessmen were more easily discredited. The public once again became sympathetic to the opinions of those critical of business and finance, and it was the critics' standards—not those of management— by which managers were finally judged. Much of the credit for the Securities Act and the later developments in the area of corporate financial publicity must be given to these critics of big business.[40]

Between 1900 and 1933, others more closely allied wtih management sought to raise the level of financial reporting, including the New York Stock Exchange, the Investment Bankers Association of America, and the public accounting profession. Of these private groups, the New York Stock Exchange was perhaps the "leading influence in the promotion of adequate corporate disclosure the world over."[41] The Exchange's direct influence, however, was limited to companies listed on the Exchange. The influence of the Investment Bankers Association and the public accounting profession was severely curtailed by the unwillingness of much of their membership to act independently of management.

The New York Stock Exchange

As early as 1869 the New York Stock Exchange's Committee on Stock List adopted a policy that companies should agree that once listed

---

[36] "Desirability of Publicity," *Journal of Accountancy*, Vol. XLIV (December, 1927), pp. 441–43.

[37] William Z. Ripley, "Stop, Look, Listen!" *Atlantic Monthly*, Vol. 138 (September, 1926), p. 380.

[38] Adolph A. Berle, Jr. and Gardiner C. Means, *The Modern Corporation and Private Property* (New York, 1933), pp. 317 ff.

[39] "Desirability of Publicity," pp. 441–43.

[40] Glover, *op. cit.*, pp. 304–305.

[41] Ripley, *Main Street and Wall Street*, p. 210.

on the Exchange they would publish some from of an annual financial report. Few companies, however, agreed to observe this stipulation. In fact, it was not until the Kansas City (Mo.) Gas Company listing agreement of 1897 that the Exchange extracted from a listed company a substantive promise to observe some minimum reporting requirements.[42] Nevertheless, from 1910 onward, the Exchange influenced improvements in financial reporting practices of listed companies.

Before 1900, so reluctant was the Exchange to enforce its reporting requirement upon industrial management that, in 1885, it created the so-called Unlisted Department. This department sought to grasp business then going to outside street markets where fewer restrictions were placed upon issuers. The companies whose stocks were noted by the Unlisted Department (mainly industrials) were not required to furnish the Exchange with financial information relevant to the issue. Nevertheless, these shares were traded with regularly listed securities, unlisted stocks being distinguished on quotation sheets only by an asterisk. In this manner "such active stocks as those of Amalgamated Copper and the American Sugar Refining Companies were dealt in on the exchange for many years without the public having any information regarding their affairs. . . . They were in effect conducted and maintained as 'blind pool.' Those in control were then enabled to use their information for speculative purposes."[43]

Subsequently, in 1910, under growing threats of government regulation, the New York Stock Exchange abolished its Unlisted Department. Thereafter, over the next twenty years, the Exchange's Committee on Stock List actively sought to improve the reporting practices of listed companies, particularly with respect to the frequency with which they published financial statements. For example, in 1916, General Motors Company agreed to publish semi-annually a consolidated income statement and balance sheet. In 1924, Inland Steel Company modified its original listing agreement and agreed to issue a public statement of quarterly earnings.

Two years later, the Exchange officially recommended the publication of quarterly reports by all listed companies.[44] Also, by this time, nearly all listed manufacturing companies had adopted the practice of issuing

[42] Shultz, *op. cit.*, p. 17.

[43] "Report of the Committee Appointed Pursuant to House Resolutions 429 and 504 to Investigate the Concentration of Control of Money and Credit," *House Reports*, 62 Cong., 3 Sess., No. 1593, p. 37.

[44] At the time this announcement was made a census showed that of the 957 companies listed on the exchange 242 were already making quarterly reports, 79 were reporting semiannually, 339 issued annual statements, and 297 companies had no agreements with the exchange respecting the issuance of such statements. Many of this last group were transportation companies which were subject to the reporting requirements of the Interstate Commerce Commission, and utility companies which were under the author ty (as to publicity) of the various state public servcie commissions. Ripley, *Main Street and Wall Street*, p. 187.

annual reports covered by an independent auditor's opinion certificate,[45] a practice made mandatory by the Exchange in 1933. Such progress was not easy, however, since as late as 1931 many an executive of a listed company held the Exchange's suggested publicity requirements to be "arbitrary and unreasonable."[46]

Unfortunately, there were limitations to the New York Stock Exchange's influence. The Exchange's control was restricted only to those corporations which sought to list securities. The securities handled on the over-the-counter markets and the securities listed on the "provincial exchanges"—Chicago, Boston, Pittsburgh—were not only beyond the New York Stock Exchange's control, but were also subject to less rigorous requirements so as to attract "local lesser corporations, more closely controlled and less susceptible to educational appeal"[47]—yet these were the very corporations where the most need for improved financial reporting existed.

The Investment Bankers Association of America

Between 1920 and 1927, the Investment Bankers Association of America on several occasions sought, through voluntary action of its membership, "to standardize the information regarding industrial securities" presented to the public, particularly that in prospectuses. The initial impetus for these reform efforts grew out of a desire on the part of some Association members to protect investors; to protect legitimate investment bankers from the growing public resentment against the sellers of fraudulent securities; and to forestall federal and state governmental regulation of securities.[48] Already, by 1920, some twenty states, alarmed by the prevalence of fraudulent stock promotions, had passed so-called blue-sky laws,[49] and on the federal level, securities bills had been placed before Congress by Representatives Edward T. Taylor, Andrew J. Volstead, and Edward E. Denison in 1918, 1919, and 1921, respectively.[50]

On at least six occasions[51] the Investment Bankers Association issued

---

[45] George O. May, "Corporate Publicity and the Auditor," *Journal of Accountancy*, Vol. XLII (November, 1926), p. 322.

[46] Richard Whtiney, "Business Honesty, Address Delivered . . . before the Philadelphia Chamber of Commerce . . . April 24, 1931" [New York, 1931], p. 9.

[47] Ripley, *Main Street and Wall Street*, p. 213.

[48] "Report of Industrial Securities Committee," *Proceedings of the Ninth Annual Convention of the Investment Bankers Association of America* (Chicago, 1920), pp. 153 ff.

[49] Jacob M. Edelman, *Security Regulation in the 48 States* (Chicago, 1942), p. 4.

[50] H. R. 188, 66 Cong., 1 Sess. (1918); H. R. 12603, 66 Cong., 2 Sess. (1919); H. R. 7215, 67 Cong., 1 Sess. (1921).

[51] See, for example, the following subcommittee reports presented in the respective *Proceedings of the . . . Annual Convention of the Investment Bankers Association:* "Report of Industrial Securities Committee," 1920; "Report of the Business Practice Committee," 1923; "Report of the Committee on Real Estate Securities," 1923; "Report of the Special Committee on Circulars," 1925; "Report of Public Service Securities Committee," 1926; and "Report of Industrial Securities Committee," 1927.

reports setting forth recommended minimum standards for financial disclosure in prospectuses. In general, these reports, three of which were related to industrial companies, called for an "adequate" and "understandable" balance sheet with some comments on such items as inventory, working capital, and depreciation policy, as well as a presentation of earnings by years.[52] In the case of holding companies, it was suggested that investors be provided with a consolidated balance sheet, a consolidated statement of earnings, and an income statement for the holding company. The Association also suggested, in the case of holding companies, that there should be readily available through annual reports and other media the following information: the securities of the subsidiary companies owned by the holding company and those owned by the public; and statements for each subsidiary company giving earnings, expenses, maintenence expenditures and reserves, fixed charges, dividends, assets, capitalization, and other liabilities.[53] In short, the spokesman for the Association said, "the banker's responsibility to the investing public rendered it essential that the public be given the same information used by the banker in assuring himself of the integrity of the company and that dictated the structure of the issue."[54]

Few of these recommendations were ever followed in practice by investment bankers or their corporate clients. The reasons for the failure of the Association's voluntary reform program were many. A number of members of the Association were "indifferent"[55] or displayed a "lack of knowledge"[56] with respect to these recommendations. Also, one banker complained that among those companies that issued securities "some of the best companies object to furnishing full information to go beyond the eyes of their [investment] bankers."[57]

In addition, a number of investment bankers still preferred to follow the nineteenth-century practice of selling securities on the basis of the investment banker's reputation alone, rather than on the merits of the issue and issuer. As late as 1923, "confidence," one investment banker said, "[was] the bulwark in the relationship between the dealer and the client."[58] Earlier, in 1918, another investment banker had stated, "the questions of brick and mortar and turnover and rate of profit and all the other fine points . . . [were] secondary considerations."[59] Other investment bankers relied upon the nineteenth-century "custom" of nondisclosure to justify the hiding of weakness in the dubious securities they offered.[60]

[52] "Report of the Special Committee on Circulars," 1925, p. 272.
[53] "Report of the Business Practice Committee," 1929, p. 294.
[54] "Report of Industrial Securities Committee," 1920, p. 153.
[55] "Report of Committee on Ethics and Business Practice," 1924, pp. 210–11.
[56] "Report of Real Estate Securities Committee," 1926, p. 248.
[57] "Report of Industrial Securities Committee," 1920, p. 166.
[58] "Report of the Publicity Committee," 1923, p. 302.
[59] "Report of Industrial Securities Committee," 1918, p. 96.
[60] See, for example, "Stock Exchange Practices," *Senate Reports*, 73 Cong., 2 Sess., No. 1455, pp. 100 ff.

Clearly, such attitudes as these were hardly likely to lead to universal voluntary acceptance among investment bankers of the Association's suggestions regarding financial disclosure. Some investment bankers, it would seem, were just as desirous as their corporate clients to foster financial secrecy.

The Accounting Profession

During the years 1900–1933, with the growing dependence of business on outside sources of capital, with the introduction of the income tax law in 1913, and with the passage of the excess profits tax in 1917, the accounting profession became an essential part of American business life. Credit-granters came to depend upon financial statements as the basis for credit decisions, and complete and accurate accounting records became necessary for income tax purposes.[61]

As a result, the public accounting profession expanded and accounting instruction was increasingly included in college curricula. In addition, in 1917 and 1930, the profession through its principal society—the American Institute of Accountants—undertook two important programs to improve corporate disclosure practices. The first was in conjunction with the Federal Trade Commission and the Federal Reserve Board; the second with the New York Stock Exchange.

Throughout most of this thirty-three-year period the primary force among accountants for improved corporate financial disclosure came from three sources: educators, individual practitioners, and the American Institute of Accountants. Around 1900, because of a growing recognition of the importance of business in American life, universities added to their curricula business courses which included accounting as a primary subject. Accounting no longer was the concern of petty teachers. University prefessors such as William Morse Cole of Harvard University, and later Henry Rand Hatfield of the University of California, W. A. Paton of the University of Michigan, and A. C. Littleton of the University of Illinois, began to probe behind accounting practice and explore its logic. The first university department of accounting, as such, was established by New York University in 1900. For the first time in the United States, accounting education was rising above the level of bookkeeping, and an ideology for accounting technology was slowly developed.

Among businessmen, perhaps a more influential group were the leading

---

[61] The introduction of corporate income taxes not only spurred businessmen to keep better accounting records and take a more active interest in financial accounting, but also led directly to the adoption of certain valuation practices for corporate accounting. For instance, the acceptance of the "last in first out" method of valuing inventory for tax purposes resulted directly in its widespread adoption in industrial financial reports.

practitioners of the accounting profession. Such men as George O. May and A. Lowes Dickinson of Price Waterhouse & Co., and Robert H. Montgomery of Lybrand, Ross Bros. & Montgomery, through their day-to-day contacts—literary and personal—with other accountants and business-men sought to raise the level of industrial financial disclosure and hasten the adoption of sounder accounting practices. In general, these men, whose early training had been in England, believed that the disclosure standards included in the English Company Acts should be adopted by American businessmen. Later, the framers of the Securities Acts exhibited a similar belief when they based the "disclosure philosophy" underlying the Securities Act of 1933 on the existing English Company Law.[62]

The genesis of the American Institute of Accountants, and its work to raise the standards of the American accounting profession can be traced back to similar earlier attempts in Great Britain before 1880. In Great Britain a vital and influential accounting profession had existed since about 1850. Beginning in the 1880's a number of these British chartered accoun-tants went to the United States, principally to audit the various British investments there. To these transplanted Britishers the first steps necessary to improve the stature of accounting in the United States appeared to be the establishment of a nationwide society of accountants, along the lines of the Institute of Chartered Accountants in England and Wales.[63]

Accordingly, the first organized body of professional accountants in the United States was formed in New York in 1886.[64] Soon after, other state and national accounting bodies were founded. Subsequently, in 1905, the contending national organizations were united to form one principal organization: the American Association of Public Accountants. Sometime later, in 1916, the association was reorganized as the American Institute of Accountants.

From 1886 onward, the American Institute of Accountants and its predecessor organizations worked along with the various state societies, to police better the standards of admission to accounting practice, to improve accounting education, and to promote Certified Public Accounting legisla-tion. So effective was the work of this organization that the accounting profession obtained national prominence in the United States by 1913.[65] It was, however, a profession without recognized standards. Audit practices varied greatly from firm to firm and there were many theories as to what constituted sound accounting.

---

[62] James M. Landis, "The Legislative History of the Securities Act of 1933," *George Washington Law Review*, Vol. XXVIII (October, 1959), p. 34.

[63] James T. Anyon, "Early Days of American Accountancy," *Journal of Accountancy*, Vol. XXXIX (January, 1925), p. 7.

[64] James D. Edwards, *History of Public Accounting in the United States* (East Lansing, 1960), p. 54.

[65] *Ibid.*, p. 101.

The first attempt of the Institute to set some auditing and reporting standards came in 1917 when it joined with the Federal Trade Commission and the Federal Reserve Board in publishing *Uniform Accounting*[66]—the most comprehensive and authoritative document related to corporate financial disclosure and balance-sheet audits yet published in the United States. Over the years, the Federal Trade Commission, in the course of its investigation of business conditions, had become disturbed over the lack of uniformity in balance-sheet audits and financial reports. As the first step toward standardization of practices relating to the compiling and verifying of corporate reports, the Commission requested the Institute to prepare a memorandum on balance-sheet audits.

The Institute's memorandum was eventually prepared by a committee under George O. May's direction, approved by the Federal Trade Commission, and given "tentative endorsement" by the Federal Reserve Board. This tentative document was then submitted to bankers throughout the country for their consideration and criticism. Later in 1917, the final draft[67] of *Uniform Accounting* was published by the Federal Reserve Board. In 1918, it was reissued under the name, *Approved Methods for the Preparation of Balance Sheet Statements.*[68] Subsequently, in 1929, it was revised by the Institute for the Federal Reserve Board, republished, and renamed, *Verification of Financial Statements.*[69]

Uniform Accounting and its later versions were widely distributed in accounting, financial, and commercial circles by the Federal Reserve Board—the main interest of the Board being to improve the quality of the financial statements submitted along with applications for bank credit. The bulk of this document related to balance-sheet audits. Its last three pages, however, presented suggested forms for comparative income statements and balance sheets. The model income statement provided for some twenty-nine income and expense items. The asset side of the proposed balance sheet called for details under the following headings: cash, notes and accounts receivable (less provision for bad debts), inventories, other quick assets, securities, fixed assets (less reserves for depreciation), deferred charges, and other assets. The liability side of the balance sheet indicated detailed information should be presented under these headings: unsecured bills and notes, unsecured accounts, secured liabilities, other current liabilities, fixed liabilities, and net worth.

Despite their prestigious backers, the recommendations outlined in *Uniform Accounting* were not quickly adopted by corporations, bankers, or the accounting profession—chiefly, because bankers, out of a fear of driving

---

[66] *Federal Reserve Bulletin*, Vol. III (April, 1917), pp. 270–84.

[67] Federal Reserve Board, *Uniform Accounting* (Washington, 1917).

[68] Federal Reserve Board, *Approved Methods for the Preparation of Balance-Sheet Statements* (Washington, 1918).

[69] Federal Reserve Board, *Verification of Financial Statements* (Washington, 1929).

away customers, refrained from insisting upon audited statements from their clients.[70] Nevertheless, progress was made over the years and by 1928 A. P. Richardson, the editor of *The Journal of Accountancy*, could report that bankers had been "induced" at last to adopt a sterner attitude which resulted in "many improvements in the manner and method of preparing statements to be used as the basis of applications for credit."[71]

Except for the recommendations pertaining to inventories and disclosure of asset values, few of these "improvements" referred to by Richardson ever found their way into public reports. Businessmen in general believed that the standard form of financial statements outlined in the Federal Reserve Board's publication called for too much information and would be used to their detriment by competitors.[72]

Encouraged by the publication of *Uniform Accounting*, the Institute directed its main educational efforts for the next nine years toward encouraging businessmen to use balance-sheet audits for credit purposes. By 1926, George O. May declared to the accounting profession that, among prominent industrial companies, the practice of having audits "had become almost universal." Now, he said, the time had come for the Institute to assume a larger responsibility and "render a higher service to the community." The new goal he proposed for the profession was the adoption by industrial corporations of the financial disclosure standards embodied in the English Companies Acts. To achieve this end, he suggested that the Institute cooperate with "such bodies as the leading stock exchange, the investment bankers and the commercial banks which grant credit." It was impractical, May believed, to consider bringing about improved corporate disclosure in the United States through direct legislation,[73] such as had happened in England.

During the next four years, the Institute undertook two cooperative efforts along the lines suggested by May. The first undertaking with the Investment Bankers Association of America in 1928 produced little. In 1930, with the long-standing urging of J. M. B. Hoxsey, the executive assistant on stock list of the New York Stock Exchange, and May reinforced by the effects of the market crash of 1929, the Institute appointed a committee to cooperate with the Exchange, "in consideration of all problems which are of common interest to investors, exchanges and accountants."[74]

Hoxsey's concern was principally for the protection of investors, of

---

[70] William B. Flowers, *Criteria for Disclosure of Post-Statement Events* (Austin, 1960), p. 10; "Value of Audited Statements," *Journal of Accountancy*, Vol. XXVIII (December, 1919), p. 454.

[71] "Cooperation with Bankers," *Journal of Accountancy*, Vol. XLVI (October, 1928), p. 286.

[72] Flowers, *op. cit.*, pp. 10–11; William B. Campbell, "Cooperation between Accountants and Bankers," *Journal of Accountancy*, Vol. XLV (January, 1928), p. 12.

[73] May, "Corporate Publicity and the Auditor," pp. 322–23.

[74] "Cooperation between Accountants and Stock Exchanges," *Journal of Accountancy*, Vol. L (October, 1930), p. 242.

whom there were some 10,000,000 in 1930.[75] "Accounting," Hoxsey told the Institute, "is a matter of convention but it is questionable whether these conventions have kepts pace with the changes in modern business conditions."[76] To date accounting had evolved, he noted, with primary emphasis on two objects: (1) to supply management with accurate information essential for the conduct of business; and (2) to provide prospective creditors with accurate information essential to the determination of credit capacity. However, he declared, the increasingly widespread ownership of corporations and the need of investors to determine the value of their investments had created a new need for "sound accounting practices" and understandable financial statements.

At Hoxsey's suggestion, the American Institute appointed a Special Committee on Cooperation with Stock Exchanges, with George O. May as chairman, to work with the New York Stock Exchange to explore the issues raised by Hoxsey. This undertaking was a significant development as it represented a change in outlook by the accounting profession. *Uniform Accounting* had been prepared with an institution concerned with the quality of credit and the recommendations contained therein made with the credit granter in mind; the new undertaking was with the New York Stock Exchange and the accounting problems were to be considered from the standpoint of those who traded in securities—that is, investors.[77]

The first results of this cooperative effort were expressed in a letter, dated January 12, 1932, from the Stock List Committee to all listed companies. The Exchange's "general attitude" was made clear on several features of annual reports: audit certificates, capital stock, surplus, treasury stock, changes in the basis of valuation of important assets, changes in depreciation policy, other income, and disclosure of accounting for foreign subsidiaries. The substance of the Exchange's proposal was that greater disclosure be made on these topics. Subsequently, Richard Whitney, the president of the Exchange, followed this letter by urging a number of the listed corporations to issue quarterly financial statements in the comparative form.

Of Whitney's actions and the need for such reforms, the editor of *The Journal of Accountancy* stated:[78]

> . . . the stock exchange is encouraging increasing candor on the part of its listed corporations. There must be a wide departure from past practice in order to meet the just demands of the investing public. . . . The public now demands information and everything which can bring about more compre-

[75] Alfred L. Bernheim and Margaret G. Schneider (eds.), *The Security Markets* (New York, 1935).

[76] J. M. B. Hoxsey, "Accounting for Investors," *Journal of Accountancy*, Vol. L (October, 1930), p. 251.

[77] May, *Financial Accounting*, pp. 43–44.

[78] "Stock Exchange Calls for Comparative Statements," *Journal of Accountancy*, Vol. LIII (February, 1932), p. 83.

hensive statements should receive hearty support. . . . American custom has a little reformation to undertake—and there is evidence that it will be undertaken.

On September 22, 1932, the Institute's special committee submitted its report to the Exchange's Committee on Stock List. The report, which was published in 1933 under the title *Audits of Corporate Accounts*, listed four principal objectives the Committee thought the Exchange should "keep constantly in mind and do its best to gradually achieve." These goals were: to bring about a better recognition by the public that balance sheets did not show present values of the assets and liabilities of corporations; to encourage the adoption of balance sheets which more clearly showed on what basis assets were valued; to emphasize the cardinal importance of the income account; and to make universal the usage by listed corporations of certain broad principles of accounting which had won fairly general acceptance. On this last point the report warned the Exchange against attempting "to restrict the right of corporations to select detailed methods of accounting deemed by them to be best adapted to the requirements of their business."[79] In addition, the report suggested each listed corporation should submit to the Exchange a clear and detailed statement of the accounting principles it observed when compiling financial statements.

This document, which was the most specific statement yet formulated on just how financial reports could be made more informative and reliable, was given "warm" approval by the Controllers Institute and the Investment Bankers Association.[80] Taking a lead from the report's recommendations, on January 6, 1933, the Exchange announced henceforth corporations seeking listing must submit financial statements audited by independent public accountants and agree to have all future reports to stockholders similarly inspected. In addition, the scope of the audit was to be no less than that indicated in *Verification of Financial Statements*.[81]

The accountant read Whitney's announcement with "a feeling of hearty gratification." Richardson, the editor of *The Journal of Accountancy*, who had campaigned long and hard for such a listing requirement, hailed the announcement as probably the "most important forward step in the history of accounting within recent years."[82]

Such joy was short lived. Within six months the envisioned role of the Committee on Stock Lists and that of the Institute's special committee in effect passed to a federal agency—first to the Federal Trade Commission and

[79] "Report of the Special Committee on Cooperation with Stock Exchanges of the American Institute of Accountants to the Committee on Stock Lists of the New York Stock Exchange, September 22, 1932," quoted in May, *Financial Accounting*, pp. 72–80.

[80] May, *Financial Accounting*, p. 57.

[81] Announcement of Richard Whitney, January 6, 1933, as reproduced in: "Stock Exchange Demands Audit of Listed Companies," *Journal of Accountancy*, Vol. LIV (February, 1933), pp. 81–82.

[82] *Ibid.*, p. 82.

then to the Securities and Exchange Commission. In 1934, many accountants, including George O. May, believed that the profession might in the future "all too easily, find itself merely the ciphering agency for vitally unreviewable bureaucrats."[83] As yet, such has not been the case.

Management and Financial Disclosure

Between 1900 and 1933, the financial disclosure practices of industrial corporations improved somewhat. Nevertheless, despite such exceptions as United States Steel Corporation, Bethlehem Steel Corporation, and General Motors Company, the financial reporting practices lagged far behind the recommendations for greater and more useful corporate financial disclosure made by critics of big business, by the New York Stock Exchange, by the Investment Bankers Association, and by the leaders of the accounting profession. Also, the numerous alternative accounting principles which had caused so much confusion during the late nineteenth century were still observed in practice.

As time passed, however, the statements of industrial corporations became more uniform as to the degree and form of disclosure.[84] By 1933, most publicly owned manufacturing corporations were publishing annual reports containing balance sheets at least as detailed as that of the American Tobacco Company shown in Table 3. Furthermore, in line with the shift of emphasis in common stock valuation techniques from the balance sheet to the income statement,[85] a sketchy income statement showing sales, several major expense items, and current profits was now usually included. Auditing by outside accountants was also becoming more common.

Yet some of the larger companies still refused to provide stockholders with written financial statements. For instance, it was the settled policy of the Singer Sewing Machine Company not to issue annual reports; information regarding the company's affairs being given verbally at the annual stockholders' meeting.[86] As late as 1927 the Royal Baking Powder Company had issued no financial statement whatsoever for over a quarter of a century.[87] In addition to the nonreporting companies, a number of large companies, such as American Woolen Company, California Packing Corporation, and National Tea Company, rendered their reports to the public well after the close of their fiscal year.[88]

[83] A. A. Berle, Jr., "Accounting and the Law," *Accounting Review*, Vol. XII (March, 1938), p. 15.

[84] Flowers, *op. cit.*, p. 11.

[85] Benjamin Graham and David L. Dodd, *Security Analysis* (3rd ed., New York, 1951), p. 391.

[86] Letter from Treasurer of Singer Sewing Machine Company, May 18, 1932. (Corporation Records Division, Baker Library, Harvard Graduate School of Business Administration, Boston, Mass).

[87] Ripley, "Stop, Look, Listen!," p. 385.

[88] McLaren, *Annual Reports*, p. 6.

There were two basic reasons for management's slow progress in improving corporate financial reporting. First, managers did not consider public reports a matter of prime importance.[89] Second, and more important, businessmen were still inclined toward financial secrecy, principally because of their fear of assisting competitors. With respect to the latter justification for nondisclosure, as early as 1900 one financial reporter had complained that this was "a familiar old argument, but it is becoming threadbare and ridiculous."[90] Nevertheless, as late as 1927, even William Z. Ripley was willing to concede that in those industries where competition narrowed down to two or three big competitors it took "a hardy perennial to stand the wind and weather of publicity alone." In other words, Ripley said, all too often, the "laggard corporation, persistent in secretiveness, lays a heavy penalty upon its progressive rivals all down the line."[91]

Financial chicanery and business custom were also responsible for corporate secrecy. Unfortunately, there were still a few industrial directors and officers who practiced financial secrecy so as to profit in their stock market activities through the use of corporate information not available to others.[92] While the motivation of management in such cases was clearly to deceive or mislead, in most instances of nondisclosure, it should be noted, corporate financial secrecy resulted primarily because it was "simply a custom that had been handed down from generation to generation to tell as little as possible."[93]

In addition, there were still few external restraints upon management's financial reporting practices. State corporation laws relating to corporate financial reports had not advanced much beyond the nineteenth-century stage. Federal law was still silent on industrial financial publicity as it was assumed this was a state matter. Also, after 1914, public opinion was "indifferent" to the attempts to improve the financial reports of industrial companies. In particular, investors, the very group the reformers sought to protect, were usually satisfied with generalities and did not request detailed financial statistics.[94]

Similarly, accounting practice placed few restrictions on industrial management. There was an inviting variety of alternatives approved by

[89] Ripley, *Main Street and Wall Street*, p. 211.

[90] "It Makes One Suspicious," *United States Investor*, Vol. XI (June 30, 1900), p. 827.

[91] Ripley, *Main Street and Wall Street*, pp. 208–209.

[92] "Stock Exchange Practices," pp. 55 ff.

[93] U. S. Congress, Interstate and Foreign Commerce Committee, House of Representatives, "Stock Exchange Regulation, Hearing, 73d Congress, 2d Session, on H. R. 7852 ... and ... H. R. 8720 ..." (Washington, 1934), p. 49.

[94] Berle and Means, *Modern Corporation*, p. 318; *Commercial and Financial Chronicle* (September 4, 1926), pp. 1200–1201; *Statement by Richard Whitney, President of the New York Stock Exchange made to the Governing Committee and the Membership in regard to the investigations of stock exchange practices by the Committee on Banking and Currency of the United States Senate, August 24, 1932* [New York, 1932], p. 31; Clinton Collver, *Industrial Securities* (New York, 1921), p. 85.

accountants and employed by businessmen. For example, there still were many different theories of depreciation. No consensus of opinion yet existed as to the degree of ownership which warranted consolidation. Frequently, no distinction was made between operating income and other income.[95] And a variety of methods pertaining to the recording of asset values persisted.[96] Such accounting freedom unfortunately tempted a number of managements to inflate reported profits through questionable adjustments to surplus and profits. These adjustments were seldom revealed to the public.[97]

Finally, the reformers were powerless to force their proposed financial reporting standards upon industrial management. Businessmen, in the absence of regulatory restraints, held the balance of power vis-à-vis the would-be reformers. Between 1914 and 1930, for instance, critics of big business lacked the necessary public support to have their ideas translated into legislation. The efforts of the Investment Bankers Association were thwarted by its own membership and the accounting profession was not yet willing to be truly independent.[98] Even the New York Stock Exchange was unable to enforce its authority upon recalcitrant listed companies. According to Richard Whitney, the exchange was hesitant to strike a stock from the list because it "imposes a tremendous penalty upon the stockholders who are innocent of wrongdoing but does not necessarily punish the officers and directors who are really at fault."[99]

Thus, as late as the 1920's, industrial management could ignore with impunity the demands for improved financial disclosure. The economic depression of 1930, the subsequent shift in the public's attitude toward business, the election of Franklin D. Roosevelt as president in 1932, and the passage of the Securities Acts in 1933–1934, brought this situation to an end. Henceforth, for most publicly owned industrial companies, the Securities and Exchange Commission became the final arbiter in matters of financial disclosure; not management.

THE SECURITIES ACT AND ITS AFTERMATH

After 1933, the federal government, through the newly created Securities and Exchange Commission, played a larger role in encouraging fuller, more reliable, and more comparable financial disclosure on the part of industrial managements. Not only did the Commission publish a number of opinions on accounting matters, it also supported the continuing efforts

[95] Hoxsey, "Accounting for Investors," pp. 259–61.

[96] James S. Schindler, "The Need for Accounting Theory and Standards: The Era of Asset Revaluations," Paper presented at the American Accounting Association Convention, August 29, 1962.

[97] A. C. Littleton and V. K. Zimmerman, *Accounting Theory: Continuity and Change* (Englewood Cliffs, 1962), p. 101.

[98] Flowers, *Criteria for Disclosure*, p. 17.

[99] Whitney, "Business Honesty," p. 10.

of the American Institute of Certified Public Accountants[100] to improve corporate financial statements along the lines originally suggested by the Institute's Special Committee on Cooperation with Stock Exchanges. Consequently, two widely acknowledged documents related to accounting standards have emerged: the 90-odd *Accounting Series Releases* of the Securities and Exchange Commission; and the 51 *Accounting Research Bulletins* of the American Institute of Certified Public Accountants published between 1939 and 1958.

Since 1933, businessmen have rapidly improved their financial reporting practices in response to the direct pressure of the Securities and Exchange Commission; to the growing reliance of bankers, investors, and the public upon the standards articulated by the accounting profession; and to management's own increasing awareness and acceptance of its public responsibility. During this same period, however, new demands have arisen for even greater financial disclosure and more uniformity in the application of accounting principles than that present in those management practices currently accepted by the accounting profession and the Securities and Exchange Commission. Sensitive to these new demands, the American Institute of Certified Public Accountants, in 1959, undertook, under the direction of its newly created Accounting Principles Board, a new program to lessen the gap between existing accounting practices and society's newly articulated financial information needs.

The Emergence, Impact, and Inadequacies of Authoritative Standards

On May 29, 1933, President Roosevelt requested Congress to enact a federal securities bill which would add "to the ancient rule of *caveat emptor*, the further doctrine, 'let the seller also beware.'"[101] The President's bill, in other words, proposed to put the burden of telling the whole truth on those connected with the sale of securities—corporate officers, investment bankers, and accountants. Congress responded to the President's request and on May 27, 1933, Roosevelt signed into law the Securities Act—"an act to provide full and fair disclosure of the character of the securities sold in interstate and foreign commerce. . . ."[102] Clearly, the past financial disclosure practices of industrial management were no longer acceptable. Now, unlike in earlier years, management could no longer afford to neglect society's demands for improved corporate publicity, for these demands were now embodied in a federal statute.

The Securities Act was originally administered by the Fedreal Trade Commission, but in 1934, the act was amended to provide for the creation

[100] In 1957, the American Institute of Accountants changed its name to American Institute of Certified Public Accountants.

[101] Special Message of March 29, 1933, as quoted in Franklin D. Roosevelt, *On Our Way* (New York, 1934), pp. 45–46.

[102] Public Law No. 22, 73 Cong., 1 Sess. (1933).

of a special body—the Securities and Exchange Commission—to assume its administration. Specifically, the Securities and Exchange Commission's task was to regulate the degree of disclosure, financial and nonfinancial, associated with new public security offerings as well as to require reports from those companies whose securities were already traded on the public security markets. Furthermore, the Commission was given broad statutory authority to state accounting rules for registered companies and to enforce them.[103]

In line with its power to prescribe accounting practices, the Commission quickly standardized the format of required financial statement it received. More important, the Commission issued, from time to time, a number of opinions on accounting principles to encourage the development of uniform standards and practices in major accounting questions. Ninety-two such releases had been published by July, 1962.[104]

These opinions, however, cover but a small number of accounting practices. In those cases where no opinion has been expressed by the Commission, its policy is to accept a registrant's accounting practice "if the points involved are such that there is substantial authoritative support,"[105] which in most instances has meant acceptance by the accounting profession. So far, these opinions of the Commission, it should be noted, apply only to those publicly available, prescribed statements which registrants are required to file with the Commission. The management representations contained in periodic reports to stockholders have not yet been placed under the Commission's control. In this latter case, the extent and reliability of disclosure are still dependent on the influence and integrity of the accounting profession and management's own sense of responsibility to its stockholders.

Increasing public interest in financial reports, the continuing cooperative attitude of the New York Stock Exchange, and the backing of the Securities and Exchange Commission has led the American Institute of Accountants to place "increased emphasis on accounting principles and consistency in their application, and of fuller disclosure of the basis on which accounts are stated."[106] First, the Institute formally adopted the recommendations made by its Special Committee on Cooperation with Stock Exchanges. Then, in 1936, the American Institute of Accountants revised *Verification of Financial Statements* and republished it under the title *Examination of Financial Statements*. This document, in contrast to its predecessors, was published under the Institute's name and applied to financial statements prepared for stockholders as well as those for credit purposes.

Next, beginning in 1939, and continuing through 1958, the Com-

---

[103] Littleton and Zimmerman, *Accounting Theory*, p. 100.

[104] U. S. Securities and Exchange Commission, *Accounting Series Releases Nos. 1–92* (Washington, 1937–1962).

[105] U. S. Securities and Exchange Commission, *Accounting Series Release No. 4* (Washington, 1938).

[106] American Institute of Accountants, *Examination of Financial Statements* (New York, 1936), preface.

mittee on Accounting Procedure of the Institute issued a series of fifty-one *Accounting Research Bulletins* touching upon a number of accounting problems and procedures. The principal objective of the bulletins was "to narrow areas of difference and inconsistency in accounting practices, and to further the development and recognition of generally accepted accounting principles." Each bulltein's opinions and recommendations "would serve as criteria for determining the suitability of accounting practices reflected in financial statements and representations of commercial and industrial companies." The authority of the opinions set forth in these bulletins rested "upon their general acceptability" among accountants and businessmen.[107] In practice, however, the bulletins' authority has been greatly strengthened by the reliance placed upon them by the New York Stock Exchange and the Securities and Exchange Commission in determining the acceptability of any questionable accounting practice.

Today, the financial reports filed by industrial corporations with the Securities and Exchange Commission and the national stock exchanges are perhaps the most comprehensive, reliable, and detailed financial statements available publicly anywhere in the world. The financial statements published in periodic reports to stockholders, while less detailed, are nevertheless a great improvement over pre-1933 reports. Yet, despite this progress, as late as 1959, Professor L. Vann Seawell of Indiana University, after a two-year study of nearly 800 published annual reports of American industrial companies concluded: "It is impossible for me to avoid a conclusion that corporate reporting to shareholders is in some respects a financial fantasy."[108] Vann Seawell's conclusion rests on the fact that the so-called "generally accepted accounting principles" upon which corporate financial statements are based have never been satisfactorily defined. The result has been that there is no general agreement among practicing public accountants as to the proper accounting treatment applicable in particularly important areas of financial reporting—such as accounting for business combinations.

In recent years, a number of prominent, influential, and responsible public accountants, security analysts, social critics, and accounting educators have become increasingly disturbed by what they perceive to be inadequacies in management's financial disclosure practices. The motives of these modern-day critics are similar to those of the earlier critics of management already discussed. Some want to protect investors from fraud and blind speculation. Others desire to make management more accountable to stockholders for its actions. A few wish to contain, or even destroy, big business. Several hope to increase the independence of the accounting profession.

[107] American Institute of Certified Public Accountants, *Accounting Research and Terminology Bulletins* (Final edition, New York, 1961), pp. 8, 9.

[108] L. Vann Seawell, "Corporate Annual Reports: Financial Fantasy," *Business Horizons*, Vol. II (Fall, 1959), p. 92.

In general, those critical of management's accounting practices today complain that accounting principles, as approved by the Securities and Exchange Commission and the American Institute of Certified Public Accountants, allow management too much latitude in determining reported profits. The result, they maintain, is that most financial statements are incompatible, if not misleading, since different managements, with the approval of the accounting profession, use different accounting principles to treat similar transactions. Therefore, these critics say, steps must be taken by the accounting profession to bring about more uniformity in the application of accounting principles. Also, because of improved investment analysis techniques or changes in the character of business operations which are of growing interest to investors, conventional financial statements must be recast to include more information in such areas as divisional sales and earnings.

To date, management has adopted some of the critic's suggestions. No management has adopted all. The principal reason given by modern management for its general noncompliance with the critic's demands is the old feeling that such information would help competitors![109]

In 1959, faced with the growing discontent over current financial reporting practices and the increasing demand for more uniformity in accounting principles, the American Institute of Certified Public Accountants dissolved its Committee on Accounting Procedure, the group that had issued the *Accounting Research Bulletins*. It has since embarked upon a comprehensive research program designed to lead to the acceptance by businessmen of a more integrated and less permissive set of accounting principles than that currently observed. If the Accounting Principles Board, the group responsible for this ambitious undertaking, cannot succeed in its task, there are some who predict that "it is quite possible that the government will promulgate accounting principles, as done in several European countries."[110] Thus, both management's reporting prerogatives and the accounting profession's newly acquired function as the principal source of authoritative accounting standards are at stake. As to what the outcome will be one can only guess.[111]

---

[109] See, for example, Alan R. Cerf, *Corporate Reporting and Investment Decisions* (Berkeley, 1961), esp. pp. 66–67.

[110] Robert N. Anthony, *Management Accounting* (rev. ed., Homewood, 1960), p. 593.

[111] The dissolution of the Committee on Accounting Procedure and the creation of the Accounting Principles Board did not lessen the authority of the *Accounting Research Bulletins*. These Bulletins were to remain in force until specifically cancelled by the Accounting Principles Board. As of December, 1962, none of the Bulletins had been cancelled. In addition, the Accounting Principles Board had issued one opinion of its own related to the accounting treatment of the revised depreciation lives permitted for tax purposes by the Internal Revenue Service in 1962. Also, the Accounting Principles Board's research staff had issued four research studies pertaining to the basic postulates of accounting, the principles of accounting, cash flow analysis and the funds statement, and leases. As yet, no action has been taken by the Board on the recommendations outlined in these studies.

SUMMARY: EVOLVING STANDARDS AND LAGGING PRACTICE

The financial disclosure practices of modern American industrial management have nearly all developed since 1933. Yet modern standards have sprung from an earlier reaction to the secrecy which surrounded the financial affairs of most nineteenth-century manufacturing firms. This reaction, which began around 1900, is the historical base upon which recent developments rest. Improvements in reporting practices came principally as the result of continuing pressure from individuals outside the managerial class for improved corporate publicity. This nonmanagement group included such diverse characters as the so-called critics of big business and leaders of the public accounting profession, and set the evolving standards by which the public evaluated corporate financial disclosures. The tempo of these critics' activities varied directly with the public attitude toward business, increasing markedly during those periods when management had fallen from popular favor.

Persistently, management's financial reporting practices lagged far behind the externally set standards, since management favored corporate secrecy and the would-be reformers were powerless to force their recommendations upon managers. Eventually, because management generally had not voluntarily adjusted its financial reporting practices to society's evolving financial informational needs (as perceived by management's critics) and amid the business disorder following the 1929 stock market collapse, the federal government intervened in the field of corporate financial disclosure in 1933.

Thereafter, some authoritative, but nevertheless permissive, accounting standards were developed by the Securities and Exchange Commission and the Committee on Accounting Procedure of the American Institute of Certified Public Accountants. To comply with these new standards industrial management rapidly improved its financial reporting practices in a number of areas. Yet, in the meantime, the demand for fuller, more reliable, and more comparable financial data once again outstripped management practice and the expressed standards of the accounting profession.

Once more, the possibility of further government intervention in industrial reporting matters is imminent, principally because of the accounting profession's inability to narrow the areas of difference in accounting principles and management's resistance to its critics' demands for improved corporate financial disclosure. Whether or not it will be necessary to expand government authority in the area of industrial accounting practice will probably depend upon the acceptance by both management and its critics of the authority and contents of the pronouncements of the Accounting

Principles Board, as well as the Board's willingness and ability to resolve the issues confronting it. In any case, the historical evolution of acceptable standards of financial disclosure among American industrial firms is far from complete.

Louis P. Galambos

6

The Cotton-Textile Institute
and the Government:
A Case Study
in Interacting Value Systems[1]

Our present form of mixed economy—a compound of private capitalism, government controls, and a social welfare system—is the product of a complex historical process that has created the central issues of American politics for almost a century. This process has involved continuous interaction between business and the government. And in the course of business-government relations, the values expressed in public policy and in business behavior have both undergone a series of important adjustments.

The following article explores certain key characteristics of the process by which these adjustments have taken place, viewed primarily from the business side. For this purpose the article examines a segment of the history of relations between the federal government and a business association, the Cotton-Textile Institute. As it developed, the Institute came to represent a particular set of values which were not uniformly shared—and in some cases were vigorously opposed—within the cotton-textile industry. Implementation of policies embodying these values also created a potential conflict between the association and federal antitrust policy. Consequently, the

[1] The larger project of which this is a part was begun as a Ph. D. thesis at Yale University and carried forward at the Harvard Graduate School of Business Administration, where I was a Business History Fellow. I am grateful for the financial assistance and direction that I received at both of these institutions, particularly for the help of David M. Potter, who was my thesis director. I have also received research funds from Rice University and the American Philosophical Society, and I appreciate the support that they have given me. I am indebted to several persons for their valuable suggestions about this article, particularly Arthur M. Johnson, Frank E. Vandiver, and Leonard M. Marsak.

Institute's officers were forced to proselytize their associative values within the industry and friendly government agencies while maneuvering to avoid conflict with government bodies representing different values. The strategy and tactics that they employed in their relations with the various areas of government are a major concern in this study since they also had an important influence upon the values of the association.

During the early 1930's, the Institute's officers were able to influence decisively the values expressed in federal antitrust policy. In 1932 and 1933, they played a major role in persuading the government to abandon temporarily the antitrust prohibition of loose combinations in restraint of trade and to experiment with a program built around trade associations. This new approach, incorporated in Title I of the National Industrial Recovery Act, was a direct product of the sort of subtle interaction in values that can best be understood when government-business relations are studied as a continuing historical process.

THE TRADE ASSOCIATIONS AND ITS OFFICERS

When the Cotton-Textile Institute, a national trade association, was organized in 1926, the textile industry was suffering from excess capacity and cutthroat competition. Rapid expansion in the South and the widespread adoption of a night shift (in a normally day-shift industry) had resulted in an intensely competitive market and profitless operations for most of the industry's firms.[2] These conditions had stirred management to search for some means of reviving their "sick" industry; the remedy that they devised was the Cotton-Textile Institute.

When first organized the Institute had a single goal: ending the depression in cotton textiles by "stabilizing" prices at a profitable level. Political representation and other associative functions were left in the hands of the existing regional trade associations. In fact, the southern members saw to it that the Institute was specifically barred from involvement in "Legislative and political questions," since southern management was afraid that the northern members might somehow use the Institute to lobby for national laws regulating working conditions. The South had much less restrictive state regulations than New England, and in 1926 southern manufacturers were not yet prepared to sacrifice this regional advantage.[3]

[2] Lloyd G. Reynolds, "Cutthroat Competition," *American Economic Review*, Vol. XXX (December, 1940), pp. 736–47.

[3] Cotton-Textile Institute, "Minutes, Organization Meeting," October 20, 1926; and *Certificate of Incorporation and By-Laws of the Cotton-Textile Institute, Inc.* (1927 ed.), pp. 13–14, Northern Textile Association MSS. These minutes and other papers subsequently cited as NTA MSS. are in the office of the association in Boston, Mass. I am indebted to William F. Sullivan, Jessie E. Vint, and Josephine A. Loughry for making these papers available and for assisting me in countless ways during my study of the materials.

Although handicapped by the restriction on political action, CTI had substantial economic resources and an excellent staff. With 447 mills (about two-thirds of the industry's capacity) supporting the organization, CTI had an income of over $300,000 during its first year of operations. By 1929 the membership had grown and the Institute was spending over $400,000 a year.[4] With this kind of financial support, the association could well afford a top-flight staff.

The first president of the Institute was Walker D. Hines, a corporation lawyer who had served as Director-General of the Railroads in 1919 and 1920. When Hines became president of CTI, the association acquired several important assets: the prestige of a public figure identified with wartime service to his country and peacetime service to the agencies of international cooperation (the League of Nations); the talents of an excellent lawyer who had worked for years in the railroad industry; the experience of an administrator who had dealt extensively with government officials and businessmen.

Hines was assisted by the Institute's Secretary, George A. Sloan, who later (1929) became CTI's second president. Sloan had served as executive-secretary of the Copper and Brass Research Association (1920–1925), a trade group which sought to create new markets for copper and brass products. In addition to this valuable experience in association work, he brought to his job at the Institute his youthful enthusiasm and a sincere dedication to the association's cooperative ideology.

Both Sloan and Hines frequently turned to the Institute's counsel, Goldthwaite H. Dorr, for advice. Dorr, like Hines, was a careful, reflective person who expressed his ideas in that precise manner characteristic of the upper reaches of the legal profession. A specialist in antitrust law, Dorr had received his LL.B. from Columbia University (1904) and had lectured at both Columbia and Harvard. On several occasions he had been special assistant to the United States Attorney-General, and during World War I had worked in the War Department.

The background and accomplishments of these three men were important factors in determining the course of CTI's relations with the government. These trade association leaders (since they were not really businessmen, one must distinguish them from business leaders) were all men who could operate in the upper levels of the nation's business, legal, and governmental framework. By education, social class, and ability, this new breed of business representative was a type carefully recruited in order to be an effective spokesman for associative values.

[4] CTI, "Minutes, Board of Directors," September 30, 1936, Goldthwaite H. Dorr MSS. These minutes and the papers, hereafter cited as Dorr MSS, were opened for my examination by Mr. Goldthwaite H. Dorr. I am very grateful to Mr. Dorr and to Mr. John K. Watson for assisting my project in this and other ways.

THE INSTITUTE'S BASIC VALUES

The basic values inherent in the Institute and its program—the values promoted by Hines, Sloan, and Dorr—were economic stability and associative self-regulation. Of course, these values were expressed as specific ends and means. Economic stability was the value incorporated in CTI's end or goal. Associative or cooperative self-regulation was the value intrinsic to CTI's means of achieving that goal.[5]

Among the manufacturers who organized and supported CTI, the first of these values was relatively secure and acceptable. Its content was precisely defined in concrete terms that each of the businessmen could understand.[6] Economic stability meant relatively stable prices which fluctuated around a norm high enough to assure profitable operations for his firm.

Associative self-regulation appeared at first to be equally acceptable and equally well defined. By joining CTI, textile manufacturers indicated that they wanted to cooperate with their fellow manufacturers in the Institute's three fundamental programs: the open-price plan of statistical exchange; the effort to improve and standardize cost accounting techniques; and a "New Uses" program aimed at enlarging the demand for cotton products. Under the open-price plan, each manufacturer sent the association statistical reports on the activities of his company. CTI compiled general reports on the industry's various products, indicating how much of each was being purchased, how much stock was piling up, and how many unfilled orders the mills had. The association then sent these reports to the participating mills, so that management could use them in setting their price and production policies. At "product group meetings," which brought together the manufacturers of a single product, the participants were able to discuss the general reports and their implications for the mills' production policies (the theme of these discussions was normally the need to cut production). The cost-accounting program called upon the manufacturer to help CTI devise a guide to sound, standard techniques of unit-cost accounting and to introduce these techniques in his own mill. "New Uses" ordinarily demanded only financial support from the mills, since this particular program was

[5] By "values," I merely mean "conceptions of the desirable that are distinctive of some human group," It is perhaps necessary to distinguish this particular concept of a value from the more commonsense idea of an ethical or moral principle. The former may involve (as it does in the case of CTI) realizable objectives, while the latter of necessity refers to objectives toward which one strives without the possibility of complete attainment. Burton R. Clark, "Organizational Adaptation and Precarious Values: A Case Study," *American Sociological Review*, vol. XXI (June, 1956), p. 328.

[6] *Ibid.*, pp. 328–29. Clark discusses several of the reasons values may or may not be secure or acceptable, and throughout this article I am using his concept of the "precarious" or insecure value.

left almost entirely in the hands of the staff at the association's New York office.

Although well-defined and apparently acceptable, associative self-regulation proved to be a relatively insecure or "precarious" value even among the mills which joined the Institute. As it turned out, members were willing to join the association and to participate in the programs, but most of them were unwilling to adopt the production and price policies that would make the plan work. They were unwilling to sacrifice policies that were, in the short term, to their own best interests in order to achieve the long-range goal of stability. Acceptance of the Institute's concept of associative self-regulation was thus only partial, even among its members. Consequently, it was necessary for the association's officers to try to convince members that they should fully commit themselves to the industry-wide outlook that was essential to the program's success.[7]

At the same time, CTI was attempting to carry its gospel to the cotton manufacturers who had not joined the organization. Outside the Institute stood about one-third of the industry (in terms of capacity), and to these manufacturers both stability and self-regulation appear to have been undesirable values. Although CTI made a vigorous attempt to reorient the value systems of these nonmembers, a significant number of the executives never supported any of the association's programs and never changed their value systems to embrace stability and self-regulation.[8] The association ultimately failed to achieve its economic objectives when it was unable to persuade the industry to accept wholeheartedly its two basic values, but this paper touches upon this subject only incidentally. The primary concern here is the interaction between CTI's values and the values expressed in federal public policy.

THE INSTITUTE'S VALUES AND THE GOVERNMENT

Between 1900 and 1926, the federal government had gradually adopted a number of policies which sought to stabilize a limited variety of economic activities. One of the objectives of the Federal Reserve System, for instance, was greater stability in the money market and in the nation's banking system. Similarly, the Transportation Act of 1920 made stabilization of the corporate structure and policies of the nation's railroads a specific

---

[7] The fact that the members had not fully accepted the obligations of self-regulation became obvious as early as the fall of 1927. American Cotton Manufacturers Association, *Proceedings*, Vol. XXXII (Boston, 1928), pp. 29, 64–65. ACMA, *Proc.*, Vol. XXXIII (Boston, 1929), pp. 86–87. CTI, "The Situation in Print Cloths," April, 1928, Dorr MSS.

[8] At its peak (August, 1932), the Institute was being supported by 88 per cent of the industry. George A. Sloan, *Sixth Annual Report of the Cotton-Textile Institute, Inc.* (New York, 1932), p. 25.

goal of public policy. In the field of labor relations the federal government had begun, hesitantly, to control certain aspects of the labor contract for special classes of workers such as railroad employees. This was a way of stabilizing working conditions which heretofore had been subject to the play of the market. During the 1920's, when CTI was organized, Secretary of Commerce Herbert Hoover was vigorously encouraging businessmen to stabilize conditions in their industries.[9]

These federal policies arose out of a general cultural environment which had begun around the turn of the century to reflect an increasing interest in stability. This interest could be seen in several facets of American life. As the giant corporation came to dominate important sectors of the American economy, businessmen thought more and more in terms of long-range goals, of stable patterns of profitmaking and growth. Equally significant was the new interest in ethnic stability. Whereas the United States had previously absorbed millions of diverse peoples, the nation decided in the twentieth century to control the flow of immigrants to preserve an existing ethnic balance. During these same years, America's territorial expansion came to a halt. After a brief flirtation with imperialism, Americans decided they were happy with their existing frontiers. Manifest Destiny had been fulfilled. Thus, long before the great depression of the 1930's, America was beginning to turn toward the institutions and ideas which favored stability over chaotic growth. This gradual shift in intellectual attitudes influenced public policy and helped to create suitable conditions for the development of stability-oriented institutions such as trade associations.

Despite this trend, the electorate and the federal government during the 1920's were still primarily dedicated (or at least felt they were dedicated) to the old style of rapid, uncontrolled growth. The rise of new industries, the relentless search for new markets, the variety of technological developments—all of these changes challenged the need for or desirability of stabilization. The great boom in the stock market was the most obvious yet viciously deceptive manifestation of popular expectations concerning economic progress; and when the President of the United States encouraged further speculation in that market, he was merely reaffirming the government's support of America's traditional optimism and expansionism. Stabilization was certainly not condemned by pubilic policy in the 1920's, but it was encouraged only in cases which were recognized as the exception, not the rule.

---

[9] Seymour E. Harris, *Twenty Years of Federal Reserve Policy* (2 vols., Cambridge, 1933), Vol. I, pp. 79–111. I. L. Sharfman, *The Interstate Commerce Commission* (4 vols., New York, 1931–1937), Vol. I, pp. 177–244. Leonard A. Lecht, *Experience Under Railway Labor Legislation* (New York, 1954), pp. 14–30. *Tenth Annual Report of the Secretary of Commerce, 1922* (Washington, 1922), pp. 29–32.

So far as CTI's other fundamental value, associative self-regulation, was concerned, public policy was generally hostile; but the courts had marked out certain forms of cooperative action which were considered acceptable. The establishment of joint traffic bureaus, cooperative insurance plans, and provisions for commercial arbitration fell into this class. In 1925 even the open-price plan for statistical exchange had been approved by the Supreme Court in the Maple Flooring[10] and Cement[11] cases. In light of these decisions, neither a statistical program nor a cost-accounting plan stood much chance of inviting adverse action by the Justice Department as long as CTI did not allow the group meetings to merge into price-fixing arrangements. So long as each member of the association continued to decide individually what his production and price policies would be, CTI could assume that the Justice Department would watch the association carefully but would probably not bring suit under the Sherman Antitrust Act.[12]

Nevertheless, in terms of the extant expressions of public policy, the federal government was basically hostile to associative self-regulation. Competition, not cooperation, was the traditional American policy, and the antitrust laws of 1890 and 1914 made most forms of associative self-regulation illegal or, at best, suspect. Efforts by trade associations to maintain price agreements or production controls had been repeatedly condemned by the Supreme Court. Even before 1890 the courts, drawing upon the common law prohibitions of monopoly and restraint of trade, had refused to consider this sort of associative agreement as a legal, enforceable contract. Although a program such as CTI was beginning might be tolerated, its promoters had little reason to expect that the Justice Department or the courts would support a plan aimed at controlling production on an industry-wide basis.

ADJUSTMENT TO THE VALUES EXPRESSED IN PUBLIC POLICY

Initially, the Institute's leaders adjusted to the realities of public policy by cautiously tailoring their program so as to minimize the risk of direct conflict. Stability *per se* was not a very dangerous idea. Therefore the association made no attempt to alter or to conceal from government officials its primary objective of stabilizing the cotton-textile industry.

Emphasis on self-regulation, however, raised the danger of direct conflict with the government. Under Hines' influence, CTI was especially circumspect in determining the specific form that the various programs in this area should take. In the statistical plan, for example, the organization

---

[10] *Maple Flooring Manufacturers' Association v. United States*, 268 U.S. 563 (1925).

[11] *Cement Manufacturers' Protective Association v. United States*, 268 U.S. 588 (1925).

[12] S. P. Simpson to W. D. Hines, July 25, 1927; G. H. Dorr to W. D. Hines, October 10, 1927, Dorr MSS.

collected information and supplied reports to members without indicating how they should use the statistics. Copies of the various reports were sent to the Department of Commerce and, in some instances, to the Federal Trade Commission; a monthly aggregate report on the entire industry was released to the press. By making at least part of the information available to buyers as well as sellers, CTI tried to meet the standards offered by the Supreme Court, which had indicated that the failure to do this might be considered evidence of an illegal restraint of trade. In the cost-accounting program, CTI focused upon the basic principles of unit-cost accounting, avoiding any discussion of the precise cost figures that the association might feel its members should use.[13] The emphasis was thus upon individual decision-making within an industry-wide organization which merely supplied the members with up-to-date information and general accounting principles.

Although holding close to the boundaries of legality (and apparently only one of the product groups experimented with direct price-fixing), CTI's officers also attempted to forestall any hostile governmental action by shaping a favorable public image of their program. This was a purely defensive maneuver. They merely sought to prevent the development of public pressure for governmental action against their organization. A Madison Avenue agency was employed to advise the association in "publicity matters."[14] Communications that might reach the press, directly or indirectly, were channeled through the association's New York office and meticulously censored. As might be expected, certain generally desirable aspects of the Institute's operations were stressed, especially the relationship between industrial stability and stability of employment.[15]

The Institute's defensive strategy also involved close cooperation with those government officials who believed in stability and self-regulation. Principally, this meant Secretary of Commerce Herbert Hoover and his

[13] In regard to the statistical program, see: CTI, "Minutes of Carded Yarn Group Meeting," July 7, 1927; P. B. Halstead, "To All Manufacturers of Narrow Sheetings," September 1, 1927; W. D. Hines to W. D. Anderson, June 25, 1929, in Donald Comer MSS. These papers were made available for my examination by the late Donald Comer of Birmingham, Alabama. When I began working on the collection, the papers were in Birmingham, but since that time they have been placed in the Baker Library, Harvard University. I am much indebted to Mr. Comer, who gave me unrestricted access to these materials. On the cost-accounting program, see: B. B. Gossett to B. B. Comer, July 2, 1927; CTI, "Minutes of Narrow Sheetings' Cost Accountants' Meeting," August 9, 1927, Comer MSS. Ward Thoron, a member from New England, felt that the association's officers were far too careful. Thoron told a convention of manufacturers in 1930 that he felt that publication of the statistics had been a mistake; he said "that any Institute, that is run by a series of officials who are afraid of going to jail, is not worth the paper its circulars are written on or the money that is being put into it. The whole object of an Institute is to make one worthy of jail and try to avoid getting in it." National Association of Cotton Manufacturers, *Transactions*, Vol. CXXVIII (Boston, 1930), pp. 99–100.

[14] CTI, "Minutes, Executive Committee," October 18, 1927, Dorr MSS.

[15] G. A. Sloan, "Memorandum for Mr. Hines," October 18, 1927; G. H. Dorr to W. D. Hines, June 25, 1928, Dorr MSS.

Department. Under Hoover's direction, the Department was encouraging trade associations to standardize products, to improve cost-accounting techniques, to promote commercial arbitration, and, in general, to eliminate what Hoover felt was waste and inefficiency in industry.[16] In his advocacy of associative self-regulation to achieve these objectives, Hoover came perilously close to suggesting that competition itself was inefficient. While he tried to go no further than the law allowed, Hoover was extremely sympathetic to the Institute's efforts to control production and to stabilize prices in cotton textiles.

Hoover had actually helped the cotton manufacturers organize the Institute. In 1925 when the industry was taking the first hesitant steps toward the formation of a national trade organization, a group of the manufacturers had conferred with Hoover and had been strongly encouraged to proceed with their plans.[17]

After this first encounter, the cotton manufacturers understandably kept in close touch with the Department of Commerce. In February, 1927, when the product groups were actually being organized, Hoover blessed CTI with a statement released through *Textile World*, a trade publication.[18] This public statement helped the Institute establish or "legitimate" its authority within the industry, but it also gave added reason to hope that the association would not be confronted with an antitrust suit.[19] Of course, Hoover's support was no absolute guarantee that another branch or official of the government would not attack the Institute's program as an unreasonable restraint of trade. But the good wishes, publicly announced, of one of the strongest Cabinet members made such an attack far less likely.

The Cotton-Textile Institute, an organization with a goal and a program involving precarious values, thus initially accommodated itself to public policy in three specific ways: (1) by shaping its program to fit the government's concept of legal self-regulation while taking all of the leeway that the association felt would be allowed; (2) by carefully controlling its public image; and (3) by utilizing its strongest ally within the government to counteract possible adverse developments in the Justice Department. During the first crucial months when the Institute's program was taking shape, these measures were successful. The association organized the industry without stirring up an unfavorable response from any branch of the government.

[16] Hoover's support for the association is clearly stated in his annual reports as Secretary of Commerce, particularly the following: *Twelfth Annual Report* (Washington, 1924), pp. 22–24; *Thirteenth Annual Report* (Washington, 1925), pp. 10–27; and *Fourteenth Annual Report* (Washington, 1926), pp. 11–27.

[17] Cotton Manufacturers Association of Georgia, *Report*, Vol. XXVI (Atlanta, 1926), pp. 65–66.

[18] *Textile World*, Vol. LXXI (February 5, 1927), p. 130.

[19] In regard to "legitimation" see Max Weber, *The Theory of Social and Economic Organization* (New York, 1947), pp. 124–32.

NEGOTIATION FOR A MINOR ADJUSTMENT IN THE GOVERNMENT'S POSITION

In subsequent months, however, CTI attempted to extend its program, and the association's leaders began to seek a modification of antitrust policy to accommodate this change. Several things favored such an adjustment. The Coolidge Administration's favorable attitude toward business was important, as was the specific support that CTI continued to receive from Hoover. Even the Assistant to the Attorney General who was in charge of antitrust enforcement found acceptable the association's goal of industrial stability. Furthermore, the new program that the Institute developed was temporary in nature, and the structure of the industry made it appear unlikely that CTI could engineer a very effective restraint of trade, with or without government permission. Another important factor, however, was the skillful representation that Hines and Dorr provided for the Institute. The Administration's friendly attitude gave CTI a natural advantage, but such advantages are seldom exploited naturally. They are exploited by men with special training, experience, and skill—men such as those on CTI's professional staff. Initially, these association leaders influenced the organization's decision to hew to a strict standard of legality; now, they helped the association nudge the Justice Department into a new position on cooperative self-regulation.

The new program became necessary because CTI's original plan failed to stabilize the industry's market. By the fall of 1927, prices were sagging badly because CTI's members had been unwilling to cut back production when sales had begun to fall off.

In an effort to deal with this situation, CTI introduced its new program in November, 1927. At a group meeting of the narrow-sheeting manufactures, Hines discussed the industry's situation and encouraged members to take action, individually, to meet the crisis. After Hines' address, one of the members who represented a large company indicated that he was going to curtail production whether anyone else did or not. Others indicated the same and the consensus was that for the immediate future mills should be closed at noon each Friday, cutting down their work week a full day. After the meeting, the officers of the product group informed the other narrow-sheeting mills of what had been done and circulated lists of the companies that were adopting the curtailment schedule. Thus, the association provided guidelines for its members' production schedules and knowledge of their immediate competitor's actions. In effect, associative activity had artificially created oligopolistic conditions in an industry characterized by price competition.[20]

[20] G. H. Dorr, "Memorandum of Conference with the Assistant to the Attorney General, Colonel Donovan, Monday, December 5, 1927;" William J. Vereen, "To Narrow Sheetings Manufacturers," December 9, 1927, Dorr MSS.

Adoption of the "Gary-Dinner technique" edged CTI over the hazy line of legality drawn by the Supreme Court's most recent decisions. The members were agreeing to adopt a common policy in order to restrict production. They had, furthermore, established a means of "policing" the agreement. Since the courts had condemned such arrangements in the past, the association was in a difficult position.

Assuming that their efforts and the Institute should not be abandoned, the association's officers were forced to choose between several possible courses of action. They could simply proceed with the new program, taking the chance that the government would not bring suit, or if it did, would not be able to win its case. This was the way the legal boundaries of associative self-regulation had been established in the past. They might, on the other hand, seek to change those boundaries by pressing for new legislation. Or, being less ambitious, they might try to arrange a *modus vivendi* with the Justice Department, an "accommodation" that would change the government's antitrust policy in their case without really establishing a legal precedent. The choice was obvious. Legislative action was ruled out by the association's bylaws. An antitrust suit would scare members away from the association. The most promising course of action was to seek an understanding with the antitrust division of the Justice Department.

Dorr and Hines visited the Assistant to the Attorney General, Colonel William ("Wild Bill") Donovan, in December, 1927.[21] Dorr opened the conference by carefully outlining for Donovan the industry's general condition and the difficulties that the Institute had experienced in organizing the mills for constructive action. Next, he invoked the authority of the Secretary of Commerce. Echoing Hoover's recent remarks, he pointed out that the cutthroat competition in cotton textiles had important effects both within and without the industry. There was, he said, "an inevitable *violent* adjustment of production to demand confronting the industry if no *orderly* adjustment were made." Hines then outlined in some detail the Institute's program and the means of achieving "*orderly*" curtailment that had been introduced at the recent meeting of the manufacturers of narrow sheeting. It was likely, he indicated, that other branches of the industry would take similar action in the near future. Hines also made further use of Hoover's support. Before the narrow sheeting mills had met, Hines said, a representative from the industry had discussed the problem with Secretary Hoover; indeed, that very day Hoover had assured Dorr and Hines "that . . . that Department regarded what was being done as sound economics." Hoover had told them that he would be happy to talk to Donovan about their program.

Colonel Donovan was sympathetic but cautious. He served an Admin-

[21] The following account of this conference is taken from G. H. Dorr," Memorandum of Conference with the Assistant to the Attorney General, Colonel Donovan, Monday, December 5, 1927," Dorr MSS.

istration which felt that the business of America was business, and like Herbert Hoover, Donovan was inclined to favor what he felt was the business point-of-view. He was, nevertheless, by virtue of his position specifically charged with the enforcement of the antitrust laws. Consequently, he sparred lightly, searching for an opening more favorable to the antitrust division. Would it not be possible, he asked, to use the Institute's program as a test case, under circumstances that would be favorable to the association?

Donovan still had not yielded what Dorr and Hines wanted, so they deftly parried his offer. CTI's authority within the industry was too weak to withstand court action, Dorr said; he was explaining the situation fully in the hope that Donovan would give him a frank statement of the government's position. In the present emergency, Hines quickly added, any government action against the association would be a "serious matter."

By this time Donovan apparently felt that he had given adequate expression to his role as antitrust enforcer. He could not, he said, guarantee that the antitrust division would not take action in the future. On the other hand, he could not see "any necessity for making a test case of the general questions on the basis of what was being done." There was, he felt, no need "to restrain what it had been outlined was being done in the emergency." Despite his qualifying phrases, Donovan had created with the Institute an implicit agreement which adjusted public policy to associative self-regulation in this specific situation.

Compromising to Win a Major Adjustment in the Government's Position

In pursuing its program during the early 1930's, CTI was able to take advantage of the fact that the general industrial depression made economic stability one of the specific goals of public policy. In order to bring about a significant relaxation of the prohibition of self-regulation, however, the Institute's officers still found it necessary to plan their strategy carefully. Recognizing that a blatant attempt to institute a stronger system of production control might arouse the Justice Department, they compromised by tying production control to a program incorporating humanitarian values which were attractive to government officials and the general public. Such a compromise required the manufacturers to espouse ideas that many of them had long opposed. But that was the price of an aggressive plan for associative self-regulation.

The compromise introduced by CTI in 1930 was a plan for the elimination of night work for women and children. Since women were an important part of the work force in cotton textiles, the plan, if adopted, would make it difficult for mills to operate a night shift. The association hoped that this in turn would force the mills to cut back on production. Although a mill could run at night by using men, wage costs would be higher and the advantage of the second shift considerably reduced. The companies adopting the plan were asked to sign a pledge; thus, CTI would be able to give each of the cooperating mills strong assurance that its competitors, specifically named, were adhering to the industry-wide policy.[22]

In effect, the night-work proposal placed the cotton-textile industry affirmatively behind an idea that had in the past aroused vigorous opposition throughout the industry, especially in the South. For years reformers had been pressing for child-labor legislation and for laws limiting the work week for women. In New England such legislation had been passed, despite the vigorous opposition of the manufacturers. But the southern states had not followed suit. Past attempts to deal with the problem through national legislation had been unsuccessful. So it was a significant development when the industry, North and South, altered course by voluntarily promoting the popular idea of improving working conditions for women and children.

The Institute's leaders had anticipated that the Justice Department would not look with favor on a program built around written pledges and a common production policy, and this was one of the reasons that the plan's humanitarian aspects were so important.[23] And so far as CTI's relations with the federal government were concerned, the night-work plan achieved its objective. Not a sound was heard from the Justice Department. In fact, the association was able to enlist the active support of the Hoover Administration. Sloan and Hines stayed in close touch with the Department of Commerce while they were planning the night-work campaign.[24] In early 1931, when Sloan was experiencing difficulty in presuading some of the mills to join, he arranged a meeting with President Hoover and Secretary of Commerce Robert P. Lamont; after the conference, he announced to the press that:[25]

> The President had evinced deep interest in the type of cooperative work being done by the cotton-textile industry and was particularly impressed with the constructive efforts to stabilize employment for men and women

---

[22] W. D. Hines to D. Comer, January 25, 1930, with enclosed "Memorandum;" CTI, "Meeting of the Board of Directors," September 24, 1930; CTI, "Minutes of the Meeting of the Executive Committee," October 14, 1930, Comer MSS.

[23] The advantages of this particular form of agreement are carefully stated in W. D. Hines to D. Comer, January 25, 1930, Comer MSS.

[24] W. D. Hines, "Memorandum for File," February 7, 1930; G. A. Sloan, "Memorandum for Board of Directors," October 1, 1930; G. A. Sloan to D. Comer, October 17, 1930; G. A. Sloan to R. P. Lamont, October 31, 1930; R. P. Lamont to F. A. Sloan, November 3, 1930, Comer MSS.

[25] G. A. Sloan to D. Comer, February 10, 1931, Comer MSS. *Textile World*, Vol. LXXIX (February 21, 1931), p. 881.

through the new tendency to concentrate normal operations on the day shift. He wished for the movement every success, especially in view of its humanitarian aspects.

Secretary Lamont gave even more direct assistance. He sent personal letters to leading northern and southern manufacturers expressing the Administration's firm support for the plan.[26]

Later that year and again in early 1932, CTI called on the executive branch for help. In January, 1932, the Secretary of Commerce called a special conference between government officials and a group of prominent bankers and textile manufacturers.[27] At the meeting, Lamont bluntly told his visitors that the government wanted stability and the government wanted the night-work plan to succeed.[28] A few weeks later, when some of the uncooperative executives still refused to join, Lamont sent Sloan a telegram explaining how disappointed the Secretary was to hear "that women and minors are still being employed long hours at night in a few cotton mill centers." Lamont said that he earnestly hoped "that the gains made . . . during the past two years through constructive voluntary cooperation and particularly in better stabilizing employment for men and women alike on the day shift will be preserved and expanded."[29] Although the Institute was never able to crack the resistance of all of the non-cooperators, this was certainly not for the want of support from the government.

It is essential to remember, however, that members of CTI as well as the government had adjusted their value systems in order to achieve this compromise. Within the industry this development seems to have had the important and lasting effect of softening the opposition to social control of working conditions. George Sloan made the night work program a veritable crusade, with CTI's members themselves playing a decisive role in the efforts to persuade the entire industry to join.[30] This sort of campaign inevitably influenced the attackers as well as the attacked. It conditioned management to accept the heretofore alien idea that working conditions should in some manner be controlled with a social objective in mind. This helps to explain the industry's behavior in 1933, when the manufacturers

[26] R. P. Lamont to T. M. Marchant, February 12, 1931; R. P. Lamont to Henry F. Lippitt, February 12, 1931, Records of the Department of Commerce, RG 40, 87481, Box 675, National Archives (hereafter NA).

[27] The correspondence file of the Department of Commerce contains material concerning the conference: RG 40, 83057, Boxes 546–547, NA. Also see G. A. Sloan to Herbert Hoover, January 27, 1932, RG 40, 87481, Box 675, NA.

[28] G. A. Sloan, "Special Memorandum," January 26, 1932, Comer MSS.

[29] R. P. Lamont, telegram to G. A. Sloan, February 24, 1932, RG 40, 87481, Box 675, NA.

[30] G. A. Sloan to D. Comer, with enclosure, October 29, 1930, and January 3, 1931; D. Comer to W. D. Hines, January 16, 1931, Comer MSS.

voluntarily introduced into their NRA Code a ban on child labor.[31] It also helps to explain the support that many southern manufacturers subsequently gave to efforts to improve state laws controlling working conditions.[32] A significant result of CTI's strategy in implementing the precarious value of associative self-regulation was thus an adjustment in the industry's general value system, introducing the new concept of social control of working conditions.

LOBBYING FOR A NEW DEAL ON SELF-REGULATION

Although politically successful, the night-work plan failed to solve the industry's economic problems, and CTI's officers set out to change public policy to the end that the government would help the associations enforce their programs. In order to give the officers a free hand, the Institute's members voted in October, 1932, to remove the bar on political action.[33]

There were several reasons for the Institute's officers and members to be optimistic about the chances of selling self-regulation as the best means of achieving industrial stability. In the first place, the economic crisis which hung over the nation in 1932 made stability extremely desirable; some new means of achieving this goal seemed to many Americans to be absolutely necessary. Furthermore, a variety of other industries had been experimenting extensively with trade associations. Large-scale associations like CTI had been created in many of the nation's leading manufacturing industries. Since the leaders of many of these organizations were also calling out for a new antitrust policy, CTI's officers could depend on having considerable support in their efforts to change the government's position on self-regulation.

The possibility of reversing public policy was also enhanced by the groundwork that Dorr and Hines had already done. Neither man could officially speak for the association on political matters before October, 1932; they had nevertheless undertaken their own personal campaign to reorient federal antitrust policy. In 1931 they had begun to address their concept of self-regulation to a small number of leaders, an elite, in the higher

---

[31] G. A. Sloan to J. J. Manning, July 17, 1933; "Statement of Cotton Textile Industry Committee," June 27, 1933, Comer MSS. NRA, "Official Transcript of Hearing No. 1," Transcripts of Hearings, 1933–1935, RG 9, Box 7152, NA.

[32] George H. Lanier to Scott Roberts, January 14, 1931; G. A. Sloan to D. Comer, March 27, 1931; D. Comer to W. K. Moore, April 6, 1931; D. Comer to Governor B. M. Miller, May 29, 1931, Comer MSS. ACMA, *Proc.*, Vol. XXXV (Boston, 1931), p. 26. For the "unreconstructed" attitude toward such laws see: Cotton Manufacturers Association of Georgia, *Report*, Vol. XXXI (Atlanta, 1931), p. 30; and *ibid.*, *Report*, Vol. XXXII (Atlanta, 1932), p. 72.

[33] CTI, "Minutes, Executive Committee," October 18, 1932; CTI, "Minutes, Annual Meeting," October 19, 1932, Comer MSS.

reaches of the legal profession,[34] the business world,[35] and government service.[36]

Instead of campaigning for broad public support, Hines and Dorr attempted to influence policy by influencing the sort of men that the late C. Wright Mills labeled the "power elite." Hines was very active in the United States Chamber of Commerce, and in March, 1932, he began to correspond with James Emery of the National Association of Manufacturers.[37] He and Dorr also drew together a small group of influential lawyers who were interested in the antitrust question. They started to exchange ideas with Gilbert H. Montague, a New York attorney who was Chairman of the Committee on the Federal Trade Commission and the Anti-Trust Laws of the Merchants Association of New York. In April they were joined by William Church Osborn, another lawyer who was influential in business circles and in New York politics.[38]

In the spring of 1932, George Sloan was drawn into the effort to recast public policy. In April, he was called to Washington for a conference with Secretary of Commerce Lamont. Lamont said that he would pass Sloan's ideas on self-regulation along to President Hoover, who he felt would like to see something of this sort done. But the possibilities of action, Lamont warned, were poor.[39] A few months later Sloan was invited to Washington for a talk with Hoover. In this meeting, the President agreed with Sloan "that some way must be found in our scheme of economic planning to strengthen cooperation among those units which are endeavoring to promote the best interest of a given industry." Hoover also suggested that they needed to devise some means of encouraging "a more reasonable attitude on the part of those who have persistently ignored all constructive plans and policies."[40] He did not, however, have any specific ideas about how this might be accomplished.

As Sloan discovered, his talks with the Administration were like the

[34] Hines' talk before the Taylor Society in Philadelphia (April, 1931), was reported in the New York *Times*, May 1, 1931, and cited by Justice Louis D. Brandeis, in *New York Ice Co. v. Liebmann*, 285 U.S. 307, note 51. Also see, Milton Handler (ed.), *The Federal Anti-Trust Laws: A Symposium* (Chicago, 1932), pp. 75–95, 101–104.

[35] U.S. Chamber of Commerce, "Minutes, Board of Directors," January 23, April 29, and June 26, 1931; "Minutes, Executive Committee," March 21, 1931. These and other records of the Chamber subsequently cited are in the office of the U.S. Chamber of Commerce, Washington, D.C.

[36] Attorney General William D. Mitchell to G. H. Dorr, May 14, 1931; G. H. Dorr to William D. Mitchell, August 18, 1931, Dorr MSS.

[37] U. S. Chamber of Commerce, "Minutes, Board of Directors," June 26, 1931, and September 23, 1932. James A. Emery to W. D. Hines, March 29, 1932; John M. Redpath (U. S. Chamber of Commerce) to G. H. Dorr, November 22, 1932, Dorr MSS.

[38] Gilbert H. Montague to W. D. Hines, March 9, 1932; William C. Osborn to W. D. Hines, April 19, 1932, Dorr MSS.

[39] G. A. Sloan to W. D. Hines, April 27, 1932, Dorr MSS.

[40] G. A. Sloan, "To the Board of Directors," September 19, 1932, Comer MSS.

other "no-business" conferences that the President held in 1931 and 1932: they created the appearance of great activity, without requiring the President to do anything.[41] Experimentation with associative self-regulation in the style suggested by Sloan and others was a radical move, too radical for Hoover. The President wanted solutions which appeared to stay within America's framework of traditional values. He could give Sloan a sympathetic audience. But that was about all that he had to offer.

After the Institute's leaders were authorized to undertake political activities, Hines and Dorr made a direct attempt to persuade the judiciary to accept their concept of associative self-regulation. In December, 1932, they filed a brief with the Supreme Court as *amici curiae* in the Appalachian Coals case,[42] which involved a joint marketing agency established by a group of competing coal producers. In the brief that Dorr and Hines (assisted by Wilson Compton)[43] submitted, they dealt primarily with the economic aspects of this sort of concerted action by a group of competitors. This type of activity, their brief said, did not necessarily contravene the antitrust laws. These laws were directed toward preserving "an effectively functioning competitive system in industry," and such agreements might actually support that purpose. This was possible because the competitive system would not function properly unless there was active competition among buyers as well as sellers. "If this duality of competition is destroyed by a monopolistic combination either among buyers or among sellers, then the competitive system, certainly so far as furnishing any protection to the public is concerned, is destroyed in that industry. . . ." The "duality of competition" could, furthermore, be disrupted by conditions other than monopoly: "A great overplus or marked shortage as compared with the accustomed needs of the community will be quite as devastating to the protective functioning of the competitive system . . . as a monopolistic combination would be." Therefore, the Institute's representatives argued, an effort to deal with the problems of overproduction or extreme shortage through self-regulation might actually contribute to the smooth functioning of the competitive system.[44]

On March 13, 1933, the Court handed down its decision in the Appalachian Coals case. Although it was impossible for Dorr and Hines to tell how effective their brief had been, they could not help but be satisfied with the decision, since it sharply altered the Court's position on cooperation

[41] John K. Galbraith's, *The Great Crash, 1929* (Boston, 1955), pp. 144–46, gives an engaging description of this type of conference.

[42] *Appalachian Coals, Inc., et al v. United States*, 288 U.S. 344 (1933).

[43] Compton was also a trade-association officer and the brief was submitted on behalf of the two associations he represented, as well as the Institute.

[44] *Brief of Walker D. Hines, Goldthwaite H. Dorr, and Wilson Compton, As Amici Curiae on Behalf of the Cotton Textile Institute, Inc., Window Glass Manufacturers' Association, and National Lumber Manufacturers Association* (New York, n.d.), pp. 4, 7–9, 11, 13–27.

among competitors. Speaking for the majority, Chief Justice Hughes found that the joint selling agency of the coal producers was not in violation of the Sherman Act. In his careful inquiry into the economic structure of the industry, Hughes described distress selling and other manifestations of cutthroat competition as "evil conditions" which the producers had a right to correct through concerted action. In a passage that seemed to reflect Dorr's economic philosophy, Hughes observed that "the existing situation prompted defendants to make, and the statute did not preclude them from making, an honest effort to remove abuses, to make competition fairer, and thus to promote the essential interests of commerce." The decision announced, in effect, that the judicial branch of the government had adjusted its value system, finding justification now for stabilization through cooperative self-regulation.[45]

Meanwhile, the Institute's officers had begun to lay the groundwork necessary before expanding their relations with the executive branch. In December, George Sloan and a subcommittee from CTI met with General Hugh Johnson, "of Mr. Bernard Baruch's office," to discuss the farm problem. Correctly anticipating that a cooperative attitude would pay dividends later, the association's representatives were initially receptive to the proposals made by Johnson, Raymon Moley, and others.[46] During these same months, other members of Hines' and Dorr's informal group were undertaking similar activities. Henry I. Harriman of the United States Chamber of Commerce and Gilbert Montague were discussing business associations with various members of Roosevelt's Brain Trust. Montague, after consulting with Hines, sent a memorandum on antitrust to Rexford G. Tugwell and Adolf A. Berle, Jr.[47]

The men with whom Dorr, Hines, and Sloan were cooperating were drawn into a more formal alliance when they made their first and last attempt to sell the idea of self-regulation to the legislative branch. James Emery of the National Association of Manufacturers precipitated this development by arranging a meeting between the House Judiciary Committee and the several industrial and association leaders who had been speaking out for self-regulation.[48] When the group confronted the Judiciary Committee on February 8, 1932, the businessmen found the representatives skeptical about association programs which to their minds smacked of price fixing. Neither Hines (whom the group elected as its spokesman) nor the

---

[45] 288 U.S. 372–78.

[46] G. A. Sloan, "Memorandum to Executive Committee," December 21, 1932, and "Memorandum to Board of Directors," January 13, 1933, Comer MSS.

[47] Rexford G. Tugwell, "Notes from a New Deal Diary," January 14, 1933, Franklin D. Roosevelt Library (hereafter RL), Hyde Park, New York. Gilbert H. Montague to W. D. Hines, January 31, 1933, Dorr MSS.

[48] James A. Emery to W. D. Hines, December 22, 1933, and January 31, 1933, Dorr MSS.

other members of the group were prepared to answer the specific questions the representatives asked, and the meeting concluded on an indeterminate note. Out of their experience at this conference, however, the members of the industry group drew two important conclusions: First, that it was useless to approach Congress, since the initiative in measures of this magnitude would rest with the newly elected Administration. Second, that it was futile to talk about self-regulation in general terms. In order to succeed in making this value a public-policy goal, they had to present a specific and carefully drafted bill.[49]

Dorr was given primary responsibility for drafting a specific proposal. Assisted by Walter G. Merritt, a New York attorney, and Rush C. Butler, a prominent Chicago lawyer who was chairman of the Commerce Committee of the American Bar Association, Dorr was able to put together a bill by the middle of February. This proposal followed closely the economic philosophy expressed in the Appalachian Coals brief. The bill stated that the "national economic emergency" was the result "of a general shrinkage in consuming power and a general overdevelopment of the facilities of production and distribution." To counter this emergency, the bill provided for an Economic Emergency Board consisting of the Secretaries of Commerce, Labor, and Agriculture. During the emergency, the Board would encourage associations to establish agreements in regard to production, sales, and distribution, with the antitrust laws suspended insofar as these understandings were approved by the Board.[50]

Dorr and Hines now attempted to persuade Roosevelt and his advisers to accept this specific proposal. On February 18, they saw Adolf A. Berle, Jr. and discussed the matter with him at considerable length. They left a copy of their proposed bill and supporting memoranda with Berle, whom they found appreciative of "the gravity of the problem" and willing "to consider some such method of dealing with it."[51] Berle carried their ideas to Roosevelt, who apparently reacted positively to the general idea of industrial self-regulation.[52] After again discussing the bill with Berle, Dorr and Hines decided to reconvene the industry group to unify them behind the specific measure drafted by Dorr's subcommittee. A conference and consensus seemed essential because several members of the group were already

[49] G. A. Sloan, "Memorandum to Board Members," February 8, 1933, and "Memorandum to Members of the Board," February 18, 1933, Comer MSS. "Statement of W. D. Hines to the conference with the House Judiciary Committee," February 8, 1933; and "Memorandum by WDH," March 16, 1933, Dorr MSS.

[50] G. H. Dorr to Rush C. Butler, February 10, 1933; *Draft of Proposed Bill to Create an Economic Emergency Board and for other Purposes, with Memorandum,* February 17, 1933, Dorr MSS.

[51] W. D. Hines to A. A. Berle, February 21, 1933; W. D. Hines to Gilbert H. Montague, February 21, 1933; G. H. Dorr to Rush C. Butler, February 28, 1933, Dorr MSS.

[52] A. A. Berle to W. D. Hines, February 23, 1933; W. D. Hines to A. A. Berle, February 24, 1933, Dorr MSS.

in contact with Roosevelt's counselors, and there was the danger that they might give the President-elect conflicting advice.[53]

When the industry group reconvened on March 8, it was soon apparent that there were strong differences of opinion about the amount of government regulation that should be accepted. William Osborn was suspicious of the bureaucratic controls that might be spun out by the Emergency Board. James Emery of the NAM and Robert P. Lamont, who was now president of the American Iron and Steel Institute, were extremely critical of the measure proposed by Dorr's subcommittee. Emery was worried about the labor unions; they would, he thought, take advantage of government authority to gain new power. Lamont felt that businessmen should be more cautious about asking for government interference. They should consider and reconsider, he said, "what industry might lose by getting tied in with bureaucracy." C. E. Bockus of the National Coal Association seconded Lamont's fears. Bockus also doubted whether the plans for self-regulation should be forced on the producers who did not elect to join. John Redpath, who represented the Chamber of Commerce, was not worried about government controls, but he did take exception to the fact that Dorr had drafted an emergency measure. Instead of a temporary experiment with industrial self-regulation, Redpath wanted the government to abandon permanently the antitrust prohibition of concerted action by competitors.

Although there were several members who strongly supported the Dorr bill—including Gilbert Montague and J. Harvey Williams, a Chicago tool manufacturer—about the only things that the entire group could agree on were the need for unanimity and the necessity of carrying their ideas directly to F.D.R. himself. They gave to J. Harvey Williams the hopeless task of uniting the various associations and industries behind a single proposal, while Hines was commissioned to speak to F.D.R.[54]

At this crucial point, the task of uniting the group behind a single bill was further complicated by the Supreme Court's announcement of the Appalachian Coals decision. The Court's new tack encouraged those who wanted a permanent relaxation of the antitrust laws to strike out on their own. Gilbert Montague drew away from the group and began to work independently in behalf of his own version of a permanent bill.[55] The Chamber of Commerce was even more determined to push for permanent relief from antitrust, and Silas H. Strawn called another meeting in the

[53] W. D. Hines, "Memorandum for Mr. Dorr," February 13, 1933, Dorr MSS; Rexford G. Tugwell, "A New Deal Diary," February 12, 1933, RL.
[54] W. D. Hines, "Memorandum," March 8, 1933; J. Harvey Williams to Rush C. Butler, March 10, 1933, Dorr MSS. At this and other meetings of the group interested in a new approach to antitrust, it is significant that the majority of those in attendance were not businessmen in the strictest sense of the word; they were lawyers and professional association leaders.
[55] W. D. Hines, "Memorandum," March 16, 1933, Dorr MSS.

hope that he could at last pull them together behind this proposal. At the meeting held on March 27, however, this hope was blasted. Although the participants all felt that there was a need for self-regulation, the assembled representatives of the organized forces of industry seemed determined to defy the stereotyped picture of a monolithic business community. They left the conference in disarray.[56]

By the end of March, 1933, the once-impressive group was hardly a group any more. Although the members continued to communicate with one another and continued to cooperate in a limited sense, individually they were descending upon the Roosevelt Administration with their own plans for associative self-regulation.[57]

Despite the fracturing of his group, Hines proceeded with his plans to meet the President. He had already sent to the White House a memorandum outlining his position. In this brief for self-regulation, Hines sketched in Dorr's economic analysis of the "duality" of competition; he pointed out that in the Appalachian Coals decision the Supreme Court had, in a limited way, approved cooperative measures to stabilize prices. What was needed now, Hines said, was "drastic affirmative action" with strong government leadership. On the basis of his experience with the textile industry and his "contact with a group of representatives of a wide range of industries," Hines suggested that they had to have "the immediate leadership of the Administration."[58]

After his talk with the President on April 11, Hines was discouraged. Even though the antitrust question was "getting red hot" and the Black 30-Hour Bill was forcing Roosevelt's hand, the President was hesitant to commit himself. Hines found Roosevelt basically sympathetic to the idea of self-regulation under government leadership, but F.D.R. was apparently not eager to experiment with this radical new approach to the recovery problem. Like Hoover, Roosevelt was leery of tampering with traditional values. As he explained to Hines, the antitrust question "was a highly controversial matter the consideration of which would take many weeks." The President said very emphatically "that it ought not to be brought up at the present session of Congress."[59]

Despite Roosevelt's caution in his interview with Hines, developments in the next few days suggest that the exponents of self-regulation had been far more successful with the President than they had thought. At his press

[56] "Anti-Trust Conference," March 27, 1933; John M. Redpath to G. H. Dorr, April 13, 1933, Dorr MSS.

[57] Robert L. Lund to Louis McHenry Howe, March 29, 1933, President's Personal File 8246, RL. Henry I. Harriman to W. D. Hines, April 3, 1933; John M. Redpath to G. H. Dorr, April 13, 1933, Dorr MSS.

[58] W. D. Hines to M. H. McIntyre, March 23, 1933, with enclosed *Draft of Points for White House*, Official File 466, RL.

[59] W. D. Hines to Henry I. Harriman, April 14, 1933, Dorr MSS.

conference on the day after he met Hines, Roosevelt indicated that the Administration might be interested in a production-control program that would spread work throughout an industry instead of allowing it to be concentrated in the hands of a few producers.[60] A few days later he was even more specific.

In his press conference on April 14, Roosevelt described the problem that the cotton-textile industry had encountered in its cooperative programs. If the government set up minimum wage boards, he said, they would encounter the same problem—the resistance of a small percentage of non-cooperators. If they could find some constitutional means of dealing with this minority, the President said, he would favor it.[61] Like the association leaders, F.D.R. now described the non-cooperators in associative action as villains and the majority, the producers who wanted stability, as heroes. Instead of looking at the competitive process as a self-correcting mechanism in which the hardest competitors played a vital role, the President was inclined to favor cooperative methods of eliminating cutthroat competition. Both the executive and judicial branches of the government had thus adopted the fundamental equation that CTI had been promoting: economic stability was desirable, and associative self-regulation was the best means of stabilizing industry.

Although CTI's leaders played a very important role in this successful effort to persuade the executive branch to accept the associative values, the Institute's officers certainly did not achieve this result by themselves. The general trade-association movement in American industry provided the essential background for their efforts. Roosevelt had been familiar with this movement long before 1933. He had served, in fact, as the president of a trade association, the American Construction Council, in the 1920's. This experience undoubtedly helped smooth the way for the numerous association leaders who, along with CTI's officers, were proposing a new anti-trust policy. With CTI, the Chamber of Commerce, and hundreds of other trade organizations calling for a similar change in public policy, Roosevelt was assured of widespread business support for this new approach to antitrust.

Shortly after the press conference on April 14, the Administration had three teams at work drafting a bill that would implement these values. Senator Robert Wagner headed one of the groups. Another centered around Hugh Johnson. A third around John Dickinson, the Assistant Secretary of Commerce. Gilbert Montague, who by this time was again supporting Dorr's emergency measure, was helping Senator Wagner.[62] CTI's leaders had been in touch with Hugh Johnson since December, 1932, and they had

---

[60] Press Conference No. 11, April 12, 1933, RL.

[61] Press Conference No. 12, April 14, 1933, RL.

[62] Arthur M. Schlesinger, Jr., *The Coming of the New Deal* (Boston, 1959), p. 96. Gilbert H. Montague to John Dickinson, May 3, 1933, RG 40, 94694, NA. Schlesinger's volume (pp. 96–98) contains the best available description of the drafting of the bill.

been assured of the support of Bernard Baruch, Johnson's "patron."[63] For some weeks, Montague and Harriman had been in close contact with Dickinson, who favored the Chamber's specific proposals.[64] Whatever form the final bill took, it was thus fairly certain that it would include some provision for associative self-regulation and a temporary abandonment of the antitrust policy on loose combinations.

At this juncture, however, Dorr, Hines, and Sloan were not at all certain about what was happening in Washington. Consequently, they continued to sell their program. Dorr outlined his views on associative production control before a meeting of the American Bar Association's Committee on Commerce. Hines stayed in touch with Harriman, Montague, Emery, Osborn, and several other members of their erstwhile group.[65]

Both Dorr and Sloan were speakers at the annual convention of the United States Chamber of Commerce in Washington on May 3–4. This meeting was, in effect, a giant rally for industrial self-regulation. Sloan was there to receive for the Institute the annual award of the American Trade Association Executives. Since the award was given, along with the customary speech, by Secretary of Commerce Daniel Roper, Sloan had a chance to talk to Roper about "self-regulation of industry backed up by government support." Sloan also presented his views to Secretary of Agriculture Henry Wallace and to John Dickinson, with whom he discussed the bill that was being drafted.[66] Dorr presented a paper on "The Effects of the Anti-Trust Laws under Conditions of Depression." Recognizing that many businessmen were skittish about government interference, he elaborated on the necessity of having government leadership so that the recalcitrant minority could be brought into line. He also bowed to the Administration's recently expressed interest in minimum wages, pointing out that concerted action was needed in regard to wages as well as production.[67]

By this time, however, the Administration had already endorsed self-regulation as an acceptable value. John Dickinson, who followed Dorr on the Chamber of Commerce program, assured the audience that "within the administration there is at the present time very active consideration going forward in connection with these problems, and that the point of view that has been so ably expressed by Mr. Dorr is receiving the most sympathetic consideration."[68] President Roosevelt, who addressed the

[63] W. D. Hines, "Memorandum for Mr. Dorr," February 13, 1933, Dorr MSS.

[64] W. D. Hines to Gilbert H. Montague, April 18, 1933; Gilbert H. Montague to W. D. Hines, April 20, 1933; W. D. Hines to G. H. Dorr, April 25, 1933, Dorr MSS.

[65] G. H. Dorr, "Mr. Dorr's Talk—April 12, 1933"; Henry I. Harriman to W. D. Hines, April 19, 1933; W. D. Hines to William C. Osborn, April 19, 1933; W. D. Hines to James A. Emery, April 19, 1933, Dorr MSS.

[66] U.S. Chamber of Commerce, "Minutes, 21st Annual Meeting," May 3, 1933. G. A. Sloan to D. Comer, May 4, 1933; CTI, "Minutes, Executive Committee," May 8, 1933, Comer MSS.

[67] U.S. Chamber of Commerce, "Minutes, 21st Annual Meeting," May 4, 1933.

[68] Ibid.

Chamber that evening, reaffirmed his support for "an orderly industrial system" in which the majority within an industry would, with government backing, bring "minorities to understand that their unfair practices are contrary to the sound public policy of the nation."[69] Three days later in a Fireside Chat, Roosevelt outlined in greater detail the bill that was being drafted. To illustrate how the measure would work, F.D.R. again used the example of the one particular industry which had obviously impressed him with its concern for the public welfare: cotton textiles.[70]

Although it was now clear that the Administration had committed itself to associative values, the Institute's officers made one more strategic move to ensure that the government would not change course. On May 8, CTI's Executive Committee launched a program to impose voluntary limits of two forty-hour shifts a week on all of the nation's cotton mills.[71] Two days later the association had received a large number of favorable reactions, and George Sloan wired Roosevelt that one-third of the industry had already lined up behind the plan the President had described in his Fireside Chat.[72] What better proof could there be of the practicability of industrial self-regulation?

On May 15, 1933, the National Industrial Recovery Bill was presented to Congress. The bill contained many provisions with which CTI's officers had had nothing to do; it contained several provisions which they definitely opposed. But the fundamental objective of reversing decades of antitrust policy and winning government support for industrial self-regulation was achieved in Title I of the NIRA. For the Cotton Textile Institute, NIRA was simply an extension of the association's previous experience in business-government relations. In this fourth stage of CTI's negotiations, the values proposed for public policy had been changed with support from the highest levels of government. But once again the trade association had had to compromise, adjusting its own value system. Along with self-regulation, CTI accepted NIRA's Section 7(a), with its support for unionization. Although minimum wages had long been opposed by the industry, the Institute's officers now insisted that minimum wages were an essential part of the recovery program. A compromise on important values had again taken place as a direct result of interaction between business and the government.

In Conclusion

While the story of CTI's contacts with the federal government throws new light on the origins of NRA, the material presented above may warrant

[69] *Ibid.*

[70] Transcript, The President's Fireside Chat, May 7, 1933, RL.

[71] CTI, "Minutes, Executive Committee," May 8, 1933, Comer MSS.

[72] G. A. Sloan, telegram to Franklin D. Roosevelt, May 10, 1933, Official File 372, RL.

a few general conclusions about the way in which business values have been shaped in modern America. Judging from CTI's experience, public policy has had important indirect or secondary effects on the values of the businessman; this was certainly the case with the night-work program. As businessmen and their representatives negotiated with government officials, they modified the goals of public policy but at the same time absorbed several new concepts. Although these new values were only indirectly related to the issue at hand—the question of whether women should work at night was certainly not an antitrust problem—they were nonetheless important. They were values which helped the businessman accommodate himself to an environment in which he was held to be accountable to the public for many of his actions. These compromises thus facilitated the businessman's adjustment to a twentieth-century economy which included government controls and a social welfare system, as well as private capitalism.

This study also suggests that the slow and erratic manner in which such important policies as antitrust have been implemented may actually have had a salutary effect. Reformers and business leaders have repeatedly called for definitive, unequivocal definitions of antitrust and other policies. But examined in terms of the evolution of business values, such definitions might have had unfortunate results. By stopping the process of negotiation and compromise, they would have hardened business resistance to any form of social control or welfare system. Such definitions would have ruled out the kind of compromise on values which were so important in the case of CTI. Thus, they might actually have slowed or prevented the process of adjustment to public policy that CTI and other business organizations experienced.

An examination of the Institute's relations with the government also indicates that trade-association leaders (as distinguished from the businessmen they represent) have probably had a special role in shaping business values. In this particular case they acted as intellectual brokers between the government (and society) and the businessmen. They tailored their policies with an eye to the government's position as well as the industry's economic plight. In this way they helped to set up a series of essential compromises.

Finally, CTI's history amply illustrates that historians must somehow stop looking at business and the government as monolithic groups. Within the cotton-textile industry, the businessmen were divided on basic issues: and when Dorr and Hines attempted in 1933 to unify several industries, the business and association leaders were never able to line up behind one specific measure. Similarly, within the government there was a wide range of attitudes about antitrust and the associative values. The executive, judicial, and legislative branches were never in complete agreement. Even within the executive branch, there were crucial differences of opinion about stability and self-regulation. This case implies that unless the historian begins to look at the subtle process of interaction between subgroups and individuals within the business community and within the government, he can never really understand the manner in which public policy and the values of American businessmen have been shaped in the twentieth century.

Sidney Fine

7

The Ford Motor Company
and the N.R.A.

Perhaps no company during the two years the National Industrial Recovery Act was in effect (1933–1935) received as much publicity or was the object of as much concern on the part of its competitors and of the federal government as the Ford Motor Company.[1] To a considerable degree, the attention focused upon it stemmed from the fact that although the N.I.R.A., in theory, contemplated the partnership of industry, government, and labor in the stabilization of the economy, the Ford Motor Company refused to sign the code its industry adopted, failed to supply the federal government with proper certification that it would comply with the code, and successfully resisted the inroads of unionism in its plants.

In approving the N.I.R.A. on June 16, 1933, President Roosevelt stated that "History probably will record the . . . Act as the most important and far-reaching legislation ever enacted by the American Congress." In addition to authorizing the expenditure of $3.3 billion for public works, the N.I.R.A. sought to stimulate re-employment by a shorter work week and to augment purchasing power and production by the increase of wages and payrolls. Quite apart from these immediate goals, the statute pointed, in the long run, to the stabilization of economic activity through the cooperation of government, business, and labor. To this end, businessmen, through their trade associations, were permitted to control "destructive" competition free, on the whole, from the restraints of the antitrust legislation. To balance this concession to the business community, the right of employees to organize and to engage in collective bargaining was proclaimed.

[1] The preparation of this article was facilitated by grants to the author from the John Simon Guggenheim Memorial Foundation and the Horace H. Rackham School of Graduate Studies of the University of Michigan.

The N.I.R.A. permitted trade or industrial associations to draw up codes of fair competition whose provisions were to become "the standards of fair competition" for the trade or industry concerned when the codes had been approved by the President. On his own initiative or on complaint, the President could himself prescribe a code for a trade or industry for which a code had not already been approved. The President was also authorized to enter into agreements with or to approve voluntary agreements between and among persons engaged in a trade or industry, trade or industrial associations, or labor organizations. Moreover, when the President found that "destructive wage or price cutting" or other practices contrary to the purposes of the act were being carried on in any trade or industry, he could license the business enterprises concerned in order to make a code or agreement effective, and no person in that line of endeavor could then operate without a license. The President was permitted to suspend or revoke a license for violation of its terms.

Every code, agreement, and license approved or issued under the statute had to stipulate, according to the famous Section 7(a), that employees were to have the right to organize and bargain collectively through representatives of their own choosing and were to be free from employer "interference, restraint, or coercion" in designating such representatives or in self-organization; that no employee and no one seeking employment was to be required as a condition of employment to join a company union or to refrain from joining, organizing, or assisting a labor organization; and that employers were to comply with the maximum hours of labor, minimum rates of pay, and other conditions of employment approved or prescribed by the President.

Despite the drastic character of many of its provisions, the N.I.R.A. was not without ties with earlier programs and ideas. The policy of combating unemployment by shortening the hours of labor was, after all, traditional with organized labor. The guarantee of the right of collective bargaining in the N.I.R.A. was modeled after Section 2 of the Railway Labor Act of 1926 and the policy declaration of the Norris-LaGuardia Act of 1932. The Federal Trade Commission and the Department of Commerce had for some years prior to 1933 been assisting trade associations in drawing up codes of fair competition, and the United States Chamber of Commerce during the depression had sought legislative sanction for codes which would combat destructive wage and price cutting.

On the other hand, there is no question that the N.I.R.A. not only expanded enormously the concept of interstate commerce but that it also permitted the federal government to play a more prominent role than it previously had in the allocation of resources, the organization of production, the determination of wages and hours, and the working out of relations between labor and management. Unusual discretionary power was, moreover, delegated in the statute by the Congress to the President, and the licensing provision of the act gave the chief executive "the power of life or death over business enterprises." It is thus not altogether surprising that the N.I.R.A. was ultimately declared unconstitutional by the United States Supreme Court in a 9 to 0 decision.

It must, however, be noted that the N.I.R.A. made possible alternative lines of action and that the powers it granted were not all used. The National Recovery Administration, as it turned out, relied entirely on the initiative of trade and industrial associations in the formulation of codes, and the drastic licensing clause was never invoked. The codes, to be sure, included many provisions which were objectionable to believers in a competitive economy, but generally speaking, these were provisions that the trade associations themselves wished to have included rather than practices imposed upon them by the N.R.A.[2]

When the N.I.R.A. became law, the Ford Motor Company was but thirty years old.[3] Capitalized originally at a nominal figure of $150,000, but with only $28,000 of this sum in the form of cash, the company, without drawing on any outside source for additional funds, had become one of the nation's greatest business concerns, with total assets in 1929 of $925,612,419. It was being strongly challenged by the competition of General Motors and Chrysler by the end of the 1920's, but in 1930 Ford was still responsible for 40.33 per cent of the new passenger car registrations in the United States. The depression years of the Hoover administration, however, hit the Ford Motor Company more severely than its two great rivals. Its share of new passenger car registrations dropped to 17.54 per cent during the first quarter of 1933, and whereas the company had realized a total net profit after taxes of over $131 million in 1929 and 1930, it suffered a total net loss of over $107 million in 1931 and 1932.[4]

For all practical purposes, the Ford Motor Company, as far as the

[2] For the origin, character, and administrative history of the N.I.R.A., see Leverett S. Lyon et al., The National Recovery Administration (Washington, 1935); Lyon et al., Government and Economic Life (2 vols.; Washington, 1939–1940), Vol. II, pp. 1,035–1,061; Charles F. Roos, NRA Economic Planning (Bloomington, Ind., 1937); Raymond Moley, After Seven Years (New York, 1939), pp. 184–191; and Irving Bernstein, The New Deal Collective Bargaining Policy (Berkeley, 1950), pp. 20–39.

[3] For the history of the Ford Motor Co. and Henry Ford before 1933, see Allan Nevins and Frank Ernest Hill, Ford. The Times, the Man, the Company (New York, 1954); and Nevins and Hill, Ford: Expansion and Challenge, 1915–1933 (New York, 1957).

[4] Nevins and Hill, Ford. The Times, the Man, the Company, pp. 237–238; Federal Trade Commission, Report on Motor Vehicle Industry, 76th Cong., 1st Sess., House Doc. No. 468 (Washington, 1939), pp. 649, 657; Ward's 1939 Automotive Year Book, p. 36. Although the company was originally capitalized at $150,000, only $100,000 in stock was actually issued. The statistics given for Ford for the 1920's and 1930's include the Lincoln Motor Co. The average number of payroll employees at the Rouge plant dropped from 101,069 in 1929 to 32,514 in 1933, and the average weekly rate of wages of these employees from $36.97 to $23.58. The minimum daily wage paid by Ford was cut from $7.00 to $4.00 during the same years. F.T.C., Report on Motor Vehicle Industry, p. 668; Nevins and Hill, Ford: Expansion and Challenge, p. 588.

general public was concerned, was indistinguishable from the man who had given the company his name. For almost two decades before 1933, no other business figure loomed so large in the public view as Henry Ford. It was Ford who had successfully fought the Association of Licensed Automobile Manufacturers in the great Selden patent suit, Ford who had become the world symbol of mass production, Ford who had proclaimed the five-dollar day. Always one to do the unexpected, Ford had reacted to the onset of the depression in 1929 by raising wages and expanding plant construction. "If every one will attend to his own work," he had declared, "the future is secure."[5] The immediate future was far from secure, however, and the Ford Motor Company was soon feeling the full impact of the business downturn.

The depression persuaded many businessmen that measures like the N.I.R.A. were necessary to revive the economy, but there was little reason in 1933 to expect that Ford would view with favor legislation which called for the stabilization of the economy through the cooperation of government, business, and labor. Ford, it had already been demonstrated, was simply not the sort of person who could work well in harness. As he later said, he had decided at the beginning of the century, after his experience as superintendent of the Detroit Automobile Company, "never again to put myself under orders," and then in 1919 he had bought out the minority stockholders in the Ford Motor Company and had thus gained total control of the concern. Rugged individualist that he was, Ford was hostile to organization and had stated his belief that "People are never so likely to be wrong as when they are organized."[6]

A believer in self-help and self-reliance, Ford did not look to government to solve the economic problems of the nation even in a great depression. It was unlikely, moreover, that one who had fought the A.L.A.M. in the Selden patent suit and who had refused to joint his fellow automobile manufacturers in the National Automobile Chamber of Commerce would look kindly on legislation that encouraged the activities of trade associations. Above all, Ford was almost certain to oppose legislative and administrative actions which might lead to the establishment of unionism in his plants. Ford had, as a matter of fact, attained fame for his farsighted wage and hour policies, and certainly in 1914 and for a few years thereafter, the Ford Motor Company had "the most advanced labor policy in the world"; but Ford did not believe that organized labor should play any part in the shaping of that policy. In his view, labor unions were simply "predatory"

---

[5] Nevins and Hill, *Ford: Expansion and Challenge*, pp. 529–530, 573–575, 598–600.

[6] Henry Ford, in collaboration with Samuel Crowther, *My Life and Work* (Garden City, New York, 1922), p. 36; Nevins and Hill, *Ford: Expansion and Challenge*, pp. 105–113, 536.

organizations and were "part of the exploitation scheme."[7] To be sure, prior to 1933, unionism was conspicuous in the Ford plants and in the auto industry in general only because of its absence, but, encouraged by Section 7(a), the American Federation of Labor soon began to establish federal locals in the plants of the automobile industry. The A.F. of L. failed to make any impression on Ford's great Rouge plant, but, as we shall see, A.F. of L. federal locals sought to bargain with the Ford Motor Company after strikes broke out in September, 1933, in the Ford assembly plants in Chester, Pennsylvania, and Edgewater, New Jersey.

II

Although the National Automobile Chamber of Commerce, the trade association of the automobile manufacturers, had ascertained in off-the-record talks with government officials even before the N.I.R.A. became law that the non-member Ford Motor Company would have to abide by a code of fair competition drawn up by the industry even if it was not a party to it,[8] the organization preferred that any decision as regards a code should be made in conjunction with Ford. Taking advantage of the fact that the Lincoln Motor Company was a member of the N.A.C.C., President Alvan Macauley appointed Edsel Ford, Lincoln's president, to the committee he established late in May, 1933, with Alfred P. Sloan, Jr., as chairman, to consider the impending recovery bill in its relationship to the auto industry.[9]

Following the report of the Sloan committee to the June 15 meeting of the N.A.C.C., the auto manufacturers decided to establish a code committee to analyze the N.I.R.A. and to determine if a code was necessary. Macauley thought that the Ford Motor Company should be represented on this committee also, and Edsel Ford agreed on June 21 that Herman L. Moekle, who was in charge of Ford's auditing department and whose name the N.A.C.C. had suggested, could accept this assignment. The

[7] Nevins and Hill, *Ford. The Times, the Man, the Company*, pp. 522–567; Nevins and Hill, *Ford: Expansion and Challenge*, pp. 353, 493–494, 535–539. For the change in Ford's labor policies after 1921, see Nevins and Hill, *Ford: Expansion and Challenge*, pp. 349–354, 508–540, 589–591. Nevins and Hill point out that by 1923 "the Ford factory . . . became just like any other factory," but they insist that "working conditions . . . remained good until the end of the nineteen-thirties."

[8] Pyke Johnson, "An Analysis of the Position of the N.A.C.C. under the National Recovery Act," May 23, 1933, Roy Chapin Papers, Michigan Historical Collections; P. Johnson to Chapin, June 2, 1933, and attached report of interview with General Hugh S. Johnson, Chapin Papers.

[9] Chapin to P. Johnson, May 25, 1933, Alfred Reeves to Sloan *et al.*, June 8, 1933, Chapin Papers; N.A.C.C. General Bulletin No. G—1603, May 27, 1933, O. P. Pearson Papers (in Mr. Pearson's possession).

committee decided at its first meeting on June 22 to work on the terms of a suitable code for the industry rather than to attempt to decide whether the auto manufacturers should actually submit a code.[10]

After several sessions the committee agreed on the provisions of a code to be submitted for the consideration of the N.A.C.C. members on July 25 and the N.A.C.C. directors the next day. The minutes of the code committee's meetings do not tell us precisely what role Moekle, who was soon joined by Louis Colombo, a Ford attorney, played in the committee's deliberations.[11] Alfred Reeves, the vice president and general manager of the N.A.C.C., wrote Edsel on July 21 that the two men had "contributed invaluable help," but since the N.A.C.C. wished Ford to sign the code, it was natural that Reeves should take this line. As Moekle later recalled his part in these events, his objective was simply to keep the industry "as free as possible of controls," which coincided with the view of the other members of the committee.[12]

The participation of the Ford Motor Company in the code-making process ceased when the code committee on July 25 submitted its draft to the N.A.C.C. Ford did not join with the N.A.C.C. in presenting the code to General Hugh S. Johnson, the Administrator for Industrial Recovery, and did not participate in the conferences on the code that preceded the public hearing, in the public hearing itself, or in the post-hearing conferences that led to the President's approval of the code on August 26. The obstacle to any further Ford cooperation was clearly Henry Ford himself. Moekle and Colombo recommended acceptance of the code as "the best kind of agreement that could come out of that law," and according to Ernest G. Liebold, Ford's business secretary, "Everyone around, including Edsel," thought the company should sign.[13]

Anxious to enlist Henry Ford's support for the N.I.R.A., Johnson had decided shortly after the passage of the act to discuss the subject with Ford in person. "I want to talk to you about the whole show," he told Henry on the telephone on June 22. Two days later, Johnson secretly flew to Dearborn and explained to Henry and Edsel the purposes and character of the

[10] Reeves to E. Ford, June 12, 1933, Reeves to H. Ford, June 15, 1933, E. Ford to Reeves, June 21, 1933, Accession 203, Box 3, Ford Archives; Minutes, Meeting, June 22, Committee on N.I.R.A., N.A.C.C., Acc. 203, Box 6, Ford Archives.

[11] There are copies of the minutes of the June 22 meeting in Acc. 203, Box 6, Ford Archives, of the June 29 meeting in Acc. 203, Box 13, Ford Archives, and of the July 11 meeting in the Pearson Papers.

[12] Reeves to E. Ford, July 21, 1933, Pearson Papers; "The Reminiscences of Mr. Herman L. Moekle" (Mar., 1955), Vol. II, pp. 148–150, Ford Archives. Actually, as Moekle reported to B. J. Craig after the code committee's first meeting, "There was a strong sentiment in the committee that no code at all should be filed, if such a thing is possible." Memorandum for B. J. Craig, June 23, 1933, Acc. 203, Box 3, Ford Archives.

[13] "Reminiscences of Moekle," Vol. II, pp. 149–151; "The Reminiscences of E. G. Liebold" (Jan., 1953), p. 1,406, Ford Archives.

N.I.R.A.[14] Johnson came away from the conference thinking that Henry Ford would support the N.I.R.A. "to the limit and even beyond." The reason for Johnson's erroneous estimate of the situation is clear. In explaining the act to Henry, he had apparently emphasized its immediate objectives, the re-employment of labor through the reduction of working hours and the stimulation of purchasing power through the fixing of minimum-wage levels. Ford could easily endorse these objectives since he quite properly regarded himself as a pioneer in this area. "It was only what I had been practicing all my life," he later wrote to Charles Edison. It was thus possible for Ford on July 15 to praise General Johnson and to state that "what he [Johnson] wants is not Government control of business; he wants the best business principles of the best businessmen to become the rules of all business."

Johnson obviously did not stress in his conversation with Ford the possible implications of Section 7(a) and the likelihood that the codes of fair competition that the act contemplated would include price and production controls. It is no doubt for this reason that Liebold later remarked, "I don't think at that time Mr. Ford knew what the N.R.A. was," and that William J. Cameron, Ford's spokesman, doubted that Ford "understood the full drift of it."[15]

As the time for the final approval of the auto code approached, Ford began to have second thoughts about the N.I.R.A. He undoubtedly learned through Moekle of the N.A.C.C.'s fears concerning the threat which 7(a) posed to the open shop and perhaps also became aware of the restraints on competition included in the codes which the various industries of the nation were submitting. Thus, when Josephus Daniels urged Ford to sign the code, Cameron replied: "There can be no doubt . . . that proposals are being made in the name of recovery that have nothing to do with recovery, and that seriously affect the fundamental American idea. We doubt that it is necessary to scrap America in order to achieve recovery."[16]

In particular, Ford, like the other auto manufacturers, was anxious not to "scrap" the open shop that prevailed in his plants, and he feared that Section 7(a) would have precisely this effect. His secretary, Frank Campsall, replied to a complaint about Ford's refusal to sign the code that,

[14] The *Detroit News* discovered that Johnson had been in Dearborn, but William J. Cameron persuaded the paper not to publish the fact. Hugh Johnson correspondence folder, Acc. 52, Box 8, Ford Archives.

[15] Hugh Johnson correspondence folder, Acc. 52, Box 8, Ford Archives; H. Ford to Charles Edison, Oct. 6, 1933, Acc. 52, Box 8, Ford Archives; drafts of Cameron statements, Acc. 52, Box 8, Ford Archives; "Reminiscences of Liebold," p. 1,407, Ford Archives; "Third Interview with Mr. W. J. Cameron by Owen Bombard on June 9, 1952," p. 149, Ford Archives; Johnson, *The Blue Eagle from Egg to Earth* (Garden City, New York, 1935), pp. 235–236; *Detroit Free Press*, July 16, 1933. Cf. the version of the conference in Harry Bennett, *We Never Called Him Henry* (New York, 1951), p. 96.

[16] Cameron to Daniels, Aug. 21, 1933, Acc. 285, Box 1550, Ford Archives.

quite apart from its recovery features, the N.I.R.A. "contains a section which in effect makes obligatory the unionization of industry." From Ford's point of view, collective bargaining, in Cameron's phrasing, was simply "a smooth sounding name for the labor racketeer." Ford comforted himself with the thought that he made better bargains for his men than any labor organizer could. "We have bargained *for* our men; we have never been compelled to bargain *against* them, nor they against us."[17]

Even more important than the threat of unionization, Ford stated in explaining his refusal to sign the code, was the extensive government control of business which he saw implicit in the N.I.R.A. The Ford Motor Company, he informed the public on June 25, had achieved "industrial decencies" without "regulation or compulsion" or " 'gentlemen's agreements.' " Under the N.I.R.A, however, Ford insisted a few months later, "every detail of our operation can be placed under control of a committee one-third of whom are politicians and one-third of whom are labor leaders." If he signed the code, Moekle recalled, "He felt it would be giving away the control of his own business. . . ."[18]

Ford, as a matter of fact, was too much alarmed at the threat the N.I.R.A. posed to his business. Although the statute, as noted, had drastic implications and although many of the codes included provisions which were obnoxious to Ford, it was possible, as the N.A.C.C. demonstrated, to have a code which ignored price and production policies entirely and confined itself to the subject of wages and hours and the mandatory provisions of Section 7(a). Even with respect to the latter, the N.A.C.C. was able to gain approval in its code for a statement that "employers in this industry may exercise their right to select, retain, or advance employees on the basis of individual merit, without regard to their membership or nonmembership in any organization."[19] Also, as Ford must have known, he could not escape the terms of his industry's code by refusing to sign the document. Once the President approved the code, Ford was obligated by the N.I.R.A. to observe its provisions whether he liked them or not. By refusing to sign, Ford merely indicated his displeasure with the statute and placed himself in a more advantageous position to challenge it in court or in the press.

Hearing that the N.A.C.C. approval of a code was being held up by the organization's fear of Section 7(a) and by Ford's apparent unwillingness to sign the code, Johnson flew to Detroit on July 27 to talk with the N.A.C.C.'s directors. While in Detroit, he spoke to Edsel on the telephone and, in his usual pungent manner, asked him "what the hell was the matter." When Edsel replied that the company did not like Section 7(a), Johnson

[17] Campsall to Augustus L. Richards, Aug. 10, 1933, Acc. 52, Box 8, Ford Archives; Cameron drafts in Acc. 52, Box 8, Ford Archives; *New York Times*, Aug. 6, 1933.

[18] H. Ford to Edison, Oct. 6, 1933, Acc. 52, Box 8, Ford Archives; "Reminiscences of Moekle," Vol. II, p. 150, Ford Archives; *Detroit News*, June 25, 1933.

[19] The code of the automobile manufacturing industry is in N.R.A., *Codes of Fair Competition*, Vol. I (Washington, 1933), pp. 253–266.

sought to de-emphasize the importance of this part of the act, and he informed Edsel, as he was to inform the N.A.C.C. directors, that Section 7(a) was not inconsistent with the maintenance of the open shop. Edsel apparently pressed Johnson for a written promise that the section would not be applied to the Ford Motor Company, but this far Johnson would not go.[20]

The N.A.C.C. directors expressed to Johnson their concern about Ford's reluctance to associate himself with the code. "We want every advantage and every disadvantage equal," Walter Chrysler explained. On the one hand, the directors were troubled by the advantage in cost which the lower wages he then paid gave Ford and, on the other hand, were apprehensive that Ford, with his penchant for the dramatic, would take some action that would embarrass them. "If that baby," said Chrysler, "should go to 30 hours a week and $1.00 an hour and he signs that Clause VII it will put us in a hell of a position." Johnson informed the directors, however, that if Ford did not sign the code, his cars could not display the Blue Eagle, the symbol of compliance with the N.I.R.A. "I woudn't like to go out and sell any product in the United States that didn't have that bird on it," Johnson declared. He also assured the auto executives that he would not permit Ford to "upset" the industry's price structure.[21]

As a matter of fact, Ford had no intention of upsetting the industry's price structure, and, despite some press speculation, he was not preparing to "soar far beyond" existing hour and wage standards in the industry. He was also apparently untroubled by the thought that his failure to sign the code would prevent him from displaying the Blue Eagle. "Hell," Liebold remembers him saying, "that Roosevelt buzzard! I wouldn't put it on the car."[22]

Thus, when the auto code went into effect on September 5, 1933, the Ford Motor Company was not among the concerns that signed assent forms. This fact, plus the soon-to-be-noted refusal of the federal government, for a time, to purchase Ford cars, produced a flood of letters to the National Recovery Administration and a lesser number to Ford in criticism or in praise of Ford's action. One of Ford's critics thought him nothing less than a "traitor," and another described him as "mentally twisted, unbalanced and prejudiced." The president of the Ford Owners Alliance, who claimed two hundred thousand members, wrote on September 1 that all

[20] Special Meeting of N.A.C.C. with General Johnson held in General Motors Building, July 28, 1933, Chapin Papers; Johnson, *Blue Eagle*, pp. 236–237; Ford to Edison, Oct. 6, 1933, Acc. 52, Box 8, Ford Archives.

[21] Special Meeting of N.A.C.C. with Johnson, July 28, 1933, Chapin Papers. During Sept., 1933, the first month that the code was in effect, the average hourly earned rate for factory employees in the Rouge was $.5947 as compared to the industry average of $.656. Records of the N.R.A., National Archives, Record Group 9, Box 669 (henceforth, records from this group will be designated N.R.A.); George Myrick, "An Economic Survey of the Automobile Industry" (1936), Vol. III, p. 52, N.R.A. Box 8309.

[22] *Detroit Free Press*, Sept. 2, 1933; "Reminiscences of Liebold," p. 1,406, Ford Archives.

members would soon display windshield stickers stating "My last Ford supports N.R.A." But Ford also had his defenders, one of whom denounced this "Jewish-Johnson-Baruch-Wall Street persecution," and another of whom deplored the government's attack on "the nation's greatest benefactor." Ford drew praise, in particular, from businessmen who saw him as a symbol of opposition to government regulation and collectivism and to the New Deal. One of Ford's defenders, who congratulated him on his stand against "the present damned rotten Administration," even composed a bit of doggerel for the occasion:[23]

> NRA me down to sleep
> I pray Johnson my code to keep;
> If I should bust before I wake
> AF of L my plant will take.

Many of Ford's critics wanted the federal government to demonstrate that it was bigger than Henry Ford and, in the words of one of them, to "Turn the hose on Henry."[24] Actually though, as long as Ford complied with the automobile code, there was little the federal government could do to chastise him for his recalcitrance other than to refuse to award government contracts to the Ford Motor Company or to Ford dealers and, similarly, to urge the public not to purchase Ford products. At his press conference of August 29, Johnson, when asked if he intended to "'crack down'" on Ford, replied: "I think maybe the American people will crack down on him when the Blue Eagle is on other cars and he does not have one."[25] Public authorities in various jurisdictions and some individuals promptly responded to Johnson's suggestion by announcing their refusal to purchase Ford products.[26]

While the federal government during September, 1933, pursued a policy of "watchful waiting" as regards Ford, the Detroit industrialist took two actions which were at least in part designed to offset public criticism of his refusal to sign the auto code. On September 5, the day the code went into effect, Ford announced that his employees would receive wage increases ranging from $.40 to $1.00 a day. Ten days later the company made it known that employment would be given to 5,000 Wayne County veterans. Neither action, however, had any great impact from a public-relations standpoint. The other auto manufacturers had already increased wages by a comparable or greater amount, and the hiring of the veterans brought

[23] File of letters in Folder 11, N.R.A. Box 656; N.R.A. letters on F.M.C. attitude, Acc. 390, Box 10, Ford Archives; Jerome T. Harriman to Ford Motor Co., Sept. 1, 1933, George Gould to Ford, July 19, 1934, Acc. 38, Box 75, Ford Archives; various letters in Acc. 6, Boxes 150, 166, Acc. 23, Box 12, Acc. 38, Box 73, Ford Archives.

[24] Folder 11, N.R.A. Box 656.

[25] *Detroit News*, Aug. 30, 1933.

[26] *New York Times*, Sept, 1, 2, 12, 13, 14, 1933.

prompt charges from unemployed Ford workers who were also veterans that they were being discriminated against.[27]

Obviously antagonized by Ford's unwillingness to sign the auto code, Johnson was anxious to have the federal government proclaim its refusal to purchase Ford products. He found sanction for a boycott policy in Executive Order 6246 of August 10, 1933, which stated that the recipients of government contracts were to comply with the applicable provisions of the code of their industry or trade.[28] Although the order did not require a contractor to sign the applicable code and did not deal directly with the question as to whether the seller of a product could be denied a contract if the manufacturer of the product fell under the order's ban, Johnson contended that as long as Ford did not sign the code, the federal government should not purchase vehicles from Ford dealers even though the latter might be fully complying with the dealers' code. "To let Mr. Ford escape the consequences of this Act because his dealer has a Blue Eagle," Johnson wrote on September 22, "would be to allow a billion dollar corporation hide behind the skirts of a thirty thousand dollar company." Concurring in Johnson's view of the matter, President Roosevelt remarked at his press conference on October 27 that the federal government should buy goods manufactured not only in accord with N.R.A. standards but "by people who have gone along with the general agreement." "It is the article rather than the person you buy it through," the President declared. ". . . we have got to eliminate the purchase of Ford cars."[29]

At a press conference of his own on October 27, Johnson declared that if the Ford Motor Company did not submit the wages and hours data required of it by the auto code, he would bring this fact to the attention of the Attorney General. This moved Ford to reply, in a statement prepared by Cameron, that "Before assuming the airs of a dictator, he [Johnson] should fortify himself with evidence that Henry Ford has refused compliance with Government requirements." "We suggest a code of fair publicity for Mr. Johnson's interviews."

Johnson retorted that he had not said that he had evidence of any Ford violation of the code, but that Edsel had told him that the company would not "submit" to a code that required collective bargaining. At all events, Johnson stated, Ford was not eligible to receive government contracts, a conclusion that the President supported.

[27] *Detroit Free Press*, Sept. 7, 16, 24, 1933; *New York Times*, Sept. 6, 7, 14, 26, 29, 1933; *Detroit News*, Sept. 6, 7, 16, 24, 1933; "Reminiscences of Moekle," Vol. II, p. 155, Ford Archives.

[28] Jordan D. Hill, *Relationship of N.R.A. to Government Contracts and Contracts Involving the Use of Government Funds*, N.R.A. Division of Review, Work Materials No. 49 (Washington, 1936), pp. 3–4.

[29] Johnson to Daniel Roper, Sept. 22, 1933, Official File 466, Box 2, F.D.R. Library, Hyde Park (henceforth, Official File will be designated O.F.); Press Conference #64, Oct. 27, 1933, pp. 382–383, F.D.R. Library.

Counterattacking again, Cameron stated that Ford had complied with the code "in every respect" and exceeded it "in all its real recovery features." Ford had not bid on any government contracts, and if Ford dealers had, it was only because government departments insisted that they do so. By refusing to award contracts to Ford dealers, Johnson was simply proposing to injure the taxpayer by having the federal government pay higher prices for motor vehicles produced by companies that paid lower wages than Ford did.[30]

Ford's publicity blasts against Johnson were followed the next day by a protest to Comptroller General J. R. McCarl from Ford dealer R. P. Sabine, the head of the Northwest Motor Company of Bethesda, Maryland, that his firm had been denied a government contract for several hundred trucks for the Civilian Conservation Corps although it was the low bidder and was complying with the dealers' code. The Comptroller General on November 10 rejected Sabine's contention that the federal government, in effect, could not go behind dealer compliance to require compliance by the manufacturer, but at the same time he ruled that there was nothing in the N.I.R.A. or the auto code that required a company actually to sign a code or to signify its intent to comply. The fact that Ford had failed to take such action was "not controlling here," and unless the contrary was proved, and it had not been, it had to be assumed that Ford was complying.[31]

The crucial question thus was not whether Ford had signed the code but whether he was complying with it. The answer was not long in coming. Five days after the Comptroller General's ruling, N.R.A. Deputy Administrator Karl J. Ammerman reported that "To the extent of our information, the Ford Motor Co, has, save in respect of certain technical particulars which we consider immaterial, complied satisfactorily with the Code. . . ." Ammerman's conclusion was based on a study of the wages and hours reports that Ford had submitted to the N.R.A., and there is, indeed, no question that Ford scrupulously observed the wages and hours provisions of the code throughout the life of the N.I.R.A.[32] Whether he similarly observed the requirements of Section 7(a), which were embodied in Section VII of the

[30] *Detroit News*, Oct. 27, 28, 1933; *New York Times*, Oct. 28, 1933. Johnson, after this exchange of verbal blows with Ford, traded in his Lincoln for a Cadillac. *New York Times*, Oct. 29, 1933.

[31] *New York Times*, Oct. 26, 31, 1933; *Detroit News*, Nov. 21, 1933; McCarl to Secretary of Agriculture, McCarl to Secretary of Commerce, Nov. 10, 1933, Acc. 52, Box 8, Ford Archives.

[32] Ammerman to Johnson, Nov. 15, 1933, and attached letter for Rexford G. Tugwell, N.R.A. Box 654. The wages and hours reports of the Ford Motor Co. to the N.R.A. are in N.R.A. Box 669. In an effort to embarrass the N.R.A., Ford, on Nov. 3, 1933, made an ostentatious display of his compliance by announcing that "in compliance with the new prohibition against work in this Country," Rouge employees, then working 40 hours per week, would be laid off in shifts for 7 days at a time so that their average weekly hours of employment for the effective period of the code should not exceed the stipulated 35-hour limit. Johnson correctly interpreted this action as a response to the seasonal drop in automotive production. Ford plants in the U.S. produced only 7,142 cars and trucks in November. *Detroit Free Press*, Nov. 4, 5, 1933; N.R.A. Release No. 1556, Nov. 4, 1933, Acc. 622, Ford Archives.

code, is, however, another matter. Publicly, the N.R.A. never charged Ford with failure to comply with Section 7(a), but, as we shall see, the Compliance Board of the N.R.A. eventually concluded that Ford had violated the section's requirements.

At all events, the Comptroller General's ruling of November 10 opened the way to the award of government contracts to Ford dealers. On December 1, 1933, the Secretary of Agriculture awarded Sabine a contract for over 800 trucks for the C.C.C., and by March 1, 1934, approximately one million dollars in government contracts had been granted to Ford dealers.[33] The contest between Ford and the N.R.A. was by no means over, however. On March 14, the day after the Ford Motor Company had announced its return to the five-dollar day, the President issued a new executive order (6646), which specified, with obvious reference to the Ford case, that the federal government would not contract for materials "in whole or in part, produced or furnished by any person who shall not have certified that he is complying with each code of fair competition that relates to such articles, materials, or supplies. . . ."[34] Thus, a signed certificate of compliance by Ford was essential if Ford dealers were to receive government contracts.

In submitting a bid to the Department of Commerce on March 30, 1934, the Northwest Motor Company certified its compliance with the dealers' code but stated that it could not make representations concerning the various manufacturers who had a part in fabricating the product it was attempting to sell, and to require it to do so was "unfair and unjust." The Comptroller General, however, ruled against Sabine on May 17. Sabine thereupon secured a court order temporarily restraining the government departments concerned from rejecting his bids, but on May 24 Justice Daniel W. O'Donoghue of the Supreme Court of the District of Columbia denied the company a temporary injunction, declaring, "It would seem unreasonable that the President should be compelled to contract with any company, no matter how wealthy or how powerful, if that company is thwarting the Recovery Act and defying the government to enforce it."[35]

[33] *Detroit News*, Dec. 2, 1933, May 6, 1934. The extent to which the Northwest Motor Co. actually represented the Ford Motor Co. in submitting bids for government business has been a matter of some uncertainty. According to E. C. Simons, who was employed at the time in Ford's Washington District Sales Office, the Ford Motor Co. ceased direct bidding on government contracts as the result of Executive Order 6246. Sabine thereupon requested and received permission from Henry Ford "to engage in Government selling." Simons was instructed "to render every assistance possible" to Sabine but "to avoid any action that could be construed as participation by the Ford Motor Company in the direct sales." Until Sabine became "better established," the Ford Motor Co. aided him in financing sales to the government, and Simons did "most of the work of preparing the bids and processing the orders." Simons indicates that the Northwest Motor Co. sold 828 vehicles to the federal government in 1933; 1,518 vehicles in 1934; and 3,833 vehicles in 1935. Statement of E. C. Simons, Feb. 11, 1958, Ford Archives.

[34] Hill, *Relationship of N.R.A. to Government Contracts*, pp. 17–18.

[35] *Ibid.*, pp. 38–42; *New York Times*, May 18, 20, 25, 1934; *Detroit News*, May 6, 14, 18, 25, 26, 1934.

Despite this ruling, Ford stubbornly refused to sign a certificate of compliance, and for several months Chevrolet virtually monopolized the federal government's purchase of small cars and trucks.[36] However, although Executive Order 6646 remained in effect, the federal government eventually relaxed its ban on the purchase of Ford products. It first deviated from the requirements of the executive order by permitting the purchase of repair and replacement parts for Fords already in the government service, an obvious necessity unless the federal government was prepared to replace all its Fords. For a time the N.R.A. authorized the purchase of such parts only on the basis of emergency exceptions to 6646, but, lest it "would look as though we were backing down," no general exception to the order was made for this purpose until January 16, 1935.[37]

The Compliance Division of the N.R.A. became aware in October, 1934, that government departments were beginning to purchase new Fords on the strength of certificates of compliance furnished by dealers, but Johnson advised the Division "not to make an issue of this" because of negotiations then under way which it was hoped would result in Ford's certification of his compliance. Whatever the nature of these negotiations, however, they did not result in Ford's altering his stand in any way, although Sabine late in October tried to persuade the N.R.A. to accept as the equivalent of a certificate of compliance a telegram dated January 5, 1934, from Ford's sales manager, W. C. Cowling, to the Secretary of the Interior in which Cowling stated that Ford had complied with the code and would continue to do so. Sabine did not explain how a wire dated January 5, 1934, could contain a reference to Executive Order 6646, dated March 14, 1934.[38]

Despite Ford's refusal to compromise and in the face of objections from Chrysler, the purchase of Fords by the federal government continued. It was announced on February 19, 1935, that the Department of the Interior had purchased 35 Fords and the Department of Agriculture about 400, and a few days later the War Department, anxious to widen the competition in the bidding for its contracts, requested Ford to bid on a $4 million order for the C.C.C.[39]

[36] *Detroit News,* June 26, Aug. 6, 1934. Ford claimed that he refused to sign a certificate of compliance because this meant to "waive his constitutional rights and accept Gen. Hugh S. Johnson as both judge and jury in any dispute that might arise." *Detroit News,* June 27, 1934. Ford, however, refused to sign a certificate of compliance even after Johnson left the N.R.A.

[37] H. J. Collins to Administrator, N.R.A., June 11, 1934, Frank Healy to Blackwell Smith, June 25, 1934, Healy to Sol Rosenblatt, Dec. 6, 1934, Administrative Order GC-73, Jan. 16, 1935, N.R.A. Drawer 1798; Healy to Donald Nelson, Nov. 6, 1934, N.R.A. Drawer 642.

[38] Healy to George Lynch, Oct. 12, 1934, Healy to S. Clay Williams *et al.,* Jan. 3, 1934 [1935], N.R.A. Drawer 642; Sabine to Williams, Oct. 22, 1934, N.R.A. Box 3; *Detroit News,* Nov. 22, 1934. There is a copy of the alleged Cowling telegram in N.R.A. Box 677.

[39] Executive Assistant, Division II, to W. A. Harriman, Nov. 26, 1934, N.R.A. Box 34; *Detroit Free Press,* Feb. 20, 26, 1935.

All in all, Ford's refusal to sign a certificate of compliance did not seriously affect the sale of Ford cars and trucks. It is true that Ford lost out on the possibility of gaining his share of several million dollars of government business, particularly between March and October, 1934, but the civilian purchase of Ford products suffered not at all. It would appear that the nation's motorists agreed with Will Rogers when he remarked, "You can take the rouge from female lips, the cigarettes from the raised hands, the hot dogs from the tourists' greasy paw, but when you start jacking the Fords out from under the traveling public you are monkeying with the very fundamentals of American life."[40] Indeed, whereas the Ford Motor Company (including Lincoln) had suffered a net loss of $7,888,718 after taxes and accounted for only 21.5 per cent of the total new passenger car and truck registrations in the United States in 1933, in 1934 it made a profit of $21,362,118 after taxes and increased its percentage of total new car and truck registrations to 28.8. Ford triumphantly announced on November 1, 1934, that the depression was over for him and that this would be true of the nation as a whole "if American industrialists would just forget these alphabet schemes and take hold of their industries and run them with good, sound American business sense."[41]

III

Particularly during the early months of the Ford-N.R.A. controversy, there was speculation in the press concerning the possibilities of a meeting between President Roosevelt and Henry Ford to discuss N.R.A. problems. Roosevelt certainly desired such a meeting, but the various attempts to bring the two men together all came to naught.

When George J. Atwell wrote the President late in September, 1933, that Ford was anxious to visit with him, the Chief Executive instructed his secretary, Marvin H. McIntyre, to reply that the President would be glad to talk with Ford, "but that he has never even suggested that he would like to see the President."[42] Not wishing to leave this important matter to chance, Charles Edison, son of Ford's long-time friend, Thomas A. Edison, and active in N.R.A. work in New Jersey, tried his hand at about this time at arranging a meeting between the President and the industrialist. His effort elicited a long letter from Ford on October 6 in which the motor king indicated that he had "deep respect" for Roosevelt "personally and as President" and that

---

[40] Cited in William A. Simonds, *Henry Ford, His Life—His Work—His Genius* (Indianapolis, 1943), p. 247.

[41] Federal Trade Commission, *Report on Motor Vehicle Industry*, p. 649; *Ward's 1939 Automotive Year Book*, pp. 42, 46; *New York Times*, Nov. 2, 1934.

[42] Atwell to F.D.R., Sept. 29, 1933, F.D.R. to Mac, Oct. 3, 1933, O.F. 3217, F.D.R. Library.

he credited him "with an earnest and religious desire to do everything possible to ease the situation of this country. . . ." Indeed, Ford remarked that he had "to make a sharp distinction . . . between the President and the N.R.A." because he could not believe that Roosevelt had conceived that "complicated and impractical plan."[43]

Upon reading this letter, the President, Edison informed Dearborn by phone, remarked, "Oh, he doesn't get it at all. I wish he would let me talk this over with him." The next day, in a letter which he had drafted with McIntyre's aid and which the President had edited, Edison wrote that it appeared to him that the two men were willing to meet but that each thought the other should request the meeting. Edison felt it necessary to remind Ford that Roosevelt "is, after all, the President of the United States." The feeling of the President for Ford, Edison thought, was "a very friendly one. I noted no note of antagonism, beyond his statement made with a smile that 'If Henry will quit being a damn fool about this matter and call me on the telephone I would be glad to talk with him.' " Ford, however, did not make the call, and Edison had to concede, "As a Clearing House, I guess I'm something of a flop."[44]

A few weeks after Edison's unsuccessful effort, Ford's former business associate, Senator James Couzens, informed the President that Ford would like to visit with him. Roosevelt, therefore, on Novemebr 7, 1933, invited Ford to the White House "as an old friend whom I used to know in my Navy days." Ford declined the invitation, however, allegedly because he feared that his visit would be construed as an effort on his part to persuade the government to buy Ford cars.[45]

Roosevelt renewed the invitation in responding to birthday greetings which Ford wired him on January 30, 1934. "We all admire the directness with which you are attacking the nation's problems," Ford wrote, "and we are all the grateful beneficiaries of your immeasurable services in maintaining a courageous spirit amongst all the people." In reply, Roosevelt said that he would "like very much" to have Ford visit him any time he was in Washington.[46]

Assuming the initiative once again, Roosevelt, late in October, 1934, decided to invite Henry and Edsel Ford and their wives to the White House to talk about plans to relocate urban dwellers in "country communities" and to locate smaller industries in small towns. This time Mrs. Roosevelt intervened and informed Presidential Press Secretary Steve Early, that she thought "it would be a 'stupid political mistake' to have them here, invited

---

[43] Ford to Edison, Oct. 6, 1933, Acc. 52, Box 8, Ford Archives.

[44] Text of phone conversation with Edison [Oct. 7, 1933], Edison to Ford, Oct. 8, 9, 1933, Acc. 52, Box 8, Ford Archives.

[45] F.D.R. to Ford, Nov. 7, 1933, President's Personal File 680, F.D.R. Library (henceforth, President's Personal File will be designated P.P.F.); *Detroit News*, Nov. 26, 1933.

[46] Ford to F.D.R., Jan. 30, 1934, F.D.R. to Ford, Feb. 23, 1934, P.P.F. 680, F.D.R. Library.

by you." It was her view, Early informed the President, that "Ford did more than any other man to wreck NRA; to have him here would be to encourage NRA opposition and discourage the friends of NRA."

Undoubtedly because of Mrs. Roosevelt's objections, the President decided to delay the invitation to Ford until after the Congressional elections. The letter was sent on November 8, and the Fords were invited not to the White House but to Warm Springs. Henry and his wife were unable to come because of the state of Mrs. Ford's health, but Mr. and Mrs. Edsel Ford visited with the President on November 24.[47] Whether Edsel and the President discussed N.R.A. problems is not known, but what does appear clear is that Edsel's father not only refused to sign the code for his industry but was unwilling even to discuss the matter with the President of the United States.

IV

The answer as to whether or not the Ford Motor Company conformed to the requirements of Section 7(a) is to be found in the events growing out of the labor disturbances that occurred in late September, 1933, at the Ford assembly plants in Chester, Pennsylvania, and Edgewater, New Jersey. The trouble at Chester began on the morning of September 26. The principal grievance of the men appears to have been the decision of the company, announced on September 22, that the work week would be reduced from five to four days without any increase in the base pay of $4.00 a day. There was no union in the plant, and there had been no effort on the part of the men to present any demands to the local management. At about 10:00 a.m. on the 26th there was a commotion at the rear end of the chassis line occasioned by a few men who threw down their tools and shouted to the other workers to follow them out of the plant. This sudden action caused a shutdown of the chassis line. Superintendent A. M. Harris then appeared and, when he failed to persuade the employees congregated about the line to return to their jobs, ordered the workers out of the plant. Approximately twenty-five hundred persons were employed in the plant at that time.

Outside the plant, where the men were milling about, a committee of employees representing the various departments in the plant was formed to present demands to the plant management. The committee entered the plant and informed Harris that the workers wanted a seven-hour day, a five-day week, and a minimum wage of $5.00 per day. There is a difference of opinion as to whether other demands were also presented. Harris informed the committee that the matter would have to be referred to company head-

<hr />

[47] Confidential memo for the President from S. T. Early, undated, attached to F.D.R. to Ford, Nov. 8, 1934, P.P.F. 680, F.D.R. Library; Ford to F.D.R., Nov. 16, 1934, McIntyre to Ford, Nov. 21, 1934, Acc. 285, Box 1676, Ford Archives; *Detroit News*, Nov. 25, 1934. The following notation appears at the bottom of Early's memo: "Hold till after Cong. elections. S.E."

quarters in Dearborn. He advised the committee to have the workers back at their jobs by 12:00 noon, but since it was already 11:20 a.m., he changed the time of return to 7:30 the next morning.[48] Harris then called Dearborn and was instructed to post a sign that the plant was closed indefinitely.[49] This decision was made without any knowledge as to whether the workers would return to work the next morning.

When the committee reported the results of its meeting with Harris to the workers outside, the decision was made to organize an A.F. of L. local. An A.F. of L. representative was called in, and an application for a charter was made. Apparently, a substantial number of workers pledged that they would join the union, but only a few hundred actually paid initiation fees. The A.F. of L. organizer who had been summoned got in touch with the National Labor Board the same evening, and the N.L.B. instructed James F. Dewey, a Department of Labor conciliator and a Chester resident, to proceed to Chester to arrange a settlement.[50]

When the workers arrived at the plant on the morning of the 27th, prepared to return if their demands were met or, perhaps, pending mediation by the N.L.B.,[51] they, of course, learned that the plant was closed indefinitely. Dewey arrived on the scene within a few hours and went into the plant. He was kept waiting for 45 minutes and was then informed by a stenographer that Plant Manager F. A. Atcheson would not see him until he had received permission to do so from Dearborn. Dewey told the stenographer to inform Atcheson that if he would not see him in five minutes, he would refer the issue to Washington. Dewey was thereupon ushered into Atcheson's office and advised the plant manager that if the company would meet with the committee and with him, the matter could be settled in five minutes. The men could return to work, and any unresolved issues could be taken up with Dearborn. Atcheson called his superiors in Dearborn and then

[48] The workers' version of the events of Sept. 26 is presented in Thomas J. Dunphy *et al.* to Wagner, Oct. 11, 1933, N.R.A. Drawer 641; transcript of conference in Handler's office, Dec. 4–5, 1933, Case 105, Records of the National Labor Board, Record Group 25, National Archives, Drawer 17 (henceforth, records in this group will be designated N.L.B.); and N.R.A., Ford Motor Co., Transcript of Hearing Held at Chester, Pa., Mar. 3, 1934, N.R.A. Drawer 642. Harris' version is in Statement Dictated by Mr. A. M. Harris, Mar. 1, 1934, Acc. 52, Box 12, Ford Archives. The grievances of the workers are summed up in Dunphy *et al.* to Wagner, Sept. 27, 1933, N.R.A. Drawer 641.

[49] Harris statement, Mar. 1, 1934, Acc. 52, Box 12, Ford Archives.

[50] Transcript of Handler conference, Dec. 4–5, 1933, pp. 2, 5–6, Case 105, N.L.B. Drawer 17; N.R.A., Transcript of Chester Hearing, Mar. 3, 1934, pp. 9–10, 25–26, 87–88, N.R.A. Drawer 642; memorandum based on information supplied by Michael J. Gandiello, Oct. 16, 1933, N.R.A. Drawer 641. The N.L.B. was created by the President on Aug. 5, 1933, to adjust "differences and controversies" arising out of the President's Re-employment Agreement. It also began dealing with "differences and controversies" arising under the codes, although it was not specifically authorized to do so until Dec. 16, 1933.

[51] There is conflicting evidence as regards the intention of the workers on the morning of the 27th. See Dunphy *et al.* to Wagner, Oct. 11, 1933, N.R.A. Drawer 641; transcript of Handler conference, Dec. 4–5, 1933, p. 6, Case 105, N.L.B. Drawer 17; N.R.A., Transcript of Chester Hearing, Mar. 3, 1934, p. 89, N.R.A. Drawer 642; *Chester Times*, Sept. 26, 1933.

informed Dewey that the plant was closed and that he could not discuss the situation with either Dewey or the employees' committee. At Dewey's request, Atcheson phoned this information to Senator Robert F. Wagner, the chairman of the N.L.B. Dewey, who regarded the company's attitude as "very arbitrary and unfair," presented the situation to the N.L.B. the next day and recommended "drastic action."[52] For a time, however, Wagner was no more able than Dewey had been to persuade the company to negotiate with the employees and a representative of the N.L.B.[53]

The company decided to reopen the plant on October 16, and approximately eight hundred workers were summoned by invitation to report on that date. The union insisted that many of these men had not been on the payroll on September 26, but apparently only seven of those summoned were new employees.[54] It should of course be noted that in the view of the Ford Motor Company, the workers who remained away from their jobs at Chester, and also at Edgewater, thereby severed their connection with the company and had to apply for re-employment if they wished their jobs back, whereas the N.L.B. regarded strikers (and certainly workers who had been locked out) as continuing in the status of employees.[55]

On October 14 the N.L.B. wired Atcheson that it had been charged that some employees were being discriminated against in the reopening of the Chester plant and that the company had refused to bargain and that therefore a hearing would be held on October 17, to which Ford was invited to send a representative. Ford replied on October 16 that the company had been advised by counsel that it had no obligation to attend any hearing but that it could say there had never been discrimination against Ford employees because of union affiliation and that the company had not refused to meet duly authorized employee representatives.[56]

[52] Dewey testimony, transcript of Handler conference, Dec. 4–5, 1933, pp. 8–9, Case 105, N.L.B. Drawer 17; Dewey to Leiserson, Sept. 27, 1933, N.R.A. Drawer 641.

[53] Wagner to H. Ford, Sept. 29, 1933, Liebold to Wagner, Oct. 3, 1933, Leiserson to Liebold, Oct. 5, 1933, N.R.A. Drawer 641.

[54] A. J. Bait to H. C. Doss, Oct. 20, 1933, Acc. 52, Box 8, Ford Archives; Atcheson to Doss, Oct. 26, 1933, Acc. 52, Box 12, Ford Archives (Doss, who was assistant to the Ford sales manager, served as the liaison man between Dearborn and the Chester and Edgewater plants during the period of the labor disturbances); Dunphy et al. to Wagner, no date, N.R.A. Drawer 641; undated memorandum dealing with the reopening of the plant, N.R.A. Drawer 641; Chester Times, Oct. 14, 1933; Philadelphia Inquirer, Oct. 15, 1933. Some of the workers were apparently asked to sign a card certifying the signer as one of the "Loyal Ford Employees" of Chester. Company officials denied knowledge of this. Dunphy et al. to Wagner, undated, N.R.A. Drawer 641. One of these cards is in N.R.A. Drawer 642.

[55] For the N.L.B.'s position, see Lewis L. Lorwin and Arthur Wubnig, Labor Relations Boards: The Regulation of Collective Bargaining under the National Industrial Recovery Act (Washington, 1935), p. 174. There is a copy in Acc. 52, Box 12, Ford Archives, of the communication sent to the Chester employees, following the shutdown of the plant, terminating their services with the company.

[56] Wagner to Atcheson, Oct. 14, 1933, Ford Motor Co. to Wagner, Oct. 16, 1933, N.R.A. Drawer 641; Wagner to Ford Motor Co., Oct. 17, 1933, Atcheson to Doss, Oct. 18, 1933, Acc. 52, Box 12, Ford Archives.

Although there was no hearing on October 17, Dewey was able to arrange a conference between the employees' committee and the plant management on October 25. Actually, the conference involved no real discussion of issues since Atcheson was utterly without any authority to make any decisions. He even had to consult with Dearborn before rejecting the committee's request to engage a stenographer. The main purpose of the meeting was to provide the men with an opportunity to present their demands. Worried about the re-employment of those not yet called back to work and advised to concentrate on this subject by Dewey, the committee asked that those not working be returned without discrimination; that those who could not be reinstated at once because of lack of work should be re-employed before new workers were engaged; that men on the payroll who were not working September 26 should be discharged to make room for those who had been "locked out"; and that after full operations had been resumed or as soon as any of the committeemen had been re-employed, a conference should be held to discuss wages and other grievances, with regular meetings to follow.[57]

The reply to these demands was worked out in Dearborn and was handed by Atcheson to the employees' committee on November 10 without comment and without discussion. The company stated that it always judged applications for work on the basis of merit alone and without discrimination and that its policy was also to rehire "former" employees on this basis. No one then working, the company declared, would be discharged for reasons other than lack of work or incompetence. Finally, a system of regularly scheduled meetings was "unnecessary to the continuance of just relations between the Company and the employees" since the management was "ready at all reasonable times to hear individual employees or their representatives on matters that properly pertain to the relations between them." Instructed to report to Dearborn on the effect of this communication on the workers, Atcheson was able to state in a few days that he had learned through an "agent" that most of the active union men now realized that they had been defeated and were prepared to return to work.[58]

Anxious for the assistance of the federal government, the employees' committee presented its case to the N.L.B in a conference conducted by Milton Handler, the N.L.B.'s general counsel, on December 4 and 5.[59] A few days later, Handler, in response to a phone call from the acting secretary of the union, who appears to have been a Ford labor spy, indicated that the employees had been in error in walking out before any demands had

[57] Atcheson to Doss, Oct. 26, 1933, Acc. 52, Box 12, Ford Archives; Meeting of Strikers' Committee and Chester Branch Officials, Oct. 25, 1933, Acc. 52, Box 12, Ford Archives; memorandum by Benedict Wolf, Oct. 23, 1933, N.R.A. Drawer 641.

[58] Doss to Atcheson, Nov. 8, 1933, and attached reply to workers' demands, Atcheson to Doss, Nov. 14, 1933, Acc. 52, Box 12, Ford Archives.

[59] Transcript of Handler conference, Dec. 4–5, 1933, Case 105, N.L.B. Drawer 17.

been subimitted and that the evidence they had presented did not indicate any violation of the N.I.R.A. by Ford.[60] Discouraged by this report and by their inability to secure any material aid from the A.F. of L., the workers voted to disband their local union and to return its charter.[61] Their case was eventually turned over to the Compliance Division of the N.R.A., and a hearing was held by the Compliance Board on March 3.[62] The Ford Motor Company refused to attend the hearing, insisting that no specific complaint had been filed against it and claiming that it had not violated Section 7(a).[63] The conclusions of the Compliance Board will be noted below.

The facts in the Chester case make it clear that what had begun as an unorganized strike soon developed into a lockout. There also seems little doubt that the company practiced discrimination in its re-employment of those who had walked out. As late as the first of March, 477 employees had not been re-employed even though the total number at work on that date exceeded the number at work on September 26.[64] Since those denied employment were persons whose merit had already presumably been tested by their former service for the company—some of them were employees of long standing—the failure of the company to re-employ them suggests that factors other than merit influenced the decision. The fact that active union leaders were not rehired strengthens this inference.[65]

Above all, the company's conduct raises the question as to whether anything which can be described as collective bargaining actually took

[60] Memorandum by Handler, Dec. 7, 1933, N.R.A. Drawer 641; #45 to George J. Schmidt (Chester factory service head), Nov. [Dec. ?], 7, 1933, Acc. 52, Box 12, Ford Archives. Internal evidence strongly indicates that the latter report, only a typed copy of which is available in the Ford Archives, was actually made on Dec. 7. If this is so, #45 was Ed Hoffman, acting secretary of the Chester local, who later was chairman of the Com-munist-led Ford Workers' Protective Association against Discrimination, an organization formed by former Chester employees after the A.F. of L. local dissolved. According to #45's report, Handler advised that the men should return to work. Handler, who names Hoffman as the man who questioned him, states that Hoffman thought that under the circumstances the men should return to work.

[61] Dunphy to Healy, Feb. 22, 1934, N.R.A. Drawer 641; *Chester Times*, Mar. 5, 1934.

[62] The National Compliance Board, consisting of the Compliance Director and a member each from the N.R.A.'s Labor Advisory Board and Industrial Advisory Board, heard cases involving violation of a code.

[63] Exchange of correspondence between William H. Davis and G. C. Royall and Ford Motor Co., Feb. 27–Mar. 4, 1934, N.R.A. Drawer 642; N.R.A., Transcript of Chester Hearing, N.R.A. Drawer 642; *Chester Times*, Mar. 5, 1934.

[64] "Payroll Data" attached to typed sheet with heading, "March 1st, 1934," Acc. 52, Box 12, Ford Archives. Section 7(a) did not specifically forbid an employer to discriminate against union members, but it was so interpreted by the N.L.B. Lorwin and Wubnig, *Labor Relations Boards*, pp. 167–168.

[65] The president of the A.F. of L. local still had not been re-employed as late as Feb. 22, 1934. Dunphy to Healy, Feb. 22, 1934, N.R.A. Drawer 641. Two of the members of the employees' committee had worked for the company for over 10 years. Meeting of Strikers' Committee and Chester Branch Officials, Oct. 25, 1933, Acc. 52, Box 12, Ford Archives.

place at Chester. Atcheson's authority was limited to transmitting the workers' demands to Dearborn and the company's replies to the workers. At no time was there any real discussion between labor and management, any of the higgling and haggling one associates with bargaining, nor was there any effort on the company's part to reach a collective agreement. Collective bargaining, to be sure, was undefined in Section 7(a), and it remained for a succession of government labor boards to clothe it with meaning; but, nevertheless, it is difficult to regard what went on at Chester as collective bargaining even if the term is defined in the loosest possible sense. Of course, it must also be noted that the employees considerably weakened their case against the company by walking out before they had made any effort to discuss their grievances with the management.

The labor trouble that had developed at Chester on September 26 spilled over to the Ford assembly plant at Edgewater two days later. Unlike the situation at Chester, an A.F. of L. federal local had been formed at Edgewater prior to the strike. The first organizational meeting had been held on August 22, 1933, and the Ford management had a full report of what took place.[66] Indeed, throughout the strike, Ford was kept unusually well-informed by its labor spies of the union's activities.[67]

In the weeks following the August 22 meeting, Neill S. Brown, the plant superintendent, called in several of the men prominent in the new union and questioned them as to whether the formation of an A.F. of L. local was in the best interests of the employees, although Brown later claimed he made it clear that the existence of the union was of no consequence to Ford. The secretary of the local, however, stated that Brown had hinted that the presence of the union might cause Ford to close the Edgewater plant.[68] Even if the latter allegation was untrue, Brown's actions do not seem entirely consistent with that self-organization of employees guaranteed by Section 7(a).

On the morning of September 28 approximately twelve hundred Chester workers appeared at the gates of the Edgewater plant, having made the 125-mile trip from Chester by auto, and began picketing aggressively.

---

[66] T. M. Manning to E. Ford, Aug. 24, 1933, and enclosed report of Aug. 22 meeting, Acc. 6, Box 154, Ford Archives. Manning sent this report to Edsel as a means of soliciting business for the Manning Industrial Service. Edsel's secretary, A. J. Lepine, replied to Manning on Sept. 11: "The Ford Motor Company service department has covered meetings such as you mentioned, and the Company is not in the market for outside service," Acc. 6, Box 154, Ford Archives.

[67] See the numerous reports of strikers' meetings in Acc. 52, Box 12, Ford Archives.

[68] Stenographic Report of Conference Held at the Office of the Ford Motor Car Co., Edgewater, Oct. 19, 1933, pp. 2–3, Acc. 52, Box 12, Ford Archives; Albert F. Wickens affidavit, undated, N.R.A. Drawer 642. The day of the first meeting, the foreman of the export department warned the workers in his charge that those attending would be discharged. William Herford affidavit, Nov. 11, 1933, N.R.A. Drawer 642.

They had decided on this action because of unconfirmed reports that as the result of the labor disturbance at Chester, Ford planned to transfer Chester export contracts to Edgewater. As a consequence of this picketing, approximately five hundred Edgewater employees did not enter the Edgewater plant that morning. They were joined by other employees during the course of the day, and within a few days the number of workers in the plant had been reduced from 2,044 to 395. The union later claimed that sixteen hundred of the strikers were union members.[69]

As at Chester, the workers quit their jobs at Edgewater without having presented any formal demands to the plant management. The men did have their grievances against the company, however, and some of them were troubled by reports that Chester work would be transferred to Edgewater. Some of the men were thus predisposed to respond favorably to the Chester picketing, which triggered the Edgewater strike.[70]

At its inception, the strike was not a union action. As a matter of fact, on the morning of the 28th, four of the union leaders approached Brown and advised him that it was not an authorized walkout and asked permission, which was granted, to remonstrate with the men outside the plant. They failed, however, to persuade the workers to return. At an afternoon meeting of the strikers, the union leaders and A.F. of L. representative Hugh V. Reilly also failed in efforts to discourage the men from calling a strike. The next morning the strike committee requested the New Jersey N.R.A. to mediate the dispute and informed that agency that the strike demands were a seven-hour day, a five-day week, and a minimum wage of $5.00 a day, recognition of collective bargaining through representatives of the workers' choice, permission to leave the plant during the 30-minute lunch period, and the return of all the workers without discrimination when the other demands had been adjusted. The Ford Motor Company refused, however, to accept the offer of the New Jersey N.R.A. to mediate.[71]

On October 4, three Bergen County clergymen, after visiting with the strike committee, carried the strike demands to the Edgewater management. They learned that the demand concerning lunch would be met,

---

[69] *New York Times*, Sept. 29, 1933; Brown to Doss, Nov. 21, 1933, Acc. 52, Box 12, Ford Archives; In re: Striking Employees of Edgewater, New Jersey, Plant of Ford Motor Co. Informal Hearing Held before Harry L. Tepper, Nov. 29, 1933, p. 3, N.R.A. Drawer 642.

[70] Stenographic Report of Oct. 19 Conference, pp. 24–29, Acc. 52, Box 12, Ford Archives; Ford Conference at [New Jersey] State Headquarters, Oct. 19, 1933, pp. 8–13, N.R.A. Drawer 642.

[71] Transcript of Shorthand Notes of Conference at the Office of the New Jersey Recovery Board, Oct. 18, 1933, pp. 12–13, 18–26, N.R.A. Drawer 642; W. M. L[eiserson] memorandum, Sept. 29, 1933, N.R.A. Drawer 642; J. T. Ingram report, Sept. 29, 1933, Acc. 52, Box 12, Ford Archives; Stenographic Report of Oct. 19 Conference, pp. 11–15, Acc. 52, Box 12, Ford Archives; *Newark Evening News*, Sept. 29, 1933.

that the matter of recognition would have to be decided in Dearborn, and that the strike leaders "would be forever banned."[72] A few days later in a phone conversation with Edsel Ford dealing largely with the employment of workers at the plant, Plant Manager E. A. Esslinger stated, "When we hire we will take men from other parts of N[ew] Jersey and not local men." He also informed Edsel that he had refused to meet the strike committee, which led Edsel to say, "Be careful—section 7A of code."[73]

As at Chester, the N.L.B. attempted to mediate the dispute, and Senator Wagner arranged a meeting in the offices of the New Jersey N.R.A. for October 18. Acting on the advice of the prominent attorney, Congressman James M. Beck, Louis Colombo advised Brown to attend the meeting and to deny any unfounded charges against the company but to confine himself to that and to refer all all other matters to Dearborn.[74]

As advised, Brown appeared at the New Jersey N.R.A. headquarters on the morning of the 18th, but when it was suggested that he meet with the strike committee, which was present in another room in the building, Brown refused and said his instructions were to meet only with the "N.R.A. Labor Board." After calling Dearborn, however, and after being presented with a formal request from the strike committee, Brown agreed to meet with the committee in the Edgewater plant the next day.[75]

At the October 19 plant meeting the strike committee formally presented its demands. Brown replied that all policy issues would have to be referred to Dearborn but that he could state that the workers could have 45 minutes for lunch, during which time they could leave the plant. Most of the discussion related to the question of the re-employment of the strikers. Brown pointed out that despite the fact that letters had been sent out terminating the service of the strikers, 300 strikers had already been re-employed. He insisted that no employee had been "blackballed," but he noted at the same time that not all strikers were regarded as employees any longer.[76] Reilly summed up the workers' reaction to the conference when he informed the New Jersey N.R.A. that Brown was "asking the fellows to buy a yellow brick."[77]

The reply to the strikers' demands was worked out in Dearborn, and Brown was instructed on October 31 to transmit the company's answer to

---

[72] Thomas H. Wright, "Why Ford's Men Strike," *Christian Century*, Vol. L (Nov. 29, 1933), pp. 1,501–1,502.

[73] Conversation of E. Ford and Esslinger, Oct. 9, 1933, Acc. 52, Box 12, Ford Archives.

[74] Memoranda of phone conversations between Colombo and Beck, Oct. 17, 1933, Doss to Brown (dictated by Colombo), Oct. 17, 1933, Acc. 52, Box 12, Ford Archives; *New York Times*, Oct. 19, 1933.

[75] Transcript of Oct. 18 Conference, pp. 3–11, 30–50, N.R.A. Drawer 642.

[76] Stenographic Report of Oct. 19 Conference, Acc. 52, Box 12, Ford Archives. It is difficult to reconcile Brown's statements at this conference with Charles Edison's report to the White House on Oct. 21 that Ford would treat the workers as striking employees. K. memo for McIntyre, Oct. 21 [1933], O.F. 407–B, Box 18, F.D.R. Library.

[77] Ford Conference at State Headquarters, Oct. 19, 1933, p. 17, N.R.A. Drawer 642.

the strike committee "without any formal meeting for the purpose of discussing same." Brown presented the company's unsigned statement to the committee the next day. The statement claimed that three of the four demands were already company practice. The lunch demand had previously been more than met, recognition of collective bargaining was required by Section 7(a), and the workers would be re-employed without discrimination, each applicant for employment being considered "strictly on the basis of merit." As regards the wage-and-hour issue, the company stated that its wage rates were the highest for the same class of work in the "metropolitan industrial district," that wages would be increased as business conditions permitted, and that the 40-hour week would be maintained when the law and business conditions permitted.[78]

To the workers, the Ford reply was a "delayed ambiguous statement" that met unequivocally only their demand concerning the lunch hour. There was no guarantee that the idle strikers would be re-employed or that meaningful collective bargaining would take place.[79] The strikers' counsel, J. Glenn Anderson, had already filed a petition with the President accusing Ford of refusing to bargain and complaining that working conditions at Edgewater were deplorable, and Anderson was soon to file a supplementary petition which further elaborated the strikers' grievances.[80]

Since the Ford statement had noted that recognition of the right to bargain was company practice, the strike committee informed Edsel by letter on November 9 that it was prepared to meet with any duly authorized Ford representative to discuss the strikers' demands. Edsel replied on November 21 that Brown was authorized to meet with the committee and that "proper consideration" would be given to whatever committee members had to say.[81] The kind of "consideration" the strikers could expect was indicated the same day in a letter Brown sent to his superiors in Dearborn. Brown noted that of the 1,400 men working in the plant at the time, only 25 were union members. "We checked the men very carefully," Brown declared, "and do not intend to take back all the men that are out on strike [approximately 600]. However, if any of these men can prove their sincerity and loyalty to the Company, we will be glad to consider their case. Frankly speaking, we do not believe there will be over 50 more men now out on strike that we will again use in the plant." The strike, Brown thought,

[78] Doss to Brown, Oct. 31, 1933, and attached statement, Acc. 52, Box 12, Ford Archives; typed sheet dated Nov. 1, 1933, Acc. 52, Box 12, Ford Archives. The press reported that Senator Wagner regarded the company's reply as evidence that Ford was bargaining collectively with the strikers. *New York Times*, Nov. 3, 1933.

[79] Report of strikers' meeting, Nov. 2, 1933, Acc. 52, Box 12, Ford Archives; *Newark Evening News*, Nov. 2, 3, 1933.

[80] "In the District of the State of New Jersey to the Honorable Franklin D. Roosevelt," and supplementary petition with same title, N.R.A. Drawer 642. For Brown's comments on the petitions' charges, see Brown to Doss, Nov. 21, 1933, Acc. 52, Box 12, Ford Archives.

[81] Strike committee to E. Ford, Nov. 9, 1933, E. Ford to Wickens, Nov. 21, 1933, N.R.A. Drawer 642.

had been "a blessing in disguise" because it had helped to "break up the cliques" in the plant.[82]

Following the receipt of Edsel's letter, the strike committee arranged a meeting with Brown, which was held on November 27. Brown accepted the committee as representing only the men still on strike, whose number was estimated by him as 400 and by the strikers as 1,200, and claimed that he represented the men back at work. The committee concentrated on the questions of collective bargaining and the re-employment of the strikers and did not take up the grievances enumerated in the petitions submitted to the President. Reilly asked Brown if he would take back the strikers as a group and then permit the employees to determine by an election whom they wished to represent them in collective bargaining. Brown replied that he would take back individuals as needed, according to merit, but that he would not re-employ the strikers as a group and that the company would have nothing to do with an election. He would not lay off anyone then at work to make room for the strikers, and he would not set a date by which time the strikers would be re-employed. The strike committee complained to the New Jersey N.R.A. two days later that it was Ford's purpose "to carry on with gestures as long as possible in order to defeat the ultimate purpose for which the men are striking, namely, to bargain collectively with the Ford Motor Co., through their chosen representatives."[83]

The failure of direct negotiations to satisfy the striking Edgewater workers caused the N.L.B. to take a hand in the matter once again. "Why don't you take these poor fellows that are still out on strike back to work?" Senator Wagner asked Brown on December 11. Brown assured Wagner that he had not refused to deal with anyone applying for re-employment and that the active unionists who had approached the company had been taken back in every case. Brown informed Dearborn that he had tried to be "very careful" in talking with Wagner so that "no undesirable publicity might be given in connection with the showing of the new cars."[84]

When the N.L.B. failed to follow up Wagner's call to Brown with any positive action, President William Green of the A.F. of L. stepped into the dispute and on December 21 presented a statement of the facts in the case to Johnson. Green accompanied his brief with a letter in which he charged that Ford had violated Section 7(a) and requested that he be compelled to comply with the law and to bargain with the union with a view to effecting

[82] Brown to Doss, Nov. 21, 1933, Acc. 52, Box 12, Ford Archives. Brown noted that 75 per cent of the strikers lived in Kearny and Bayonne and that it was unlikely that the company would "ever secure the right type of worker as long as we continue to pick men from these communites. We believe by going to the better communities, north and west of the plant, we will secure a much better class of worker. . . ."

[83] Brown to Doss, Nov. 28, 1933, and attached report of Nov. 27 meeting, Acc. 52, Box 12, Ford Archives; Tepper Hearing, Nov. 29, 1933, pp. 2, 7–8, 10–11, N.R.A. Drawer 642.

[84] Brown to J. Crawford, Dec. 12, 1933, Acc. 52, Box 12, Ford Archives.

a settlement providing for the return of the strikers. Johnson, in turn, referred the matter to the N.R.A.'s Compliance Division for investigation.[85] A few weeks later both Green and William Davis, the National Compliance Director, advised Reilly that the men should return to work pending the N.R.A.'s disposition of the case. The strikers, their ranks depleted and the attendance at their meetings dwindling, as Ford's labor spies had reported, called off the strike on January 8.[86]

On January 17 Davis advised the Ford Motor Company of the complaint that had been filed with the N.R.A. alleging violation of Section VII of the automobile code. Replying for the company on February 2, B. J. Craig, the company secretary, informed Davis that the company had not violated Section 7(a) of the N.I.R.A. or Section VII of the code, that it had engaged in collective bargaining whenever requested by its employees to do so, that the men on strike had left the company's employ voluntarily, and that those who applied for re-employment would be re-engaged when production warranted in accordance with the company's rights as guaranteed by the code's merit clause.[87]

Davis, who regarded Edgewater as "a border line case well handled by the company and badly handled by the men," decided that the conflicting versions of the strike events presented by the company and the strikers required further examination. The Compliance Board accordingly scheduled a hearing for February 23, but the Ford Motor Company, regarding its answer of February 2 as sufficient, refused to attend. Thus, no one was present at the hearing from Ford to challenge the workers' account of their grievances against the company. As in the case of the Chester affair, however, one may well question whether anything more than the form of collective bargaining had been observed by the Ford Motor Company at Edgewater and whether it had not practiced discrimination in the re-employment of the strikers. As late as February 2, for example, although there were several hundred more persons employed at Edgewater than at the time the strike began, 350 of the strikers had still not been returned to their jobs despite the fact that over 200 of them had applied for reinstatement.[88]

After studying such evidence as was available to it regarding both the Chester and Edgewater labor disturbances, the National Compliance

[85] Report of strikers' meetings, Dec. 13, 18, 1933, Acc. 52, Box 12, Ford Archives; Green to Johnson, Dec. 21, 1933, and Brief of Facts on Behalf of the Striking Employees of the Edgewater, New Jersey, Plant of the Ford Motor Co., N.R.A. Drawer 642; *Newark Evening News*, Dec. 18, 1933; *New York Times*, Dec. 27, 1933.

[86] Doss to Cameron, Jan. 8, 1934, and attached report of strikers' meeting of Jan. 8, 1934, Acc. 52, Box 12, Ford Archives; Wickens to Davis, Jan. 18, 1934, N.R.A. Drawer 642; *Newark Evening News*, Jan. 9, 1934.

[87] Davis to Ford Motor Co., Jan. 17, 1934, Craig to Davis, Feb. 2, 1934, N.R.A. Drawer 642.

[88] Davis to Johnson, Feb. 5, 1934, Davis to Ford Motor Co., Feb. 15, 17, 1934, Craig to Davis, Feb. 2, 20, 1934, N.R.A. Drawer 642; National Compliance Board, Hearing on Ford Motor Co. Strike at Edgewater, Feb. 23, 1934, N.R.A. Box 7264.

Board on March 15, 1934, informed Johnson that the Chester affair had been a lockout designed to break up the self-organization of the employees and to stop collective bargaining and that it had been followed up at Chester and Edgewater by the company's refusal to bargain and by discrimination in re-employment "with the result that all organization of employees within these plants and all collective bargaining has been eliminated." The Board recommended that the case be referred to the Attorney General with the request that he institute proceedings against Ford in order to compel him to abide by the law.[89]

From a public-relations standpoint, it was felt within the N.R.A. that it was unwise to give the case any publicity unless the government was sure of victory. Charles Michelson, director of the N.R.A.'s Public Relations Division, advised against any publicity until the Attorney General was prepared to proceed "with speed and vigor." He contended that the effect on the N.R.A. would be "inestimably bad" if it became known that the case had been referred to the Attorney General and that nothing had come of it or if a grand jury, after hearing the evidence, refused an indictment. Johnson agreed that "absolutely no publicity is to be given this case,"[90] and, as a matter of fact, the public was never made aware of the fact that the Compliance Board had recommended prosecution and that the possibility of implementing this recommendation had been the subject of considerable controversy within the government.

The Justice Department, like the N.R.A. Public Relations Division, was unwilling to prosecute unless it was certain of victory, and it did not think that the available evidence (the Justice Department, of course, had no record of the exchange of communications noted above between the Ford Motor Company and the branch plants) was likely to produce this result. "You will appreciate," Assistant Attorney General Harold Stephens wrote Davis on March 16, "that a suit against the Ford Motor Company would be of such national importance and would be so ably and vigorously defended that it should be based only upon the clearest and highest proof of violations of the section involved. The proof referred to must necessarily be of such evidentiary value as to render the Government's position on the facts impregnable." In subsequent communications Stephens pointed out that the auto code's merit clause would make it difficult to prove that discrimination had been practiced and that the behavior of the workers at both plants would weaken the charge that the company had refused to bargain with its employees.[91]

Despite objections from the Justice Department, J. C. Randal, a

[89] National Compliance Board to Johnson, Mar. 15, 1934, N.R.A. Drawer 642.

[90] Johnson to Davis, Mar. 24, 1934, and enclosed memorandum of Michelson, Mar. 19, 1934, N.R.A. Drawer 642.

[91] Stephens to Davis, Mar. 16, 1934, N.R.A. Drawer 642; memorandum from J. W. Randal to Johnson et al., Apr. 17, 1934, N.R.A. Drawer 642.

Compliance Division attorney, strongly urged that the case be pressed to a decision. He was convinced that the evidence added up to a prima-facie case of conspiracy on the part of the Ford Motor Company to violate Section 7(a). "No person," he wrote, "can read the records in these cases without being convinced beyond any doubt, reasonable or otherwise, that the Ford employees were *restrained, coerced,* and *interfered* with in their efforts to organize for their mutual benefit and protection." Unless demurrer were sustained, he believed the "barring jury fixing, it is impossible to lose the case on the facts, even given only mediocre trial talent." He pointed to the procedural advantages and the heavier penalty that could be imposed if the government proceeded by indictment for conspiracy rather than for the substantive offense alone.[92]

No doubt Randal was influenced, at least in part, to take the position he did because of his strong bias against Ford. "High pressure publicity and pious professions to the contrary notwithstanding," he stated in a memorandum on the case, "Ford is, and has been, as ruthless an exploiter of labor and small business as this country has ever known." It is not surprising that Blackwell Smith, the Compliance Division's associate counsel, thought Randal's conclusions "intemperate." Like Stephens, he did not think the evidence strong enough for the government to proceed. He welcomed the prospect of having "a really tough, big fellow to go after," and if it could have been done without publicity, he would have been willing "to proceed against him on a complaint and develop our case in court," but he thought this would be "a bit foolhardy" under the existing circumstances.[93]

In a final effort to convince his superiors and the Justice Department, Randal prepared a detailed summary of the case, which he presented to Franklin S. Pollak, the Compliance Division's counsel, on or about April 23, but the Justice Department was not swayed by this brief.[94] It continued

---

[92] Randal to Davis, Mar. 15, 1934, N.R.A. Drawer 642; memorandum from Randal to K. Johnston, Apr. 2, 1934, memorandum from Randal to Johnson *et al.*, Apr. 17, 1934, N.R.A. Drawer 642.

[93] Memorandum from Randal to Johnson *et al.*, Apr. 17, 1934, Smith to A. G. McNight Apr. 17, 1934, N.R.A. Drawer 642.

[94] Randal to Pollak, Apr. 23, 1934, Pollak to William G. Rice, Aug. 28, 1934, Randal, In re: Ford Motor Co., N.R.A. Drawer 642. In the Detroit area, complaints that Ford was violating Section 7(a) were brought to the attention first of the Detroit Regional Labor Board and then after Mar. 25, 1934, of the Automobile Labor Board, although the latter was not too sure it had any jurisdiction over Ford since Ford had not been a party to the settlement that led to the board's establishment. The complaints involved the issue of discrimination because of union activity and were nearly all lodged by members of the Mechanics Educational Society of America, an independent organization of tool and die makers, which had organized some of Ford's workers. Several workers were reinstated when their allegations were referred to the company by one of the boards noted above. In one unusual case, the company, although unwilling to reinstate the M.E.S.A. member alleging discrimination, agreed to hire in his place any union member the M.E.S.A. suggested. The case was settled on this basis. See Cases 46 and 78 in D.R.L.B. Box 282 (the D.R.L.B. records are part of the N.L.B. records), and A.L.B. Drawer 3998 (the A.L.B. records are part of the N.R.A. records).

to believe that the government's "position on the facts" was not sufficiently strong to warrant the prosecution of Ford for alleged violation of Section 7(a) of the N.I.R.A.

To the end, thus, Ford was able to pursue without successful challenge his policy of minimum accommodation to the principles and purposes of the N.I.R.A. At no significant cost to himself, he had once again provided evidence of the independent character of his judgment and of his unwillingness to allow himself to be governed by the actions of his fellow automobile manufacturers or, for that matter, the wishes of government functionaries. Also, of import for the future, Ford, by his behavior during the two years the N.I.R.A. was in effect, had made it clear that the organized automobile workers were to face determined opposition in their efforts to bring unionism to the plants of the Ford Motor Company. Whatever the future might bring, however, Ford no doubt felt his judgment as regards the N.I.R.A. vindicated when the Supreme Court on May 27, 1935, declared the statute unconstitutional and thus wrote finis to one of the most interesting chapters in the early history of the New Deal.

Alfred D. Chandler, Jr.

8

Management Decentralization: An Historical Analysis

The past generation has seen three major developments in the organization of the large American industrial corporation. There have been the creation of autonomous operating units, the expansion of specialized staff and service departments, and the systematizing of the top coordinating and policy-making group. All three developments are integral and fundamental aspects of the administrative principle that goes by the name of management decentralization. Today both these methods and the broader principles of management decentralization are receiving a great deal of attention. "The principle," Peter Drucker points out, "is being expounded in articles and speeches, in management magazines and management meetings so that by now the phrase at least must be familiar to every American manager."[1]

Since the idea and practice of decentralization have become so widespread and since decentralization is certainly one of the most significant developments in American business, it seems legitimate for the historian to ask his special questions of the phenomenon. Why, when, and how did large industrial firms begin to decentralize? What firms have not decentralized and why not? How widespread has decentralized management actually become? What accounts for the difference in timing and the methods used in the administrative reorganization of different firms? What basic problems had to be solved in achieving decentralization? Why and how did these problems vary among different firms?

This article attempts to provide some preliminary answers to these

EDITOR'S NOTE: This study was supported by the Sloan Research Fund of the School of Industrial Management, Massachusetts Institute of Technology.
[1] Peter Drucker, *The Practice of Management* (New York, 1954), p. 209.

questions by examining the changes made during the twentieth century in the overall administrative structures of fifty of the nation's largest industrial concerns. The information for the study comes only from readily available printed materials such as annual and other reports to stockholders, articles in business and management journals, particularly *Fortune* and *Advanced Management,* and from the few business histories and biographies available on the companies and their managers. Since such sources can only provide brief and incomplete information, the conclusions drawn from them must be tentative. Even where the information is comparatively full, it indicates little about the informal organization of the company, which must be known if the firm's men and measures are to be properly evaluated. Valid and accurate answers to the historian's questions can only be found in the records and correspondence relating to organization problems in the files of businessmen and their companies.

Nevertheless, even within the limitations of the sources and the restrictions of space and time in any such preliminary study, some useful if tentative generalizations can be made.[2] Certainly the essential problem appears to be clearly defined. "That problem," wrote Donaldson Brown of General Motors in 1927, "is to combine the economical advantages of modern business, with as little sacrifice as possible of that intimate control and development of managerial ability that is the character of the well managed small business."[3]

There also appears to have been one widely accepted answer to this problem. This was the creation of an organization which included, first, a number of autonomous operating units whose managers handled the day-to-day operating decisions, were responsible for the financial performance of their unit, and had the line authority and staff assistance commensurate with this responsibility. (The criteria for judging financial performance of a unit here included costs, sales, return on investment, and share of the market.) Secondly, the organization built up a central advisory staff of specialists which provided services to the operating divisions and helped

---

[2] Because of the need to keep this preliminary study to a manageable length, this article will say nothing about the legal organization and its relation to the administrative structure of the companies examined. Nor will it discuss the foreign operations of these firms, for management structures in foreign countries have to be adjusted to many non-economic and non-business factors. Neither will the article attempt to describe the techniques of coordination, supervision, control, and policy formulation. It will only consider the administrative structures in which these are carried out. Nor will it refer to comparable developments in transportation, utility and financial firms. Of these the most significant were those which took place in the railroad industry before 1900. Finally, it might be well to point out that condensing into a paragraph or two the developments in overall management structure of a company over a period of years often requires overgeneralization. I hope that these generalizations are approximations of the truth; should they not be, the reader will do me a favor by indicating where they are wrong or misleading.

[3] Donaldson Brown, "Centralized Control with Decentralized Responsibilities," American Management Association, *Annual Convention Series, No. 57* (1927), p. 11.

the top executives carry out their functions, particularly that of coordinating the activities of the divisions. Thirdly, the organization included a top management group which not only coordinated but also supervised the divisions. This it did by reviewing and analyzing divisional operating and financial performance and by taking executive action on the basis of these analyses. The major functions of the group, however, were to determine goals, objectives, and courses of action for the company as a whole, to review the effectiveness of prevailing policies, and, where necessary, to adjust such policies to changing current conditions.

Although the problem and the answer were essentially the same for most large companies, the time and the way the problem arose and the answer was reached varied for each firm according to a number of internal and external circumstances. Internal circumstances, those resulting from the firm's historical development and from the personalities and experi-

TABLE 4

THE FIFTY COMPANIES

(Numbers indicate relative size according to 1948 assets.)

Multi-industry firms

Chemical	Electrical	Automotive	Rubber
8. duPont	9. General Electric	2. General Motors	32. Goodyear
15. Union Carbide	17. Westinghouse	10. Ford	37. U.S. Rubber
33. Eastman Kodak	—. Sylvania	19. International	39. Firestone
44. Allied Chemical		Harvester	62. Goodrich
& Dye		25. Chrysler	
52. Dow			

Single-industry firms

Oil	Steel	Non-ferrous materials
1. Standard (N.J.)	3. U.S. Steel	20. Anaconda Copper
4. Standard (Indiana)	12. Bethlehem	24. Kennecott Copper
5. Socony-Vacuum	29. Republic	28. Aluminum Co. of Am.
6. Texas	35. Jones & Laughlin	44. International Nickel
7. Gulf	43. National Steel	45. International Paper
11. Standard of Calif.		
16. Sinclair Oil		
21. Shell Oil		
22. Phillips Ptrlm.		
34. Atlantic Rfng.		

Market-oriented firms

Distribution	Food	Stimulants
12. Sears, Roebuck	27. Swift	18. American Tobacco
23. Montgomery Ward	30. Armour	26. R. J. Reynolds
40. F. W. Woolworth	36. A. & P.	31. Liggett & Myers
60. J. C. Penney	46. United Fruit	38. Distillers-Seagrams Corp.
	47. Natl. Dairy Products	41. Schenley Industries Corp.

ences of its managers, of course, differed with every company. External circumstances, however, were usually somewhat the same for companies doing the same type of business. The fifty companies studied here have therefore been divided into ten industrial categories. Four firms, all but one close to the top fifty in size, were included in order to make the industrial categories more representative. The other forty-six companies (see Table 4) comprise the largest industrial firms in the nation by asset size, as listed for 1948 in the Brookings Institution study, *Big Enterprise in a Competitive System*.[4] The ten industrial categories, in turn, fall into larger groupings. The business of the chemical, electrical, and some of the automotive and rubber firms cross traditional industry lines. On the other hand, most oil, steel, and non-ferrous metal firms have, at least until recently, operated within the boundaries of one industry. The distributing, food, and stimulant firms, which are more concerned with marketing than development, extraction, or production, form a third group. The fifty companies, then, will be considered by industrial categories, which will in turn be grouped under the three divisions: the multi-industry, the single-industry, and the market-oriented firms.

MULTI-INDUSTRY FIRMS

The Chemical Companies

Of the ten industrial categories represented in this study the chemical is best considered first. The rapid growth of that industry in the twentieth century and the ever-increasing diversity of its products have caused the nature of the large chemical firms' operations to change more rapidly than most. As a result, chemical managers have had to pay closer attention than many executives to adjusting the administrative structures of their companies to the changing business situation. That situation has since the 1920's been made more dynamic by the systematizing and institutionalizing of technological research within the chemical firms themselves. It was, in fact, a program of product development and diversification that led the largest of the chemical firms, the E. I. duPont de Nemours and Company, to devise one of the first clearly articulated modern types of decentralized organization for an industrial concern. Because this new structure became the model for later reorganizations and because duPont's original organization was

---

[4] A. D. H. Kaplan, *Big Enterprise in a Competitive System* (The Brookings Institution, Washington, D. C., 1954), pp. 153–54. I have not included Western Electric because it is, for all intents and purposes, an integral part of the American Telephone and Telegraph Company which not only owns it but takes nearly all its non-military production. The Brookings study did not include the Cities Service Company, undoubtedly because that firm was until 1944 a utility as well as an industrial concern.

typical of the structure then prevalent in American industry, a description of this innovation provides a useful introduction to an historical analysis of management decentralization in the United States.

The drastic reorganization of the duPont company's administrative form came in 1921.[5] Before this time the company, which until the end of World War I had concentrated on the manufacturing of explosives, was managed through a highly centralized, functionally defined organization. The Production Department handled manufacturing, the Sales Department the marketing, the Purchasing Department the buying of materials, and so forth. Department heads reported directly to the president, who made the major management decisions and carried most of the management responsibility. In planning and policy-making he was aided by an executive committee made up of himself and the department heads. The president and the executive committee also supervised the few subsidiaries that could not be easily fitted into this functional structure. In 1920 these subsidiaries included a handful of plastic and paint concerns which the company had recently purchased as part of a considered program to put the company into the manufacturing of products other than explosives.

Shortly after the Armistice, the company decided to expand greatly this diversification program, which had been set aside with the coming of the war in Europe. The president, Irenee duPont, then instituted a study of the administrative changes required. Clearly, there were manifold problems involved in adjusting the functionally defined departments to the processing and marketing of markedly different lines of products. Those problems were enhanced by the difficulty of obtaining a top management with the wide technical knowledge required to understand the intricacies of production and the complexities of marketing the different items. The company therefore decided to create five new "industrial" or product departments—the Cellulose Products, Pyralin, Paint, Dyestuff, and Explosives departments. Each department was placed under a general manager who had his own staff, who had full authority over the development, processing, and selling of his department's products, and who became responsible for the financial performance of his division.

The work of the departments was coordinated and supervised by a new executive committee which was now made up of men who were no longer concerned with the immediate operations of a specialized department but, instead, devoted their full time to managing the company as a whole. Moreover, the committee collectively rather than the president

[5] This reorganization is described in the annual report of the E. I. duPont de Nemours and Company for 1921, p. 6. The annual report for 1939, p. 21, also comments on organization. Besides these and other annual reports useful information can be found in *Fortune*, Vol. 42 (Oct., 1950), 87 ff.; William H. Mylander, "Management by Executive Committee," *Harvard Business Review*, Vol. 33 (May-June, 1955), 51–58; and William S. Dutton, *DuPont, One Hundred and Forty Years* (New York, 1942), especially Vol. IV, Chaps. 1, 2.

individually became responsible for policy-making and for overall administration. The finance committee, which included directors who had no managerial connection with the company, continued to have a veto on the executive committee's decisions, but it did not initiate or carry out policy.

The general officers on the executive committee were assisted by newly formed specialized service or auxiliary departments including engineering, sales, development, research, and accounting. These departments advised and serviced the operating departments, playing an important part in coordinating the policies and programs of the operating units. By providing all departments with expensive specialized services yet leaving the major operating responsibilities to autonomous, self-contained units, the company hoped it might combine the economies and other benefits of large-scale business while still retaining the advantages of a smaller, more intimate management. These hopes seem to have been realized, for, although new operating and service departments have been formed and old ones reshaped, the basic organization of the duPont company has remained essentially untouched during the years since 1921. Moreover, this type of organization has been increasingly adopted by other large American firms.

Union Carbon and Carbide, the second largest chemical company, reached this same type of organizational structure before 1930. It did so, however, by quite a different road. Carbide's major problem was in forming an effective coordinating, supervising, and policy-making center rather than, as at duPont, in creating autonomous operating units. Formed in 1917 as a merger of four companies (Carbide, Prest-o-lite, Linde, and National Carbon), all making quite different though chemically related products, Union Carbide expanded rapidly during the twenties through purchase of smaller firms and development of new products from its research laboratories. One of the major needs quickly became what was called "the synthesis of its management."[6]

By the end of the decade the company's more than twenty subsidiaries had· been placed in four operating "groups": carbon, gases, alloys, and chemicals. Each was managed by a vice president, who enjoyed a wide range of authority and responsibility. The work of the operating groups was coordinated by an "officers' committee" which included the president, the senior vice presidents, the treasurer, the vice presidents in charge of the different groups, and the men in charge of the major advisory service departments. As at duPont, the central service departments performed only advisory functions, while top policy-making and supervision were the responsibility of an executive committee made up of officers not directly concerned

---

[6] The quotation is from *Fortune*, Vol. 23 (June, 1941), 126. This article, which begins on page 61 of that issue, is the best single source of information on Union Carbide. It can be supplemented by the company's annual reports and by an article on the chemical industry in *Fortune*, Vol. 16 (Dec., 1937), 83 ff.

with operations. In 1941 those officers included the president, chairman of the board, two senior vice presidents, and one or two directors. Again as did the duPont company, Union Carbide has reshaped its operating divisions and groups and added new ones, particularly in the years immediately following World War II. In other words, the boundaries of the decision-making areas of the group managers have been constantly redefined with the development of new products and with changes in demand and marketing techniques. Such a flexible administrative structure, with decentralized operations and centralized control, may have played a part in stimulating the rapid growth, the increasing diversity of products, and the outstanding earnings record of both duPont and Union Carbide.

The value of a flexible administrative organization is further emphasized by the story of Allied Chemical & Dye Company. Like Union Carbide, Allied Chemical was formed by a merger. Unlike its two major competitors, however, it did not, after the merger of five chemical companies in 1920, develop new products either through further purchases or by intensive research.[7] Nor did the parent company, which was dominated by one of its founders, Orlando F. Weber, attempt to systematize the coordination and supervision of its operating subsidiaries. Rather, as was typical of the old-time holding company, its function was primarily to maintain a tight control over the price, production output, and financial policies of the operating units. Possibly this centralized, conservative, inflexible administrative structure helps to account for Allied's dividend record, which during the 1930's was much less satisfactory than its competitors', and the company's drop, between 1935 and 1948, from 26th to 42nd place on the list of America's largest industrials.

The war demands made it easier for Allied Chemical to perpetuate the luxury of its centralized organization. But with the war's end and the death of Weber in 1945, change came. The new president, Frederick Emmerich, began quietly but effectively to reshape his company's organization, following quite consciously, according to *Fortune*, the duPont model. Subsidiaries were re-formed into operating divisions, their managers enjoying an autonomy similar to department or group heads in Union Carbide and duPont. New central service departments, such as public relations and labor relations, were added and old ones were expanded. The general policy-making and supervising executive committee consisted of officers who were not directly engaged in operations. Since 1948 the company's sales and profits have expanded. The development of new products has led to the

---

[7] These five companies included the Barrett Company (formerly the American Coal Products Company), the General Chemical Company, the National Aniline and Chemical Company, the Semet-Solvay Company and the Solvay Process Company. The best available articles on the company are *Fortune*, Vol. 1 (June, 1930), 81 ff.; Vol. 50 (Oct., 1954), 119 ff. Except for recent years *Moody's Industrial Manual* gives more information than the company's annual reports.

formation of two new operating divisions. The company now appears to be regaining its position and prestige as a leader in the chemical industry.

If the experience of Allied Chemical indicates the dangers of a static and conservative management, that of the Dow Chemical Company suggests those that may arise when a management fails to pay close attention to administrative readjustment during a period of rapid growth. Before World War II this company was a medium-sized, family run, financially solid firm whose products came from one source, brine.[8] The war brought new demands and a great increase in production. Then, after the war, the company embarked on an aggressive expansion program which brought it by 1948 to 52nd place among the leading industrial firms. During much of this growth Willard Dow ruled the company with a firm, if informal, hand. He made basic policy and directly supervised the three older divisions, which were based on plant location rather than on products, and the two new product divisions, magnesium and plastics, which were created shortly after the end of the war. In 1944 he did form an "operating board" to help him coordinate the activities of the rapidly expanding geographical divisions.

After Dow's death in 1948 more attention was given to organization. The new president, Leland I. Doan, set up a three-man policy-making and supervising team, which was aided by an "inside" board of directors. More effective operational integration was attempted by the organization of coordinating committees for research, production, production economics, and engineering. At the same time, the central sales division and new labor relations and public relations departments were given the power to coordinate and control their functions among all the divisions. This proliferation of coordinating devices, the existence of two very different types of operating divisions, and the saddling of policy-making and supervisory personnel with day-to-day management duties suggests that Dow's overall administrative structure is in a transitional stage. Although its managers still echoed Willard Dow's boast that the company had and needed no organization chart, they admitted by 1952 that lines between. staff, operations, and top management structures needed to be "sharpened."[9] Possibly the growing administrative strains were one reason why the company announced in its 1954 report that it was "tapering off" its expansion program.

The administrative story of the Eastman Kodak Company differs from its competitors in the chemical industry primarily because of the firm's concentration on two or three major lines of products rather than a large

---

[8] *Fortune*, Vol. 3 (April, 1931), 58; Vol. 45 (May, 1952), 104 ff.; and the article on the chemical industry in *Fortune*, Vol. 16 (Dec., 1937), 83 ff. provide the best information on Dow. Its post-World War II annual reports are also useful.

[9] *Fortune*, Vol. 45 (May, 1952), 177. The quotation in the following sentence is from the Dow Chemical Company's annual report for 1954, p. 3.

number of lines based on a broad chemical technology. Eastman Kodak has tended to be more concerned with vertical integration, the controlling of all processes from the raw material to the ultimate consumer, than in development of new products. Significantly, its first venture into the chemical business did not come, as in the case of duPont, from a decision to diversify production, but because the film and camera works at Rochester were unable to take the full output of the Tennessee Eastman Company, which the parent company set up at Kingsport, Tennessee, to provide Rochester with celluloid and other basic materials.[10] Although Tennessee Eastman during the 1930's and 1940's enlarged its production of cellulose products to include fabrics, yarns, and plastics, it expanded less than its competitors into other areas of chemical production. Except for the making of military items, Eastman Kodak's only major expansion outside of Rochester and Kingsport was the formation, in 1951 and 1952, of Texas Eastman and Eastman Chemical Products for the purpose, primarily, of providing a source of materials and a marketing agent for Tennessee Eastman. Eastman Kodak's one other significant nonphotographic venture came in 1938 with the formation, in cooperation with General Mills, of the Distillations Products Industries, Inc. for manufacturing vitamins. After the war this unit became an operating division of the Eastman company.

Eastman's concern with integration rather than diversification has naturally affected its management structure. Its American organization today includes two major units and a minor one: Kodak, centered in Rochester, Tennessee Eastman (which manages Texas Eastman and Eastman Chemicals), and Distillations Products. Each unit is operated by a centralized, functionally departmentalized organization quite similar to that of the duPont company before 1921. Each appears to be quite independent of the other. There is no large staff or top management group with full-time responsibility for coordinating, supervising, or even making policy for the company as a whole. Should Eastman decide in the coming years to develop new lines of products by giving its chemical business priority, its organization or at least that of Tennessee Eastman will probably have to be divided into a number of semiautonomous units. If this is done, then thought will have to be given to the formation of a coordinating and controlling central office.

The experience of the large chemical firms emphasizes two important points. First, it clearly shows that the decentralized organization requires both an effective control center and well-defined autonomous parts. In the case of Allied and of Union Carbide, companies which resulted from mergers, the major problem was in forming the center. For a company

[10] The information on the Eastman Kodak Company comes more from the annual reports of the company than from an article on the firm in *Fortune*, Vol. 50 (July, 1954), 76 ff. Particularly useful were the reports for 1945, 1947, 1951, and 1952.

like duPont, which grew by adding new plants and products, the first problem was to define the parts. This, in turn, required study of the role and functions of the central headquarters. Dow and Eastman, if they continue to expand their chemical production, will soon or may already be facing the same type of problems duPont found itself confronted by in 1921. It seems likely that their answers will not be greatly different from duPont's.

Secondly, the experience of these chemical companies points up the value of a management structure which clearly differentiates between the generalist and the specialist. In the older functionally defined, centralized structure and in the older loosely federated holding companies there were none-too-many generalists and no clearcut division of function between the generalist and the specialist. In the new type of organization developed by duPont, Carbide, and Allied, the specialist was assigned primarily an advisory or service role. At the same time, the creation of product divisions permitted more operating managers to become generalists. This was because the managers of the new product divisions, unlike functional department heads, had to make decisions about production, sales, accounting, personnel, and every other type of business function. In the new structure, too, the top management came to be made up of men who made broad decisions about a large number of very different products as well as about the various business functions. The new structure, in fact, created two levels of generalists —the operating generalist who focused on the industry in which he operated and the policy-making generalist who focused on the broader national and international business economy. By requiring a larger number of operating generalists, the decentralized organizational structure provided excellent opportunities for the training of top policy-making generalists.

The Electrical Companies

The history of the large electrical firms further stresses the importance of creating a strong center as well as strong parts and of defining clearly the role of the specialist and of the operating and policy-making generalist. For General Electric, Westinghouse, and Sylvania the most serious continuing administrative problem has been the formation of an effective central headquarters. This was partly because these companies, like Union Carbide and Allied Chemical, resulted from mergers and partly because they were multi-product firms based on a broad technology rather than on one industrial process. Well before 1900, General Electric and Westinghouse were making a number of very different products, and from the first they had difficulty in coordinating and supervising these varied operations.

These difficulties became increasingly acute after World War I, when the two firms began to turn more to the production of consumer goods, particularly electrical household appliances. At the end of World War I, General Electric led the way with the formation of such subsidiary companies as the Edison Electrical Appliance Company, the Electrical Vacuum Cleaner Company, and the Radio Corporation of America.[11] It is not clear from the available evidence when these and other new subsidiaries were, like the older incandescent lamp and heavy electrical equipment units, grouped into larger operating departments. In any case coordination and some supervision of General Electric's many different operating subsidiaries and divisions was done by a number of coordinating committees and by the central staff departments of engineering, manufacturing, research, and sales. In order to carry out these functions, the staff executives often had real authority over the operating managers. The division of command and responsibility between the line, staff, and top management were, however, none too clear. For example, the responsibility for sales was usually separated from that for manufacturing. The central sales office set policy, but the actual marketing of goods, particularly consumers goods, was handled after 1926 by commercial vice presidents whose jurisdictions were regionally delimited. The sale of heavy apparatus, such as railroad and public utility equipment, on the other hand, was placed under the authority of a vice president with offices in Schenectady. The credit for making this heterogeneous administrative complex work as well as it did goes to the company's brilliant, dictatorial president, Gerard Swope. Although he had an advisory committee of top executives, all reports indicate that major administrative and policy decisions were almost always his alone.

Swope's retirement in 1940 made imperative a rethinking of General Electric's administrative structure. The reorganization plans of the new president, Charles E. Wilson, were postponed by the war and were not put into effect until 1946. The final reorganization did not occur until after Ralph J. Cordiner, who was primarily responsible for drawing up Wilson's administrative plans, became president in 1950.

In 1946 General Electric's diverse activities were divided along product lines into a number of operating divisions. Each was managed by a general

---

[11] Much has been written on General Electric. *Fortune* articles include Vol. 3 (Jan., 1931), 30 ff.; Vol. 3 (Feb., 1931), 39 ff.; Vol. 21 (Jan., 1940), 68 ff.; Vol. 25 (March, 1942), 65 ff.; Vol. 35 (May, 1947), 121; Vol. 45 (May, 1952), 132 ff.; Vol. 48 (July, 1953), 142; and Vol. 52 (Dec., 1955), 110 ff. A useful brief background can be had from the Harvard Graduate School of Business Administration's mimeographed case study on the history of the General Electric Company prepared by John Clark. The annual reports of the company suggest a good bit about the company's organization; those of 1951 and 1955 and the report to the stockholders at the annual meeting in July, 1946, mention organization specifically. There are also two detailed articles by Ralph Cordiner, the man most responsible for the company's major reorganization, one written before and one after the changes, "The Implications of Industrial Decentralization," American Management Association, *General Management Series No. 133* (1945), pp. 24–32, and "Problems of Management in a Large Decentralized Organization," same series, *No. 159* (1952), pp. 3–17.

manager who had a full staff and who was given wide latitude in operating decisions. These divisions were in turn placed into seven "groups" according to the company's major lines of business. They included appliances, apparatus, lamp, electronics, air conditioning, chemical and "affiliated companies." Coordination and supervision of the operating units were still done by the nine staff departments and by committees, of which the advisory and operations committees were by far the most important.

The reorganization of 1951 further reshaped operational units by creating seventy "product departments" within twenty newly formed "operating divisions." Even more significant was the redefinition of the functions of the central staff and executive units. Eleven new "service divisions" replaced the old staff departments. Unlike their predecessors they had no authority to determine or carry out policy. Rather their function was to provide specialized services on an advisory basis to both the operating units and the newly created "executive office," and to help both to plan and formulate policy.

The new executive office, which took over from the staff and committees the overall coordinating, supervisory, and policy-making functions, consisted of the president, the chairman of the board, and the executive vice presidents in charge of the five operating groups and the vice presidents in charge of the nine service departments. Since most day-to-day administrative decisions were made by the heads of the operating divisions, the group executive vice presidents were, like the top managers in duPont, generalists who devoted most of their time to considering the affairs of the company as a whole. However, in General Electric the chain of command was clearer than in duPont, where the division managers were accountable to a group of men (the executive committee) rather than to one specific executive. Otherwise, the leading electrical company had in a very different fashion reached much the same type of management structure as that devised by the leading chemical firm thirty years before.

Westinghouse has had to meet much the same problems as General Electric, but its current answer, while having many similarities to that of its competitor, centralizes many more operating decisions at headquarters. In the 1920's product diversification raised problems which had to be given direct attention sooner than at General Electric. This was because of the major change in command caused by the death in 1927 of Guy Eastman Trippe, chairman of the board since 1912.[12] When A. W. Robertson became chairman in 1929 he began his administrative reforms by delegating more authority and responsibility to the managers of the various plant divisions.

[12] This information on Westinghouse comes from its annual reports, supplemented by *Fortune*, Vol. 17 (Feb., 1938), 42 ff.; Vol. 48 (July, 1953), 142. Also useful was *Facts and Figures for Stockholders—Westinghouse Electrical Manufacturing Company July, 1938* (Pittsburgh, 1938). *Fortune*, Vol. 53 (March, 1956), 113 ff., describes Westinghouse's current troubles but says little on organizational structure, except that a new post, Vice President in Charge of Operations has been created.

At the same time, however, he began tightening the central controlling unit. He relied even more than did General Electric top executives on the staff departments for coordination and supervision. The heads of the enlarged research, manufacturing, and engineering departments became "responsible for coordinating these functions as applied to each division . . . as the means of preserving the uniformity and solidarity of the organization."[13] The sales department was given even tighter control over sales policy, particularly over consumers' goods, while the selling was in 1930 turned over, as had already been done in General Electric, to regional vice presidents. In 1934, with the creation of a merchandising division, sales personnel were given authority over "the related engineering and manufacturing activities, wherever the main outlet for the product involved is through merchandising channels."[14]

After World War II Westinghouse, like General Electric, went through a basic reorganization. The problem, essentially that of its competitor, was how to define more effectively the role and functions of the operating units, the staff departments, and the central controlling unit. The Westinghouse reorganization, done in large part through the services of the management consultant firm of Cresap, McCormick and Paget, was completed in 1951, at which time Mark W. Cresap, Jr., became the assistant to the president. The various operating divisions were organized more carefully around related products, and their managers obtained more authority and responsibility, particularly over sales. The ten staff departments were given an advisory rather than controlling status. Their coordinating and supervising functions were turned over to the vice president in charge of four product "groups" (apparatus, consumer products, defense products, and general industrial products) into which the operating divisions had been placed. Unlike General Electric, the group vice presidents have much more direct control over their division managers, including the power to hire and fire top personnel. Unlike the executive officers of General Electric or duPont, they also have large staffs of their own. Therefore, decision-making must certainly be more centralized at Westinghouse than it is in other electrical or chemical companies. Moreover, its top policy-making and supervisory group (consisting of the four group vice presidents, the president, his assistant, and some part-time directors on the finance and executive committee) does not enjoy the services of as many full-time generalists as do many other electrical and chemical companies.

Westinghouse's predilection for a more centralized organization is even more significant when Sylvania's success with decentralization is considered. Sylvania Electric Products, Inc. was selected for study rather than the larger Radio Company of America because it was more of a direct competitor with the two giants in the industry, because it has been the

[13] *Facts and Figures for Stockholders July, 1938*, p. 3.
[14] The annual report of the Westinghouse Electric Company for 1934, p. 10.

fastest growing of the electrical companies, and because, as it grew, it developed a wide variety of products.[15] For several years after it was founded by a merger in 1931, Sylvania remained a loose union of two almost in-dependent units making quite different products in two different areas, incandescent lamps in Salem and radio tubes in Pennsylvania. Until the coming of World War II the company had almost no centralized direction. Then in 1941, after Walter Poor, the youngest of the three brothers who founded the Salem end of the business, became executive vice president, an executive committee was formed and a central office set up in New York City with a comptroller, a director of industrial relations, and an advertising and sales office. In the following year directors of manufacturing and engineering were appointed. The authority of this central staff was constantly increased during the great expansion of the war years, which transformed Sylvania into a large, multi-product concern.

Immediately after the end of the war, the company's administrative structure was thoroughly reorganized in order to allow, as the 1945 annual report records, "the company to grow along projected lines without placing proportionately greater burdens upon top management."[16] Five product divisions were formed, headed by managers who were provided with staffs of their own. The New York headquarters staff was given primarily plan-ning, consultive, and overall coordinating duties. At first Sylvania, as General Electric and Westinghouse had done earlier, continued to centralize sales. In 1950, however, Chairman of the Board Don G. Mitchell placed, to use his own words, "line authority for sales under the several product divisions because we believe that sales and production must be coordinated to achieve the best results. . . . At the same time, however, we have retained the functional supervision of sales at headquarters for general policy, coor-dination and consultation."[17]

After 1950 Sylvania's major administrative problem concerned effec-tive top supervision and policy-making. In that year Walter Poor died and Mitchell became chairman of the board. H. Ward Zimmer took Mitchell's place as president. Zimmer, who believed the company was too loosely organized, attempted to handle most of the top management decisions himself, relying almost entirely on the assistance of the board chairman and members of an enlarged "inside" board. The resulting pressure of work was so great that it may have contributed to Zimmer's premature death in 1954. In any case, earlier in that year the company, in order "to accomplish fur-

[15] The information on Sylvania comes largely from its annual reports (those for 1945, 1950, and 1953 are especially useful), from Don G. Mitchell, "Big Business in Small Plants," *Advanced Management*, Vol. 15 (Dec., 1950), 2–5; and *Fortune*, Vol. 35 (May, 1947), 113 ff. Additional background data came from the Harvard Graduate School of Business Administration's mimeographed case study on the history of the Sylvania Electric products, Inc. prepared by John Clark.

[16] The annual report of Sylvania Electric Products, Inc. for 1945, p. 17.

[17] Mitchell, "*op. cit.*," p. 4.

ther decentralization of top management," appointed three vice presidents in charge of operations. The division managers reported to them rather than to the president, as they had done previously.[18] With a growing group of generalists making policy and providing executive supervision, Sylvania may achieve what it set out to do in 1945, continuing to expand (it now has nine divisions) without overburdening top management.

Sylvania, then, has developed an overall administrative structure which is on a smaller scale similar to that of General Electric. General Electric appears to be somewhat more decentralized than Sylvania, but both are certainly more so than Westinghouse. In Westinghouse, too, there seems to have been less conscious effort to create generalists at either policy-making or operating levels. The recent performance of the three firms indicates that decentralization of operations and the development of generalists may well have a correlation with continuing growth, profits, product development, and operational harmony.

The Automotive Companies

With some significant exceptions, the leading automotive and rubber firms differ from the top electrical and chemical concerns in that, until recent years, they tended to concentrate on a few closely related products rather than on several lines of goods based on a common technology. Several of the foremost automotive and rubber companies were also small individual or family run firms which grew large rapidly. As a result they were operated for a long time through centralized, vertically integrated, functionally departmentalized organizations. On the other hand, the two most notable exceptions to these generalizations, the United States Rubber Company and General Motors Corporation, were pioneers in the new decentralized type of management. In both these companies the duPonts played a significant role.

In fact, the basic reorganization of duPont and General Motors was undertaken almost simultaneously and by men who worked closely with each other. In 1920, the year when the duPont company was beginning to plan a readjustment of its administrative structures in order to meet the demands of a new multi-industry business, Pierre duPont went to Detroit as president of General Motors to rationalize the financial and administrative chaos left by that sanguine promoter, William C. Durant. Durant in the years after 1908 had pulled together under one roof a vast hodge-podge of automobile, truck, farm equipment, parts, and accessory plants, but had done little to integrate or coordinate this sprawling industrial empire, which in 1919 was already the fifth largest industrial concern in the country.

To Pierre duPont the challenge of General Motors was to find a struc-

---

[18] The annual report of the Sylvania Electric Products, Inc. for 1954, p. 13.

ture which would "knit more closely its different divisions in order that the greatest benefit might result from the cooperative conduct of this large business."[19] Although his problem was very different from that faced by his brother in Wilmington, his answer was much the same. The various subsidiaries were regrouped into large operating divisions based on products or, as in the case of the automobile divisions, on different price markets. In operating their divisions, the general managers in charge were given as full authority and responsibility for decision-making as those in duPont. They were advised by the central office staff departments, while an executive committee of full-time senior line and staff officers set the broad policy for the division managers and evaluated their performances. As at duPont, a finance committee including several men who were not full-time company officers had a final say on the larger matters of policy and administration. Coordination between the divisions and between the specialized, functionally defined advisory staff departments, as well as between the specialists and the operating and policy-making generalists, was effected by a large "operations committee" and, even more effectively, by smaller "inter-divisional relations committees." The latter at first included purchasing, sales, general technical, works' manager, and advertising committees. The organization Pierre created differed from the one his brother Irenee was forming in Wilmington in that the senior line officers were more specifically responsible for the operations of the different "groups" of divisions. This may have meant they tended to become somewhat more specialized than the duPont company top executives but also that the line of command from the divisions to top management was more clear than in the Wilmington company. The appointment after 1942, however, of two or more executive vice presidents has increased the number of generalists in the top policy-making unit.

Since 1921 the original divisions have been expanded and reformed and new ones have been added. The structure of the central unit has also occasionally been altered, the most important change coming in 1937.[20] At that time an attempt was made to define and allocate the three basic

[19] The annual report of the General Motors Corporation for 1921, p. 6. Other annual reports having information on overall administrative structure are those for 1928, 1936, 1937, and 1943. Also useful were Donaldson Brown, "Centralized Control with Decentralized Responsibilities," cited above, and Edgar W. Smith, "Organization and Operating Principles," American Management Association, *Handbook of Business Administration* (New York, 1931), pp. 1474–88. *Fortune*, Vol. 17 (April, 1938), 73 ff.; Vol. 18 (Dec., 1938), 41 ff.; Vol. 32 (Nov., 1945), 125 ff., provided needed background information as did Arthur Pound, *The Turning Wheel* (New York, 1934), pp. 199–202, Peter Drucker, *The Concept of the Corporation* (New York, 1946), Part II, Chap. 2, and Ernest Dale, *Planning and Developing the Company Organization Structure*, American Management Association—Research Report No. 20 (New York, 1952), pp. 98–106.

[20] See especially the annual report of the General Motors Corporation for 1937 pp. 37–38.

top management functions to three different units. The executive committee, which was transformed into the "administration committee," was to concentrate on executive supervision. The finance committee, which was turned into the "policy committee," was to focus upon policy formulation. The coordinating role of the interdivisional committees, called since 1934 "policy groups," was more clearly defined and the number of groups substantially increased. Still later, apparently because of difficulties encountered in trying to divide the top management duties by function, both executive supervision and policy formulation were returned to the old executive committee, now called the "operations policy committee." The old finance committee became the "financial policy committee" and regained its place as the final court of appeals and approver of policy through its control of the raising and allocation of funds. Today, then, the company's overall structure is much the same as it was in 1921. In recent years General Motors has served as a model for administrative reorganizations in other leading automotive concerns.

International Harvester, which was the first to decentralize along General Motors lines, did not do so until 1943. Like General Motors it was formed as a merger. Yet because it was smaller, better integrated, and oriented toward an established market—the farmer—it avoided the severe financial and administrative maladjustments that General Motors suffered before 1921. From its founding in 1902 until the late 1920's Harvester ran quite successfully as a tightly centralized, vertically integrated, functionally departmentalized organization.[21] The lean agricultural years beginning in the 1920's and the revolution in agricultural machinery caused by the gasoline engine turned the company to the development of new products and to the radical redesigning of old ones. This new emphasis on research and development and the changing nature of the market put a strain on the company's existing organizational structure. No major action was taken, however, until after the death in 1941 of Harold F. McCormick, chairman of the board, and Addis E. McKinstry, chairman of the executive committee, and after the growing complexities engendered by wartime expansion began to place even more serious strains on the existing framework.

In 1942 and 1943 the company went through a major administrative overhauling. Six product divisions were formed, Motor Truck, Industrial Power, Farm Tractor, Farm Implement, Fiber and Twine, and the Wisconsin Steel Division. The division, the 1943 annual report pointed out, "is a new unit in our Company. It differs from a department in that a department deals with only one function, such as engineering, personnel or sales, whereas a division is a group of departments, each concerned with its own

---

[21] Background information on International Harvester came from its annual reports and from *Fortune*, Vol. 8 (Aug., 1933), 21 ff. The 1928 report suggests the difficulties created by the changing nature of the company's market.

functions but all interested in the same product or group of products."[22] The Motor Truck and the Industrial Power divisions were completely autonomous, while the Tractor, Implement, and Fiber divisions had their selling functions placed under the General Line Sales Department. A vice presidency of Merchandising Services was formed to provide overall company services through its Operations Research, Credit and Collection, and newly formed Consumer Relations Department. This last combined many functions of the old advertising, sales, and executive units, and was to coordinate and improve the company's relations with its present and potential customers. Other coordinating functions were given to another new staff office, the vice presidency of Supply and Inventory, which was designated to carry out centralized purchasing and inventory control and "to provide a closer coordination of the flow of materials through the manufacturing and distributing processes." After the war, a final capstone to the structure was set with the formation of a small group of full-time generalists who had no operating responsibilities. The group included the chairman of the board, the president, and three executive vice presidents who were to supervise the divisions and formulate overall policy.

The Ford Motor Company copied the organizational structure of General Motors much more consciously and closely than did International Harvester. It did so, as is well known, only after the retirement of its founder. Moreover, because Henry Ford had held the reins so long, his company was in 1945 in a precarious position. After 1927 it made comparatively little money and steadily lost its share of the market. Ford's amazing decline and General Motors' just as phenomenal rise in the 1920's and 1930's was at least partly caused by the differences in management structure and methods. In any case, when young Henry Ford II in 1946 took on Ernest R. Breech as his executive vice president, he hired him specifically to install a General Motors type of management. Breech began at once, to use the words of *Fortune*, "clapping the G. M. organizational garment onto the Ford manufacturing frame, trimming the garment here and filling out the frame there. Nobody around Ford makes any bones about this, and indeed, one of Breech's first acts was to hand around copies of a semi-official G. M. text on decentralization."[23]

The garment needed adjustment primarily because the elder Ford had

[22] This and the following quotation are from the annual report of the International Harvester Company for 1943, p. 14. This report describes the reorganization in detail. Other reports that mention organizational changes were those for 1918, 1931, 1935, 1942, 1945, and 1946.

[23] *Fortune*, Vol. 35 (May, 1947), 88. Other useful articles are *Fortune*, Vol. 45 (March, 1952), 97 ff.; Vol. 50 (Sept., 1945), 123 ff. I have also made use of a current organization chart of the company. Keith Sward, *The Legend of Henry Ford* (New York, 1948) especially in Chap. 14, highlights the business and management costs of the elder Ford's organization methods.

been less concerned than General Motors about development of a number of products and more interested in vertical integration. The operational divisions that Breech set up in 1946, therefore, were divided into two major groups, one including five car and truck divisions and the other including nine "basic manufacturing" divisions. There was also a "tractor and implement" division and the Ford International Division. Several specialized service departments were formed to advise both divisional and central management, as well as to assist in coordinating the activities of the divisions. However, coordination appears to have been achieved primarily through several subcommittees of the large administration committee. These were similar to the General Motors policy groups. Executive supervision and policy-making, on the other hand, were concentrated in the fourteen-man executive committee, which consisted of the more important line and staff vice presidents as well as Breech and Henry Ford II.

The Chrysler Corporation, because the nature of its operations differed from both Ford and General Motors, had until very recently less need for the new model, decentralized management.[24] Small, with no great steel, glass, body, parts, and accessory plants, it was primarily an engine-making, assembling, and marketing organization. Given this type of operation, Walter Chrysler was able to run the firm with the assistance of K. T. Keller, B. E. Hutchinson, and one or two other close associates.

Since Chrysler's death, the revival of Ford, and the increasing loss of the company's share of the market, the company has been forced to give increasing thought to both product development and administrative organization. Until 1950 it remained structured along functional lines, with only a small central staff and a small top management group of five men—President Keller and the heads of the engineering, sales, production, and financial departments. In that year a new top executive group headed by Lester L. Colbert took over. In the next the staff was enlarged by expanding the research and labor relations departments and by making their chiefs vice presidents. In 1953 the managers of the auto and manufacturing divisions were also promoted to corporation vice presidencies, were given more authority over all phases of the processing of their products, and were for the first time made responsible for the financial performance of their units. During 1954 divisional authority and responsibility, particularly over sales, were increased and divisional staffs were enlarged. As the company's reorganization continues under N. W. Misch, recently appointed vice president in charge of organization, more attention may be given to the role

[24] Information about Chrysler's history can be found in *Fortune*, Vol. 2 (Oct., 1930), 73 ff.; Vol. 12 (Aug., 1935), 30 ff.; Vol. 22 (Dec., 1940), 57 ff.; and Vol. 38 (Oct., 1948), 103 ff. The information on the current reorganization comes from the annual reports of the company since 1950 and from *Fortune*, Vol. 49 (April, 1954), 127 ff.; and *Newsweek*, Vol. 46 (Aug. 22, 1955), 75–77.

and structure of the central staff and top management units. The final result will probably not be too different from the structure Pierre duPont created for General Motors thirty-five years ago and which International Harvester and Ford adopted in the 1940's.

The Rubber Companies

The leading rubber firms have remained more centralized than the major automotive firms. And where change has come, it has been more the result of diversification of product than of growth. The small companies which, like Goodyear and Firestone, grew large by concentrating on the tire business have only just begun to feel the administrative strains created by a broadening of their product lines. Goodrich, on the other hand, which has maintained over the years a policy of diversification but which has also had a large share of its total business in tires and tubes, has long wrestled with the problem of finding an adequate overall organizational structure. However, Goodrich very recently attained and Goodyear and Firestone seem to be working toward the type of decentralized organization which the oldest and most diversified of the rubber companies, the United States Rubber Company, developed many years ago.

The United States Rubber Company, in fact, had formed product divisions even before the duPont Company.[25] Its administrative history provides one of the most useful studies of the transformation of an old-fashioned "trust" into a modern decentralized operating company. The rubber trust, born in the 1890's as a combination of many firms, controlled over 75 per cent of the nation's footwear business, then the largest market for rubber in this country. Because of the relatively slow growth in the demand for rubber footwear and clothing, the company decided in 1910 to diversify its operations by developing rubber products that could be used for industrial purposes. The Development Department, which was formed to examine the potentialities of different new products, was also given the task of standardizing plant, equipment, and methods and making more effective the overall organization of the company. At this time, too, the company became better integrated vertically through the purchase of large rubber plantations in the Far East. Just as the company was beginning to diversify, the coming of the automobile assembly line caused a sudden and enormous growth in the tire business.

[25] The annual reports of the United States Rubber Company provide quite detailed references to diversification and organization. The reports for 1910 to 1914, and 1916 to 1918 all have something to say on these matters. Information on the later reorganization can be found in the annual reports for 1929, 1930, 1934, 1935, and 1938, and in *Fortune*, Vol. 9 (Feb., 1934), 52 ff. For more current organizational matters see the annual report for 1945 and *Business Week* (Dec. 11, 1948), 83–84; *ibid.* (Sept. 19, 1953), 46.

These changes in the nature of company operations led the president, Samuel Colt, to follow the recommendations of the Development Department and to place the different operating units under first two and then three product departments—the tire, the industrial goods, and the footwear and clothing departments. Each was headed by a vice president, as were the three major staff units (legal, finance, and development) and the separate department for all overseas activities. To coordinate the work of the different operating and staff departments their heads met regularly as the "operating council." Executive supervision and policy formulation were left to the president, the chairman and vice-chairman of the board, and an executive committee of "outside" directors. The only link between the full-time administrators in the operating council and the part-time policy-makers in the executive committee was the president. President Samuel Colt and his associates, who completed their new organization by 1918, failed to think through as carefully as did the duPont company managers three years later the structure and functions of the central staff and top management units. Nevertheless, the experience of the United States Rubber Company in forming product divisions may very well have been studied by the duPont company's Development Department when it was drawing up plans for that firm's reorganization.

In any case, the duPonts had a hand in the final rationalization of the United States Rubber Company's administrative structure in 1929 and 1930. After Colt's retirement in 1920, Charles B. Segar, a Wall Street financier and formerly president of the Union Pacific Railroad, became U. S. Rubber's president. Segar's interest was in expansion, not administration. Like many businessmen of the period he was more concerned with adding properties than in the effective operation of units he already controlled. His policies helped bring on serious financial difficulties for the company, which became worse after the collapse of rubber prices after 1926. In 1928 the duPont family purchased 30 per cent of the company's stock and sent Francis B. Davis and William de Kraft to New York City to reorganize its administrative and financial structures. Davis first completely revamped the company's physical plant by shutting down some plants, re-equipping others, consolidating some operations, and dispersing others. Next, he redefined the operating areas of the different product divisions and the duties and responsibilities of their managers. The division heads were apparently at this time given the full responsibility for financial performance which they did not seem to have had earlier.

Finally, Davis created a central coordinating, supervising, and policy-making unit very similar to that of duPont. The number of service and staff officers was enlarged but their duties became primarily advisory and consultive ones. A new executive committee of full-time executives, who were more generalists than specialists, became responsible for top management. A finance committee, made up predominantly of "outside" directors, had a final veto on policy and administrative decisions. The new management also revitalized the company's research and product diversification programs. Since 1931 the development of new products and the continuing integration of subsidiaries into the company's main operating structure has led to changes in old operating and staff divisions and to the creation of several new ones. On the whole, however, the basic administrative organization remains much as it was in the early 1930's.

The Goodyear Tire and Rubber Company, whose administrative story has been almost diametrically opposite to that of United States Rubber, had from its earliest days until very recently concentrated almost wholly on the tire business. In the early 1950's tires and tubes still accounted for more than 70 per cent of its income.[26] It is also a well-integrated firm, with large plantations in the Far East and Latin America, cotton plantations in the Southwest, textile mills, and close to 450 company-owned retail stores. Not only the nature of the business but also the makeup of its management has remained much the same over the past generation. It is still centralized, with functional vice presidents exerting tight control over their departments. The vice presidents in charge of the three major departments, production, sales, and finance, and the president and the chairman of the board compose the policy-making and supervising executive committee. This busy group also appears to handle much of the necessary top level coordinating and integrating functions. The turnover in these key posts has been slow. Paul Litchfield, chairman of the board, for example, at eighty still plays an active role in the company which he has dominated for more than forty years.

Nevertheless, some significant changes have been made in Goodyear's administrative structure as a growing interest in product diversification has increased the complexity of its operations. The depression first turned the company's attention to developing more intensively its industrial product lines. As new items were put into production, the sales and accounting operations of the Industrial Goods Division were in 1938 moved out of Akron and placed with that division's manufacturing activities. The central staff and executive offices, however, maintained a fairly close control over the work of the division. The war finally convinced the firm's managers of the value of the non-tire business—a change which was symbolized by the opening of a large central research laboratory in May of 1943. In 1945 airfoam, flooring, pliofilm, pliolite and plastics, and other non-tire operations were put under a General Products Division, which was given control of

[26] Aside from its annual reports, some information on Goodyear's organization can be found scattered in Paul W. Litchfield, *Industrial Voyage* (Garden City, New York, 1954). More useful was Hugh Allen, *The House of Goodyear* (Cleveland, 1949) especially chaps. 7 and 22. The percentage of sales revenue from tires and tubes is from Edward L. Allen, *Economics of American Manufacturing* (New York, 1952), 191.

the development, manufacture, and sale of these varied products. Shortly thereafter, the pliolite activities became separately managed by a similarly organized Chemical Products Division. The central staff and top executives still seem to have much to say about the day-to-day work of these non-tire divisions. It would appear to an outsider that since the product-oriented units have to be handled quite differently from the functionally defined tire departments, the central staff and executive officers in Akron may be under something of a strain.

The Firestone story parallels that of Goodyear in many ways except that Firestone seems to have remained even more centralized. Until the depression, the family run Firestone firm produced little besides tires and closely related products.[27] Also, like Goodyear, it was thoroughly integrated, owning plantations, textile mills, and more than 700 retail establishments. Since the 1930's it has turned to making other products. As the output of these grew, manufacturing expanded and became increasingly decentralized in various product units. After the Second World War these included Firestone Industrial Products Company, Firestone Steel Products Company, Firestone Plastic Companies, and the Firestone Chemical Company. Sales, however, remain carefully controlled by the central offices in Akron. So, too, have been the company's research and developmental activities. The top management group, which includes the major functional vice presidents, still closely supervises all levels of the company's business. Moreover these executives, older on the average even than Goodyear's, have, with the Firestone brothers, managed the firm for close to a generation.

The B. F. Goodrich Company has been more diversified and more decentralized than Firestone and Goodyear. As early as 1929 its annual reports referred to the "long-held policy of diversification in the manufacturing and sale of rubber articles, believing it good business not to have too large a percentage of the total volume in any one class of commodities."[28] Nor, until the past year or so, did Goodrich bother to integrate vertically through the purchase of rubber plantations. Its major problem, then, was to coordinate and supervise the different manufacturing and selling operations. To do this more effectively, its plant and overall organization were carefully studied in the late 1920's, at the same time United States Rubber was going through its major reorganization. By 1930 there were four somewhat autonomous product divisions (tire, mechanical, footwear, and sundries), each headed by a vice president. Top level supervision, policy-

---

[27] The annual reports of the Firestone Tire and Rubber Company have very little about organization. There is a bit more in Alfred Lief, *The Firestone Story* (New York, 1951), especially pp. 243–49, 342–45; the issues of *Business Week* (Oct. 28, 1950), pp. 65–67, and (July 4, 1953), p. 60, were helpful.

[28] The annual report of the B. F. Goodrich Company for 1929, p. 4. Also useful were the annual reports for 1927, 1930, 1941, 1945; *Fortune*, Vol. 21 (June, 1940), 65 ff.; and *Business Week* (May 16, 1953), pp. 140–42.

making, and some coordination appear to have been carried out by three generalists, the president and the chairman and vice-chairman of the board, who were aided by the divisional vice presidents and the treasurer and comptroller. Because it did not raise its own rubber, Goodrich's purchasing remained centralized. During the 1930's, under the pressures created by the depression, control by the central office, particularly over sales, increased. The tire and industrial products divisions and possibly the "sundries" division were divided into separate manufacturing and sales organizations. The Hood footwear division, however, seems to have continued to enjoy a large amount of autonomy, as did the new Chemical Division created shortly after World War II. The managers of the major manufacturing and merchandising divisions, however, in the postwar years still relied directly on central headquarters for all staff services and executive supervision. The top management group, which included more operating specialists than policy-making generalists, remained similar to that of a centralized organization.

The administrative strains generated by this partly centralized and partly decentralized structure were apparently the cause for a major administrative reorganization, which was completed in 1953. The annual report for that year described the organization of "two new major Divisions of the Company integrating sales, manufacturing, and the necessary staff functions. With the formation of the new Divisions the Company's operations were decentralized into six groups."[29] These groups included the Tire and Equipment, the Industrial Products, the Footwear and Flooring, the Chemical, the International, and the Canadian divisions. In the following year a Sponge Rubber Division was added. These divisions were in turn further divided into operating units defined by related products. "Corporate Staff Divisions," the 1953 report continued, "service, counsel, and render coordinating assistance to the Operating Divisions. This new organizational structure was adopted to further the continuing growth and diversification of the company's business. Through such decentralization of operations there is increasing opportunity for training and development of personnel needed for further expansion." By 1953, then, Goodrich had reached the same type of organization United States Rubber had achieved at least twenty years before.

The history of the leading rubber firms emphasizes the close relationship between the nature of a firm's business and its organizational structure. The sudden growth of the tire market caused firms which might have developed a variety of product lines based on rubber technology to concentrate on a single line of products. The United States Rubber Company, partly because it was one of the nation's largest business concerns before the tire

[29] This and the following quotation are from the annual report of the B. F. Goodrich Company for 1953, p. 5. See also the annual report for 1952, p. 17, and 1954, p. 9.

revolutionized the industry, maintained large non-tire operations and a decentralized organization. Goodrich, which grew with the tire business and also tried to diversify production, developed a partly centralized and partly decentralized structure. Expansion and diversification after World War II finally brought it to a fully decentralized organization. In the postwar period diversification has also begun to have an effect on the centralized operations of Firestone and Goodyear. They now seem to be approaching the type of compromise structure Goodrich employed until 1953.

Lessons from the Experience of the Multi-Industry Firms

A significant lesson suggested by the experience of Goodrich before 1953 and the electrical firms before 1950 is that a partly centralized, partly decentralized structure creates major administrative problems. The reason seems to be because the role and function of the top managers and the headquarters staff are not the same for a centralized as for a decentralized organization. In the large centralized firm the staff is more concerned with coordinating and inspecting the work of the different departments and less with providing specialized services and advice.[30] In a concern decentralized along product lines, the major integrating and inspection functions are performed by the division staffs. This allows the central staff to focus on providing services and advice, particularly in the fields of merchandising and production, which in the centralized firm are under the virtually complete control of operating departments. The staff in a decentralized company still has an important role in cordinating the activities of the different divisions, but it does this purely on an advisory basis, acting as a channel of communication between the different operating units and between each unit and the central management office.

The top executive officers in the centralized organization often are, like the staff, concerned chiefly with day-to-day operations. Most of the top management group are heads of functional departments, and as such must focus most of their attention on the executive supervision of their specialized units. They have comparatively little time for top-level interdepartmental coordination and almost no time for overall company policy planning and formulation. In a decentralized concern such day-to-day operations are left to the division managers who, with their own large staffs, are responsible for the financial performance of their divisions. Supervision for the top executives at headquarters then means largely the evaluation of this per-

---

[30] I am using these terms—advisory, service, coordination, and inspection—as they are defined in William R. Spriegel and Joseph K. Bailey, "The Staff Function in Organization," *Advanced Management*, Vol. 17 (March, 1952), 2–6. Also informative on this point is J. K. Louden "Line and Staff—Their Roles in Organization Structure," *Advanced Management*, Vol. 14 (June, 1949), 76–82.

formance through information provided by the staff and the initiation of executive action based on such evaluations. Since top-level coordination is less demanding in a decentralized than in a single product, integrated, centralized concern, the major function of the top managers can become the making of overall, long-range policy. Moreover, in carrying out this role they can rely on expert advice and data from the central staff.

It would appear, therefore, that when a firm like Goodyear, Dow, Eastman, or even Firestone attempts, as Goodrich and the electrical companies did before their recent reorganizations, to compromise between these two types of structures, administrative difficulties would result. For in such a compromise situation both the top management and the central staff would have somewhat ambiguous and occasionally conflicting roles to play. It would further seem that, where a choice existed, the decentralized organization, which so clearly differentiates between the duties of the specialists and the policy-making and operating generalists, would be patently preferable to the centralized type of structure.

Of the sixteen firms studied in the chemical, electrical, automotive, and rubber industries, twelve have come since 1921 to such a decentralized structure. Eight of these have done so since 1940. In all cases the new organization came as a response to the growing complexity of the firm's business. Except for Ford and Chrysler, that complexity resulted more from increasing diversity than from growth in size of business. The other four companies appear to be moving toward this same type of organization, and are doing so for much the same reasons. It may be safe to conclude, then, that once a firm develops more than a few closely related products for somewhat similar markets, the centralized type of functionally oriented organization becomes obsolete. The experience of the leading oil, steel, and non-ferrous materials firms seems to validate this proposition by emphasizing the other side of the coin, namely, that as long as a firm concentrates on a single line of goods, decentralization through the creation of autonomous product divisions may be impractical.

The Single-Industry Firms

The large oil, steel, and non-ferrous materials firms have historically been much less interested in diversification of products and much more concerned with vertical integration than the leading chemical, electrical, and even automotive firms. Because of this concern for integration and concentration on a single line of products, they have remained more centralized than the firms already studied. When they have decentralized they have usually done so on functional and regional rather than on product lines. In the steel industry the large firms remained the most centralized, while there was some decentralization among the non-ferrous materials firms and much more in the leading oil companies.

The Oil Companies

The history of the large oil firms emphasizes particularly the close relation between the nature of the business, the degree of integration, and organizational structure. During the 1920's the leading oil companies were bent on expanding output and becoming, chiefly through purchase, fully integrated, self-sufficient firms.[31] The dissolution of the Standard Oil Company (New Jersey) in 1911, the opening up of vast new oil fields, and the enormous new demand for petroleum products created by the automobile led to the formation of many new oil firms. Most of those formerly a part of the old Standard Oil group (in the top fifty in 1948, these included the Standard Oil Company [New Jersey], the Standard Oil Company [Indiana], the Standard Oil Company of California, the Socony-Vacuum Oil Company, Inc., and the Atlantic Refining Company) possessed more manufacturing and marketing than producing facilities. Companies formed in the Southwest (they included in the top fifty, Gulf Oil Corporation, Sinclair Oil Corporation, the Texas Corporation, and Phillips Petroleum) were primarily producing firms. So, during the 1920's one important group of companies was busy buying or developing producing properties, while a second group was purchasing and forming refining and marketing units. One other oil firm included in the first fifty American industrials was the Shell Oil Company, established in 1922 as a combination of Royal Dutch Shell and the Union Oil Company. Shell paid somewhat more attention, as it rapidly grew, to augmenting its refining and marketing facilities than to expanding its producing properties.

Although vertical integration continued after 1930, most of these oil companies had by then begun to achieve a fair balance between their production, processing, and marketing operations. In the 1930's further purchases were inhibited by the business difficulties growing out of the depression and an overproduction of oil. These conditions also encouraged mergers among the large companies. One result of mergers and the slowing down of property purchasing was that the leading oil firms turned their attention to rationalizing their operating and administrative organizations. This was first begun by Gulf in 1931, by Standard Oil (Indiana) and by Phillips Petroleum in 1932, by the Texas Corporation in 1933, by Socony-

[31] These very general trends are indicated by the annual reports of the large oil companies and are analyzed in part in John G. McLean and Robert W. Haigh, *The Growth of Integrated Oil Companies* (Boston, 1954).

Vacuum in 1934, and by Sinclair, Standard Oil of California, and Shell Oil in 1936.[32] Atlantic Refining did not undergo a comparable reorganization until 1949, after it had completed a major program of expansion and integration.

These reorganizations followed a general pattern. The operating units were reshuffled so that the units carrying on the same functions—production, transportation, refining, and marketing—were placed under a single division or subsidiary. Occasionally two subsidiaries carried on the same function in different geographical areas. Also, most large oil firms had a natural gas unit. At the same time separate organizations, usually subsidiaries, were formed to handle such basic services as exploration, research, and development. Gulf, under the guidance of a new president, James Frank Drake, gave the functional unit managers wide autonomy and made them fully responsible for the financial performance of their divisions. After the war the divisions themselves were increasingly decentralized. Gulf's marketing division, for example, was divided into separate, semiautonomous units for retail and direct sales. Each of these is divided according to five different types of markets. Socony, Indiana Standard, and apparently Phillips and California Standard developed similar types of functionally decentralized organizations. So, too, did the Sinclair Oil Corporation after Percy Spencer took Harry F. Sinclair's place as president in 1949.

In these functionally decentralized oil firms coordination of the operating units was handled to some extent by interdivisional committees and still more by the central staff. Coordination, in fact, appeared to be an even more important function of the staff than providing services and advice. Top management, a small group of generalists, concentrated on evaluating the performance of the divisions and on deciding overall company policy. There seems to have been much less decentralization of operational authority and responsibility in Shell, Texaco, and Atlantic Refining

[32] The information on the administrative developments of the ten oil companies studied here came primarily from their annual reports. However, the information in these reports was often so limited that it had to be supplemented by referring to *Moody's Industrial Manual*. Because of the paucity of information, the generalizations made here are necessarily imprecise.

Additional data on Standard Oil Company (Indiana) came from Paul H. Giddens, *Standard Oil Company (Indiana): Oil Pioneer of the Middle West* (New York, 1955), especially chap. 17 and pp. 636–41; on Sinclair Oil Corporation from *Fortune*, Vol. 6 (Nov., 1932), 56 ff.; Vol. 53 (April, 1956), 117 ff.; on the Texas Corporation from *A Statement to the Stockholders of the Texas Corporation from R. C. Holmes, a Director and Former President* (n.p., c. 1933), and a printed "Letter of the Stockholders" signed by eight directors of the Texas Corporation dated Dec. 20, 1933; on Socony-Vacuum Oil Company from *Fortune*, Vol. 26 (Nov., 1942), 111 ff.; Vol. 27 (Feb., 1943), 117; on Gulf Oil Corporation from *Fortune*, Vol. 16 (Oct., 1937), 79 ff.; Vol. 49 (Feb., 1954), 132; *Business Week* (Oct. 8, 1949), 64–68; Sidney A. Swensrud, *"Gulf Oil," The First Fifty Years, 1901–1951*, Newcomen Society of North America (1951), 21–23; Craig Thompson, *Since Spindletop* (n.p., n.d.), 51–54; on Shell Oil from *Fortune*, Vol. 6 (Oct., 1932), 33 ff.; on Phillips Petroleum Company from *Fortune*, Vol. 50 (Aug., 1954), 73 ff.; and on the Atlantic Refining Company, from *Fortune*, Vol. 48 (Aug., 1953), 128.

than in other oil firms studied here, although the available evidence is not clear on this point.

Since the depression Socony, Indiana, and California Standard have been shifting from a functionally defined, decentralized organization to one based on regionally oriented, fully integrated operating units. In so doing they are coming closer to the management structure which the largest of them all, Standard Oil Company (New Jersey), created in 1927. The pattern is just beginning to emerge in Socony-Vacuum. Since World War II that firm has added refining and, apparently, marketing facilities to its two large producing subsidiaries, Magnolia in Texas and General Petroleum in California. At the same time its East Coast refining and marketing units, by obtaining their crude from foreign subsidiaries, have lost their close business connections with the California and Texas subsidiaries. It would seem that in time three autonomous regional units might be formed.

The pattern becomes more clear in the case of the Standard Oil Company (Indiana).[33] After the mid-thirties Indiana Standard refined and marketed in the Midwest using crude oil produced, purchased, and transported by its Stanolind group of subsidiaries. In the South its refining and marketing were done by its Pan-American subsidiaries, while in the mountain states the Utah Oil Company handled marketing. Before 1940 Pan-American had become more of an integrated unit by developing its own production activities. Since the war, expansion, particularly in the East, led to further administrative changes which culminated in a reorganization in 1954. The American Oil Company then became the subsidiary which unified the Indiana company's operations both in the South and East. In the East, American Oil refined and marketed, receiving its crude from its own production subsidiaries in the South and Southwest. These same subsidiaries, which retained the name of Pan-American, did American's transporting, refining, and marketing in the Gulf and South Central states. The next step might well be a closer integration of operations in the Middle and Northwest by putting the Stanolind producing and the parent company's refining and marketing organizations under one management. Then the parent company could divorce itself completely from day-to-day management and concentrate on top level problems.

This is just about the type of organization that California Standard had evolved by 1955. In the 1920's Standard Oil of California was a well-integrated company whose markets and sources of supply in its home territory, the West Coast, were both rapidly growing. As it expanded production and marketing outside of California, the company had to make adjustments in its management structure. In 1937 it placed all its operations (producing, refining, and marketing) in Texas and New Mexico under the Standard

[33] See particularly the annual reports of the Standard Oil Company (Indiana) for 1933, p. 4; for 1934, p. 6; for 1937, p. 5; and for 1954, p. 8.

Oil Company of Texas. In 1941 it did the same thing in the Canadian Northwest with the Standard Oil Company of British Columbia. At the same time the management of these two units and that of the California Company, a subsidiary which carried on domestic production outside of California, was further decentralized "by the creation of separate managing boards with headquarters located in the areas of the principal operations." "This plan of management organization," the 1941 annual report continued, "was designed to develop initiative in field management by placing responsibility for decisions with them, thus minimizing duplications and freeing major executives of the parent company for constructive planning, policy formulation, and the exercise of overall control."[34]

The war and postwar expansion led to further administrative changes. Another integrated unit, Palotex, has been set up to handle operations in Oklahoma. The California Company not only enlarged its production activities but developed extensive marketing operations particularly in the East. So effective have these operations been, that a new subsidiary, the California Oil Company, was formed to build and run refineries and handle marketing on the East Coast. Finally, in 1954, the top management group divorced itself from specific operational duties by forming the Western Division, which became responsible for all exploring, producing, transportation, refining, and marketing activities in seven western states, Alaska, and Hawaii. "The Division has its own management," explains the 1954 report, "which reports to the Parent Corporation. In the latter executive functions have been reorganized to the end that more time and effort may be directed to increasingly complex national and international problems."[35] A next step might be the formation of an integrated "Eastern Division" combining the California Company and the California Oil Company.

The management structure of the Standard Oil of California has evolved many similarities to that which Standard Oil (New Jersey) formed almost thirty years ago. In the mid-twenties the Jersey Company was organized much in the way the Indiana and California companies were before 1954; that is, the parent company also carried on major refining and marketing operations as well as supervising a number of functionally oriented or regionally defined subsidiaries. During the 1920's top management became increasingly aware of the need for creating a more effective central unit. Coordination between its operating units was becoming more and more difficult and little or no time was available for overall company supervision and policy planning. Therefore, "in the interest of efficiency," the annual report for 1927 recorded, "the various major departments of the business have been segregated into different companies, each having its own executives upon whom devolve the entire management and control

[34] The annual report of the Standard Oil Company of California for 1941, p. 18.
[35] The annual report of the Standard Oil Company of California for 1954, p. 4; also the annual report for 1952, p. 3.

of their departments."[36] The most important of the newly formed subsidiaries was the Standard Oil Company of New Jersey (Esso), incorporated in Delaware, which took over the refining and marketing activities of the parent company and control of the Carter Oil Company, the largest producing subsidiary, and of other production and pipeline units. The organization of Jersey's other major domestic integrated subsidiary, the Humble Oil Company, remained about the same. Meanwhile, the Standard Shipping Company was formed to operate marine shipping; the Standard Oil Development Company became the central research and development unit; and Stanco, Inc., was created to operate a number of specialized petroleum products concerns. In the following years new service and product subsidiaries were formed and old ones re-formed. Today, Carter has its own marketing and refining units in the Central and Rocky Mountain states; Esso confines its selling activities to the eastern seaboard and southern states; Humble markets in Texas and New Mexico. Since 1927 these operating units appear to have been increasingly decentralized along functional and regional lines.

With the operations of its subsidiaries more carefully defined by this 1927 reorganization, the functions of the parent company, the Standard Oil Company (N. J.), became specifically those of coordination, supervision, and policy-making. Its directors, all full-time company officials with no operating responsibilities, concentrated on executive supervision through statistical, accounting, and budgetary controls and upon overall, often long-term, policy formulation. Its staff headed by six "coordinators" handled, as their title indicates, the major coordinating activities. The men who headed the six major functionally defined departments—production, refining, pipelines, marine transport, marketing, and economics—and the other staff specialists, played a role similar to that of their counterparts in the large chemical and electrical firms, acting as a channel of communication between the different units and top managements and providing both with specialized services and advice. Since 1927 at least one major change has been made in the organization of this top management group. That came in 1933 when many supervisory and policy-making functions were given to a small five-man committee. Other changes instituted after a thorough analysis the company made of its organization during the early 1940's caused apparently only minor readjustments in the basic administration structure. Possibly this structure, created a generation ago by Walter Teagle and his staff, was used as a model for the recent reorganization of Standard of California's central unit and will be used again in the future for similar changes in Standard of Indiana and Socony-Vacuum.

Besides rapid growth, the recent development of petrochemicals may

[36] The annual report of the Standard Oil Company (N. J.) for 1927, pp. 9–10. See also the annual report for 1929, p. 8; for 1936, pp. 3, 6; *Fortune*, Vol. 21 (April, 1940), 49 ff.; Vol. 21 (June, 1940), 61 ff.; Vol. 44 (Oct., 1951), 98 ff.

lead to a further decentralization of operations in the large oil firms. Nearly all the major oil companies have formed or greatly enlarged their chemical production since World War II.[37] Of the ten companies studied here, only Socony has not gone into chemicals. It has, instead, concentrated its research and development on nuclear power. The organizational responses of the other nine companies to chemical production cover a wide spectrum. Gulf and Texaco, looking upon the chemical business primarily as an investment and as a market for their petroleum and natural gas products, have joined with other companies to set up subsidiaries which are almost completely outside their management structure. Gulf, for example, formed in 1952 with the B. F. Goodrich Company the Gulf-Goodrich Chemical Corporation, each company owning 50 per cent. The Texas Corporation owns 50 per cent of the Jefferson Chemical Company and 49 per cent of the Coltex Corporation. On the other hand, Shell, which has been in the chemical business for more than twenty-five years, runs its chemical manufacturing and marketing business through a wholly owned subsidiary whose manager reports directly to the top management of the oil firm. Both Standard of California and Standard Oil (N. J.), which have been active in chemicals for many years, have created a number of subsidiaries to handle both the manufacturing and marketing of the different products. These subsidiaries are supervised by the parent companies' top management teams.

At the other end of the spectrum is Atlantic Refining. Although this company has been increasing its chemical output, such products are still manufactured and sold by the company's regular refining and marketing departments. This is the way it was first done in Sinclair and in Standard of Indiana. Then Sinclair in 1951 and the Indiana Company in 1952 formed a separate subsidiary for the sale and development of petrochemical lines. In both cases parent company refining units continue to manufacture the products which the chemical subsidiary sells. In Phillips, however, the process has gone a step further.[38] The chemical subsidiary, formed in 1948, was in 1952 given control over manufacturing as well as sales. It was then subdivided administratively along product lines. This change so increased the complexity of top level coordination and supervision that a separate Coordination Department was created. If, as Phillips' president anticipates, chemical operations will before long make up 50 per cent of the company's business, further changes in organizational structure seem certain. In fact, as the oil firms develop new lines of products based on a broader petroleum technology, they may turn more to decentralized operations along product

[37] The information for this paragraph comes from annual reports of these companies since World War II.

[38] See particularly *Fortune*, Vol. 50 (Aug., 1954), 73, 120–24; and *Business Week* (Dec. 31, 1949), 22–24.

as well as functional and regional lines. Such changes will, in turn, demand that increasing attention be paid to the organization and duties of the central staff and executive units.

The Steel Companies

A comparison between growth and administrative developments in the oil and steel industry is instructive. In steel, expansion has been slower and more conservative. So too have been efforts at product diversification and administrative innovation. Like any other study of the steel industry, this one falls into two parts, the story of the independents and the story of the Corporation. The story of the former focuses on relative growth, on integration, and on centralization. That of the United States Steel Corporation concerns relative decline and constant administrative difficulties.

Of the independents the Bethlehem Steel Corporation, created by dynamic Charles M. Schwab, grew most rapidly, with its greatest expansion occurring during the ten years after 1913.[39] By 1923 the company was well integrated, owning ore, coal and coke properties and some of the most efficient steel-making and fabricating plants in the nation. During the 1920's Schwab's hand-picked successor, Eugene Grace, rationalized the firm's many new properties and then in 1930 and 1931 purchased more structural steel fabrication plants on both the West and East Coasts. Grace, who in 1955 was still chairman of the board, kept a tight control over all aspects of the company's operations.

The expansion of the second largest independent, the Republic Steel Corporation, began in 1927 when the Cleveland financier Cyrus Eaton gained control of the firm. A rapid growth through mergers and purchases was temporarily stopped in the earlier 1930's by president Tom Girdler, partly because of the depression, but also because of the need for systematizing and simplifying the company's operational, administrative, and corporate structure. After this had been begun and after the worst of the depression passed, Republic began again to buy steel properties. The final reorganization, the 1937 report recorded, "coordinates operations and sales in the product divisions."[40] However, the division managers do not seem to have had autonomy, authority, or responsibility comparable to that possessed by heads of operating units in chemical or oil firms. From the

[39] There is a brief summary of Bethlehem's history in Gertrude G. Schroeder, *The Growth of the Major Steel Companies* (Baltimore, 1953), 46–51. There is some additional information in the company's annual reports and a good bit more in *Fortune*, Vol. 23 (April, 1941), 61 ff.; Vol. 47 (March, 1953), 101 ff.

[40] The annual report of the Republic Steel Corporation for 1937, p. 4. Besides its annual reports and Schroeder, *op. cit.*, pp. 51–53, *Fortune*, Vol. 8 (Sept., 1933), 52 ff., provides some data.

available information it would seem that Girdler, who in 1955 was still board chairman, and his functional vice presidents made the major operational as well as policy decisions.

The two other large steel independents on the list of the nation's top fifty industrial firms have not had Republic's and Bethlehem's predilection for expansion. The Jones and Laughlin Steel Corporation, a tightly held family firm which has confined itself almost exclusively to the Pittsburgh district, has made almost no purchases of property in this century. Its impressive increase in output has come from expanding its own plant facilities.[41] The National Steel Corporation also has done little buying since its formation as a merger in 1929 of two old established firms, Weirton Steel Corporation and the M. A. Hanna Ore Company, and the more recently founded Great Lakes Steel Corporation.[42]

Except for National Steel, the independents have had from the beginning highly centralized, functionally departmentalized management structures similar to that of the typical American industrial firm before 1920. Since the depression major administrative developments have been an enlargement of existing staff departments and the addition of new ones such as research, labor relations, and public relations. Since World War II, appointments of executive vice presidents have enlarged the top management groups. But both the central staff and the executive office have retained a close supervision over operations.

Even National Steel now seems to be developing a similar type of organization. After its formation it long remained a loose federation of the three constituent companies, with overall coordination and policy-making being carried out by a small central staff and an executive committee that included chairman Ernest T. Weir and the heads of the three major operating units. With the departure of two of these, George M. Humphrey and George R. Fink, who long managed the Cleveland and Detroit units respectively, and with the revelation of operating and managerial inefficiencies at Detroit, the company has recently gone through an important reorganization. One result of this has been to increase the size and authority of the central staff and executive offices.

Despite the growth of the independents, the United States Steel Corporation is still today much larger than any of its competitors. From the first, its major administrative problems have arisen from its size and, for a steel firm, the comparative diversity of its products. The problem of

[41] There is very little information in the company's annual reports. Schroeder, *op. cit.*, pp. 54–55, 59, has some data as does *Newsweek*, Vol. 38 (Nov. 12, 1951), 78; and Vol. 39 (Feb. 11, 1952), 66.

[42] Besides the company's annual reports and Schroeder, *op. cit.*, pp. 59–60, see *Fortune*, Vol. 3 (June, 1932), 30 ff.; Vol. 35 (May, 1947), 219. The recent changes are mentioned in the annual report of the National Steel Corporation for 1954, list of officers and pp. 8–9.

integrating, coordinating, and effectively supervising its varied and over-lapping activities, however, little troubled the Gary administration which dominated the company for a quarter of a century. To Judge Gary and his few fellow top executives, a holding company had few functions besides maintaining control over the price and output policies of its subsidiaries.

After Gary's death in 1927 serious attention was for the first time given to the corporation's operating and management structures. Gary's successor, Myron C. Taylor, began by ordering a thorough study to be made of how the company might best stop the continuing loss of its markets to competitors, adjust to the rapidly changing nature of its markets, and make the most of new technological advances, especially those in the processing of light steels and alloys.[43] Next came the overhauling of the company's physical equipment. Many plants were scrapped; in others production was reoriented towards new markets and new areas. Facilities were purchased on the West Coast and elsewhere and some new plants were built. At the same time improved marketing, production, and control methods were examined and adopted, while product and fundamental research was intensified.

Finally, although the depression and the attempts at recovery had slowed its adoption, Taylor created a new corporate and administrative structure. Many of the major subsidiaries were combined (as, for example, were the Illinois Steel Company, Carnegie Steel, and the American Sheet and Tin Plate), while others were re-formed or eliminated. The principal new operating units included three integrated, regionally oriented, steel-making divisions (Carnegie-Illinois centering on Pittsburgh and Chicago; the Tennessee Coal, Iron and Railroad based at Birmingham; and Columbia Steel on the West Coast). Other major units included subsidiaries which manufactured heavy steel products such as bridges, ships, structural shapes, oil well supplies, and wire, together with the older mining, coke, transportation, and cement-making subsidiaries. In most cases the managers of these units were given a large amount of autonomy including, apparently, financial responsibility.

To help assist in the supervision and coordination of these many units Taylor late in 1937 formed United States Steel of Delaware. This new company set up headquarters in Pittsburgh rather than in New York,

---

[43] The story of this mammoth reorganization is best summarized by Taylor himself in *Annual Meeting of the Stockholders of the United States Steel Corporation. April 6, 1938. Remarks of Myron C. Taylor* (New York, 1938), pp. 8–22. Also useful were the annual reports of the United States Steel Corporation for 1935, pp. 11–12; for 1936, pp. 12–13; for 1937, p. 15. The story of Gary's administration has been told many times in many different ways. The role played by the central unit is, however, fairly clear from the annual reports. A good brief evaluation of the corporation's management before and after the final reorganization can be found in *Fortune*, Vol. 13 (March, 1936), 59 ff.; Vol. 13 (June, 1936), 113 ff.; and Vol. 21 (March, 1940), 64 ff. Schroeder, *op. cit.*, pp. 37–39, 43–46, adds some interesting information and figures on operations.

where the parent company continued to maintain its offices. The Pittsburgh headquarters included a large central staff departmentalized by functions. Here the senior staff officers, the heads of the major subsidiaries, and the company's top officers conferred regularly to supervise operations. These executives carried out their supervising role and the staff its coordinating and service functions through "supervisory contracts" made with the steel-making and raw-materials producing subsidiaries. The top policy-making team was the executive committee of the Delaware corporation, whose members were also the senior officers in the parent company. In Pittsburgh these men may have had time for overall policy planning, but in New York they still had to supervise and coordinate the work of the non-steel-making units, including the railroads, shipbuilding, cement, and other subsidiaries with which the Delaware corporation had no supervisory contracts.

This decentralized organization failed to work as effectively for United States Steel as its counterpart did for Jersey Standard. The dual corporation setup was essentially a cumbersome one and the top executives must have been harassed by constant shuttling back and forth between New York and Pittsburgh, handling in each place problems of quite different management levels. Moreover, the units which did not have contracts with the Delaware company did not enjoy the benefits of the central's staff advice and service, nor did the top management have these same services in supervising such units. In any case another change came in 1950.

This reorganization was aimed at centralization.[44] The Delaware corporation was eliminated and a new operating subsidiary was formed. This new subsidiary, the United States Steel Company, combined the Carnegie-Illinois Company and the major coke and coal subsidiaries. Known as "Central Operations" it included over two-thirds of the corporation's basic steel-making capacity. It was organized along highly centralized lines, with the old Delaware executive and staff officers exercising a tight control over the operating departments. At the same time, according to *Fortune*, the top line and staff officers were given increased control over the divisions not under "Central Operations," including the regional, product, and transportation subsidiaries. Most of these divisions retained their research, sales, and purchasing departments, but the central staff officers became the heads of these divisional departments and visited the divisions often between the regularly scheduled monthly meetings of the Pittsburgh and the divisional executives. Pittsburgh also handled their labor and public relations, and had direct control over coordination of research, purchases, and sales. Top management, too, became more directly concerned with operations. All divisions, for example, must obtain permission from the

---

[44] This reorganization is mentioned in the annual report of the United States Steel Corporation for 1950, p. 18, and analyzed in some detail in *Fortune*, Vol. 44 (Jan., 1956), 89 ff.

New York headquarters before making any capital expenditures over $25,000. This centralization has meant an extensive enlargement of the already large staff and executive offices. Such a structure, moreover, suggests the possibility that the Executive Policy Committee, top management unit of the corporation, could become so engrossed in supervisory activities as to have comparatively little time for long-range planning or even for more immediate policy formulation.

The experience of both United States Steel and the independents would seem to suggest that steel making does not readily lend itself to decentralization, not even functional decentralization. This may be because steel companies manufacture much less for the mass consumer market than do the chemical, electrical, automotive, rubber, and even the oil firms. The steel companies must turn out products specifically tailored to their large individual customers' specifications, and marketing must be closely integrated with production. Moreover, steel manufacturing would seem to require close central control to assure the most effective flow of materials from mine to market. Even so, centralization would appear to create as many, if not more, problems than it solves.

Non-Ferrous Materials Companies

In very general terms the growth and administrative changes in the large non-ferrous materials companies have been similar to those in the leading steel and oil firms. Prior to the depression the emphasis was on integration. During the 1930's and 1940's the managers of the non-ferrous firms paid attention to systematizing overall management. However, less concentrated thought appears to have been given to administration than was the case in the oil or even the steel industries. This seems to have been because of the lack of competitive pressures. Because of the comparatively limited competition among the non-ferrous materials firms, the holding company remained longer here than in any other industry an instrument of price and production control rather than the essential coordinating, supervising, and policy-making unit of a large industrial complex.

The success of Kennecott Copper Corporation in developing an effective overall administrative structure may be partly attributed to the fact that it was a late comer to the copper business. Kennecott, organized in 1915, remained primarily a mining company until the late 1920's when it purchased a large fabricating organization, the Chase Brass and Copper Companies.[45] The depression helped turn the attention of E. T. Stannard, who became its president in 1933, to the problems of diversification and administration. The company began to go into oil, gold, and titanium

[45] The Kennecott story comes from the company's annual reports and from *Fortune*, Vol. 44 (Nov., 1951), 84 ff.

mining, with only the last-named proving relatively successful. In 1935 it increased the number of its finished products by buying the American Electrical Works. The need for effective integration and coordination of these different operations led to increasing centralization. As the firm's comparatively small refining and smelting works were located close to the mines, regionally defined operating divisions were set up in the West. Their managers reported directly to D. C. Jackling, the managing director in charge of mining. A separate management unit for the Chilean operations was given more autonomy than the domestic divisions. Responsibility for sales of finished goods was taken from the fabricating units and given to the sales department, set up in the New York headquarters office. For better coordination, Stannard created at headquarters a central purchasing and traffic department, as well as departments for research and development and for exploration. Top supervision was handled by Stannard and Jackling, assisted by the staff department heads at headquarters. Except for the creation of a Titanium Division, this organization remained about the same until the death of Stannard and two vice presidents in an airplane crash in 1949.

The new president, Charles Cox, has followed a policy of decentralization. He gave the managers of the mining division and the heads of the fabricating units more authority and responsibility. The latter were made responsible for sales as well as production. Apparently all are accountable for the financial performance of their respective units. Secondly, Cox increased the size of the central advisory and service staff, enlarging the research department and practically starting from scratch the engineering, public relations, and labor relations departments. At the same time he added to the executive office. Advised by this office and the heads of the staff departments and assisted by J. C. Kenner, vice president in charge of operations, and R. C. Diehl, president of Chase Brass, Cox now carries out top-level supervision and makes policy for this integrated and decentralized copper firm.

Cox's achievements become more significant when they are contrasted to the administrative developments within the nation's largest copper company. The Anaconda Mining Company, the old copper trust founded in 1895, began a rapid expansion in 1914 when the outbreak of war skyrocketed the demand for copper. During the war years it purchased large mining, smelting, and refining properties in Montana, Arizona, Chile, and Mexico and also acquired refining works in New Jersey.[46] Finally, in 1922, it rounded out the organization by purchase of the American Brass Company, itself a product of the great merger movement at the turn of the century. The only other major corporate addition was the formation of the Anaconda Wire and Cable Company in 1929 and 1930.

The major Anaconda subsidiaries have always remained almost

[46] The information on Anaconda is from its annual reports and from *Fortune*, Vol. 14 (Dec., 1936), 83 ff.; Vol. 15 (Jan., 1937), 71 ff.; Vol. 51 (Jan., 1955), 89 ff.

independent units. Cornelius F. Kelley, who, either as president or board chairman, dominated the company's affairs from 1918 to 1955, considered the primary role of the central office to be that of establishing price and production policy. Like Judge Gary, he troubled himself little with improving the coordination of and supervision over the different operating units. Nor was he seriously concerned with product development and diversification, although he did set up a central metallurgical research department. He also after 1934 caused purchasing and sales for non-fabricating units to be centralized in the Anaconda Sales Company. Aside from these functional departments, the company's headquarters have remained small. Even the great expansion of markets and production after the coming of the Second World War little affected the organization of this old-line holding company. Anaconda has not followed Kennecott's example in developing modern service departments. Top level coordination and supervision is handled, as it was a generation ago, by weekly meetings of the managers of the major operating subsidiaries and four senior policy-making executives. This organizational conservatism may have had something to do with the relatively slow growth of the company's income. Since 1939, *Fortune* reports, Anaconda's dollar revenue has gone up roughly 140 per cent, as compared to Kennecott's increase of 250 per cent and Phelps Dodge's rise of 290 per cent. The veteran top management, whose average age is close to seventy, should be retiring soon. When they do, a thorough administrative reorganization may be in order.

The administrative story of the International Nickel Company has many similarities to that of Anaconda, except that, since International has been less troubled by competition than the copper company, it has been under even less pressure to make organizational adjustments. International Nickel was formed in 1928 as a Canadian corporation after the collapse of a nickel cartel.[47] Since 1928 it has controlled a large share of the world's nickel production, which is concentrated in the Canadian province of Ontario. Almost immediately after its formation International purchased foundries and rolling mills in the United States and Britain. In 1936 it set up two distributing companies, one for the United States and one for Canada. It did not, however, go into the manufacture of finished goods as did the copper and aluminum companies.

International Nickel's headquarters on Wall Street have remained, like those of Anaconda and of United States Steel before 1927, relatively small. The central staff in the 1930's included little more than a research and development office and an "Information Bureau." Also like U.S. Steel before 1927 and Anaconda until 1955, its controlling executive committee was dominated by its chairman. Robert Crooks Stanley managed the concern almost single-handed from 1928 until his death in 1951. While

[47] The data on International Nickel is from its annual reports and *Fortune*, Vol. 42 (Nov., 1950), 93 ff.

chiefly concerned with setting price and production quotas, Stanley, more in the fashion of Gary than Kelley, kept a tight control over his subsidiaries. But his interest in technological improvements and product developments seems to have been even less than either of those two executives. To date there is little visible evidence that his successors are making any major change in the prevailing structure.

Until World War II, the Aluminum Company of America had as tight a grip on the aluminum trade as International Nickel has had in its industry. Alcoa, formed in 1888 as the Pittsburgh Reduction Company and financed by the Mellon family, concentrated much more than Nickel on the development and manufacture of fabricated and finished products.[48] This was particularly true after the automobile had enlarged the market for aluminum products. In the years after World War I it also completed the vertical integration of its operations, so that by the end of the 1920's it operated bauxite mines in the United States and the Guianas, four reduction and smelting plants, and eleven fabricating plants. The company's top executives, Arthur V. Davis (a founder, general manager until 1910, and president until 1928), Roy H. Hunt (son of the co-founder and president after Davis became chairman of the board), and Irving W. Wilson (who became vice president in charge of production in 1931), created an efficiently operated, centralized organization whose departments were divided on functional lines.

World War II, by greatly altering Alcoa's business situation, had some impact on its organizational structure, but not as much as might be expected. Not only did the war greatly expand the demand for aluminum and lead to the development of many new types of aluminum products, but the government's policy in disposing of its aluminum plants provided Alcoa for the first time with real competition, in the form of the Reynolds Metals Company and the Kaiser Aluminum and Chemical Corporation. To meet the new situation, Alcoa enlarged its service departments, especially research, engineering, public relations, and its important Product Planning Division. The new emphasis given to marketing led to the creation of "industry managers" to coordinate the sales in each of the different major markets. The increasing emphasis on product planning and product marketing may in time bring about a decentralization of operations along product lines. However, no major administrative change seems likely until the retirement of the veterans, Davis, Hunt, and Wilson, who as chairman of the board, chairman of the executive committee, and president, respectively, still play a dominating role.

[48] These comments on Alcoa come from its annual reports and from *Fortune*, Vol. 1 (March, 1930), 68 ff.; Vol. 10 (Sept., 1934), 46; Vol. 33 (May, 1946), 103 ff.; and Vol. 52 (Oct., 1955), 114 ff. Charles C. Carr, *Alcoa, An American Enterprise* (New York, 1952) adds almost nothing.

A fifth company, the International Paper Company, has been included here because of similarities to the non-ferrous metals firms in the nature of its business and its historical growth. The managers of International Paper, which was founded in 1898 during the merger movement at that period, remained until after the First World War largely concerned with regulation of price and production.[49] After the war the company expanded rapidly by going into the processing of newsprint in Canada, by buying and building plants in the South which made heavy paper, container board, and other "kraft" products, and by diversifying its production in the Northeast. The depression halted this expansion and, in fact, brought the company into serious financial difficulties in 1932. From that year until 1936 the company steadily lost money.

Under the aegis of a new president, Richard J. Cullen, International Paper went through a drastic reorganization somewhat similar to the kind United States Steel was going through at that same time and which United States Rubber had just been through. Old plants were eliminated, new ones started, and the company's administrative lines were radically redrawn. Three major product divisions were created, each managed by a vice president who was given "full authority," which apparently included the responsibility for the financial performance of his divisions.[50] Newsprint operations were concentrated in the Canadian Division. The southern division handled all the "kraft products" operations, while the units located in the Northeast made up the "specialty division," which was in turn divided on product lines. The central staff and executive offices seem to have exercised considerable control in coordinating and supervising the operations of the specialty division, but did not oversee the Canadian and kraft divisions to a comparable degree. Top level coordination and supervision were carried out by the senior executive officers assisted by the heads of the three operating divisions and by the vice president in charge of sales, whose main concern was with the specialty division. This structure, which seems to combine regional and functional decentralization quite successfully, has been little changed since the 1930's.

Summary: Decentralization in the Single-Industry Firms

This brief examination of the large oil, steel, and non-ferrous materials firms indicates how the growing complexity of operation affects overall organization structure, particularly the form and function of the central administrative unit. Where the top executives considered that their

---

[49] This information comes from a company publication, *International Paper Company, 1898–1948* (n.p., 1948), supplemented by company annual reports and *Fortune*, Vol. 1 (May, 1930), 65 ff.; Vol. 16 (Dec., 1937), 131 ff.

[50] The term "full authority" is used by *Fortune*, Vol. 16 (Dec., 1937), 131 ff.

work was merely to set price and production quotas, a small central staff and executive office was adequate. But when the central office became the coordinating, supervising, and broad policy-making heart of the enterprise, then the duties and the size of the staff and top management increased rapidly. Such increasing administrative pressures on the central unit often led to some decentralization of operational decision-making. And, in the oil industry, functional decentralization appears to have been the most effective answer. However, three of the non-ferrous materials firms and all the steel firms are today still essentially centralized. Since most of these firms have been dominated by veteran, conservative managements, organizational change may have been retarded and decentralization may eventually be more widely adopted, although it would appear that of all the industries steel lends itself the least to a delegation of decision-making.

Finally, as in the oil industry, when operations became national and worldwide, the regionally defined, vertically integrated operating unit provided another kind of satisfactory operating organization. In such regionally as well as functionally decentralized firms, the central staff and executive offices began to play a role similar to that of the administrative centers in the large chemical, electrical, automotive, and rubber companies, whose operations had become complex as a result of product diversification. Thus, while there has been increasing decentralization in the single-industry firms, it has been motivated by somewhat different reasons than in the multi-industry firms and has resulted in somewhat different structural forms.

The Market-Oriented Firms

In the distributing, food, and stimulant industries the operations of the leading firms are usually less complicated than those of non-ferrous materials, steel, oil, rubber, automotive, electrical, and chemical companies. Nevertheless, the administrative story of this last group of companies reiterates the lessons demonstrated by the experience of the firms already studied. Where the leading companies in these three trades have continued to stick to one line of products or to one particular function such as retail marketing, their overall structure has remained centralized. Where their business has become more complex, either through development of new lines of products or new types of functions, they have in many cases, but certainly not in all, decentralized.

The Distribution Companies

Consider, for example, the experience of the four leading distributing firms. The overall administrative structures of two top retail firms, J. C. Penney and F. W. Woolworth, have remained essentially centralized, while Sears Roebuck, after adding retailing to its wholesaling operations, began to decentralize. On the other hand, Sears' great rival Montgomery Ward remained highly centralized, even after it went into retailing.

A major administrative problem of the retail chain store has been the development of an efficient central unit. The very nature of the business makes it easy and sensible to leave a large number of decisions to the store managers. One of the very first steps J. C. Penney took after he had combined a number of retail stores in the western mountain states was to set up a central purchasing office in New York.[51] Three years later, in 1917, he added a central personnel department. After the company's major expansion between 1927 and 1929 the central offices (which by then included sales, advertising, real estate, and research and testing departments) were enlarged. At the same time more effective accounting controls were instituted by the treasurer's department. With this expansion the number of district managers, the essential link between the central office and the individual stores, grew and their duties became more clearly defined.

Penney, who always preached the doctrine of local decision-making and responsibility, continued to allow his store managers a good deal of autonomy. While the central office did the purchasing, laid out advertising, established hiring, firing, and promotion policies and practices, the managers of the individual stores selected their own merchandise, adapted advertising to their own needs, set their own advertising budget, hired, trained, and promoted their own personnel and were consulted on changes in the layout or location of their store. Because of this autonomy and because the nature of the company's business is comparatively uncomplicated, Penney's top executives have relatively little to distract them from top level supervision and policy-making. The top management group, which has remained small, includes Mr. Penney himself, as chairman of the board, the president, and the treasurer, assisted by the heads of the central departments. Thus, although J. C. Penney has an essentially centralized operating structure—that is, there is only one set of executive and staff offices in the company—decision-making has been widely decentralized.

The F. W. Woolworth Company has historically centralized decision-making somewhat more than J. C. Penney.[52] Because Woolworth had an earlier start—the amalgamation in 1911 of twelve small chains marks its beginning—it built up its central buying, sales, and financial departments sooner than its leading competitor. On the other hand, its personnel and

---

[51] The data in this paragraph come from Norman Beasley, *Main Street Merchant: the Story of J. C. Penney Company* (New York, 1948), supplemented by the annual reports of the company and by *Fortune*, Vol. 42 (Sept., 1950), 101 ff.

[52] The Woolworth story comes from its annual reports, *Fortune*, Vol. 8 (Nov., 1933), 62 ff.; Vol. 49 (April, 1954), 150; and *Sixty Years of Woolworth* (n.p., 1939).

real estate departments apparently received less attention, at least until after World War II. Woolworth, however, differed from Penney primarily in the larger authority and control it gave its regional managers. These district managers (there were eleven by 1939) had bigger staff and office forces than Penney's regional executives and kept a tighter control over the store managers, both through personal checking and by accounting devices. More operational decisions also seem to have been made in the New York office, where a small number of veteran senior executives and central department heads meet regularly as an overall supervisory and policy-making executive committee. If Woolworth's should feel a need to decentralize its organization further, it might follow Penney's example by giving its store managers more autonomy or it might, by increasing the decision-making role of its regional managers, make the region the major autonomous unit. Yet there would seem to be little pressure for either Woolworth or Penney to change their organizational structures radically unless they decided to go into some other type of distribution besides retailing.

It was just such a decision, though of a reverse nature—that is from wholesaling to retailing—that was a fundamental cause for the Sears, Roebuck and Company reorganization. In the 1920's Sears had a highly centralized organization. Its senior vice presidents in charge of purchasing, operations, and finance had direct control over the activities of the general managers in charge of the mail-order plants.[53] In 1925 Sears decided to operate retail as well as mail-order stores, and by 1929 the recently appointed president, General Robert E. Wood, realized that the old centralized structure was inadequate to handle these two quite different types of businesses. In 1929 he began a study of the problem which led in the following year to the creation of four territorial officers who had supervision of all Sears' activities within their regions. However, the lines of command and coordination between the retail and mail-order houses, the central office in Chicago, and the new territorial offices were ambiguous and confused. Given the contraction of markets because of the depression, the top executives decided to abandon temporarily this decentralized form and return to the older structure. All retail stores were then placed under one vice presidency. This department, headed by James M. Barker, was organized much like Woolworth's. Its regional district managers supervised the individual stores and reported directly to Barker. During the 1930's, however, a *de facto* return to the regionally decentralized organization was cautiously worked out by Barker.

[53] The Sears' experience is described in Boris Emmet and John E. Jeuck, *Catalogues and Counters: A History of Sears Roebuck and Company* (Chicago, 1950), 352–72. The administrative concepts and attitudes of the Sears officials are well expressed in J. C. Worthy, "Democratic Principles in Business Management," *Advanced Management*, Vol. 14 (March, 1949), 16–21.

This decentralization did not become *de jure* until after the end of the Second World War. Then five territorial vice presidencies were formed (one other had already been created on the West Coast in 1941). The manager of each was given full responsibility for the operating results of the Sears' activities in his area. He had a sizable staff to help him supervise and coordinate the work of four types of units under him. These consisted of "groups" of stores concentrated in one metropolitan area, large "A" stores, regionally defined zones of smaller "B" stores operating outside of the large urban centers, and the mail-order houses. The managers of each of these units had their own staffs of specialists and assistants, while the individual store or department managers were, in turn, given much autonomy in the making of business decisions. Except for purchasing, which remained centralized, the functional departments at Chicago now provided, on an advisory basis, specialized services and advice to the territorial units and top policy-making executives. The central unit thus became, in the words of Sears' historians, "the company's 'super-planning' group at the highest level and includes many specialists and a few very powerful executives."[54] Further integration between the senior executives and the staff and territorial vice presidents is carried out in two committees, Merchandise Policies and the Committee on Organizational Problems. The overall administrative structure of this distributing firm, then, has many similarities to that of the large decentralized manufacturing companies—notably the autonomous operating units and the careful division of labor between the top generalists, the staff specialists, and the operating managers.

If the Sears, Roebuck organization is similar in many ways to that of General Motors, that of Montgomery Ward has long been very close to the organization of the Ford Motor Company before 1946. In fact, the personalities of Sewell Avery and the elder Ford, like the organizations they created, had much in common. Montgomery Ward & Company, like Sears, went through an administrative reorganization during the early 1920's. This reorganization, again as in the case of Sears, came about largely as a result of the decision to enter the retail business.[55] At Montgomery Ward, however, the change began after rather than before the depression crisis. Beginning in 1932 Avery, first as a consultant and then as the company's president, did an impressive job in reviving Montgomery Ward's business health.

Avery's basic therapy lay in centralization. First, he drastically reshaped the policies, personnel, and even the physical plant of both wholesale and retail organizations. He next strengthened the control of functional vice presidents in charge of personnel, sales merchandising, operations, and finance. Retail stores were placed under the close supervison of regional

[54] Emmet and Jeuck, *Catalogues and Counters*, p. 365.
[55] The information on Montgomery Ward & Company is from its annual reports and from *Fortune*, Vol. 11 (Jan., 1935), 69 ff.; and Vol. 33 (May, 1946), 111 ff.

district managers—each of whom handled about 150 stores and reported to a vice president in charge of retailing. The local managers had less discretion and authority than those in Woolworth's and other chain stores. Top level coordination, supervision, and policy-making, while ostensibly performed by the department heads in committee, were from the start pretty much controlled by Avery. Possibly because of this one-man domination, the turnover of executive personnel at Montgomery Ward has been almost unprecedented. In fact, the "alumni association" of Montgomery Ward executives grew more rapidly in the 1940's than did the comparable number of Ford "graduates" of the 1920's. The recent palace revolution at Ward's, in which Avery and president Edmund A. Krieder were forced out of the company's management, may bring a change. As yet, however, there has been little indication that the new president and chairman, John A. Barr, is planning to decentralize operations.[56]

The Food Companies

Because the nature of their business differs somewhat from the large distributing firms, at least two of the leading food companies, the Great Atlantic and Pacific Tea Company and Swift and Company, have developed a sort of split type of organization which may pose problems in maintaining effective central control. The Great Atlantic and Pacific Tea Company's marketing has long been organized somewhat like Sears'. Its distributing organization consists, according to *Fortune*, of "seven geographical divisions each with its own officers, its own large measure of autonomy and subdivided into operating units of sixty to over 300 stores."[57] On the other hand, unlike Sears its purchasing is also decentralized. Because it handles many fewer types of products than Sears and often more perishable ones at that, its buying and processing are done by such autonomous divisions as the National Meat Department, National Bakery Division, National Butter Division, National Egg and Poultry Division, Coffee Division, the Atlantic Commission, Inc. (green goods, fruits, and vegetables), and the Quaker Maid Company, Inc., which cans, bottles, and otherwise processes food products and also performs such diverse auxiliary functions as the operation of laundries and printing plants. These divisions not only provide goods for the marketing units, but are also expected to advise them

[56] The recent changes at Wards are best described in *Business Week* (May 14, 1955), p. 30; (May 21, 1955), p. 34; and in *Newsweek*, Vol. 46 (Sept. 26, 1955), 84 ff. *Business Week* reasons that the large institutional investors who supported Avery against Louis E. Wolfson subsequently forced him out because of his ultra-conservative policies.

[57] *Fortune*, Vol. 36 (Nov., 1947), 104. This detailed article was supplemented by data taken from *Moody's Industrial Manual*. The annual reports say almost nothing. In 1954, according to *Moody's*, the Atlantic Provision Company, Inc., was dissolved and became a company division.

on how best to sell the products. This type of coordination appears to be carried out on an informal basis. Available literature does not make clear how the central staff further aids in coordination or how the top management carries on its functions. Nor is it certain when the present operating organization was created, although it most likely took form after the final mergers and consolidations making·up the present company were completed in 1925. In any case, there is little question that top-level supervisory and policy decisions have long been controlled by the Hartford brothers, John and George, whose family started the firm in the 1850's. Possibly with the recent death of John Hartford and the imminent retirement of his brother, George, who in 1954 was over 90, the central offices will be enlarged and their structure as well as specific functions more carefully defined.

When they set up their organization the Hartfords may have examined the experience of the largest meat-packing firm, Swift & Company. Well before the First World War Swift had separated its processing from its marketing.[58] Its "product" departments, including the beef, lamb, pork, poultry and dairy products, and canned food, delivered their goods to the warehouse of the Branch House Department or to the "car sales" agents. In the 1920's the Branch House Department handled sales in over thirty districts, each headed by a general manager assisted by a district sales manager and a fairly large staff. Areas not directly supervised by the branch house managers were covered by "car routes," whose salesmen ordered directly from the product departments. The car route agents, like the branch house managers, reported to one vice president in the Chicago headquarters. Products such as fertilizer, leather, and miscellaneous by-products which could not use these two types of marketing outlets handled their own distribution and were, therefore, fairly self-contained units. The headquarters staff and service departments seem to be more concerned with providing advice and services than with coordinating the various activities of the different operating units. Top-level supervision and policy-making seems to be carried out by the large number of vice presidents who have charge of from one to three of the operating departments. Although the published reports and articles on Swift are not clear here, this organization would seem to be a cumbersome one for the effective formulation of policy, not only because of the number of officers involved, but also because their primary concern would appear to be for departmental rather than company-wide problems. The recent appointment of two executive vice presidents may be a move to create a small controlling and policy-making top executive group made up of generalists rather than specialists. In any case,

---

[58] In contrast to the A. & P. the annual reports or "yearbooks" of Swift & Company are full and detailed. Particularly good are the yearbooks of 1929, pp. 24–31; of 1932, pp. 20–22; of 1934, pp. 20–25, and 1949, pp. 12–13. Also helpful was *Fortune*, Vol. 46 (Sept., 1952), 102 ff.

the company appears to be satisfied with its basic overall administrative structure, as it has made no major changes for more than a generation.

The story of Swift's chief competitor, Armour & Company, is somewhat different. Until recent years Armour was organized more on functional lines.[59] Before World War I its major operating units were the livestock, packing plant, sales, transportation, and foreign divisions; the major staff units were finance, treasury, and accounting. The sales department appears to have handled its function much in the same way as that of Swift. During the 1920's and 1930's product-oriented divisions developed, including poultry, leather, by-products, and a refinery division which processed and sold the company's entire production of fats and oils. In 1949 a significant step toward departmentalizing along product lines was taken when the buying and selling of each kind of meat were placed under one executive. By centralizing control over all operations involved in handling a line of products, one executive could thereby be made responsible for the financial results of his product division. Recently, too, many of the non-food products have been placed in an Auxiliaries Group, which in turn is divided into semiautonomous product divisions including soap, chemicals, curled hair, abrasives, and ammonia. Neither magazine articles nor company reports indicate, however, how the central staff and executive offices are designed and how their duties are divided. It seems reasonable to suppose that Armour headquarters are not too dissimilar from those of other product decentralized industrial concerns.

The experience of the United Fruit Company and the National Dairy Products Company emphasizes once again the close connection between the nature of a firm's business and the organization of its overall administrative structure. National Dairy, organized as a merger in 1923, has expanded steadily through continued purchases until today it has over sixty subsidiaries.[60] Because these subsidiaries were meeting the demands for perishable products in different geographic areas, there was little need to consolidate them into a centralized whole, or even into large territorially or product-defined units. The company's policy has always been, in fact, to leave its operating managers with a maximum amount of autonomy. In 1950, for example, the operating units set their own prices and production output, did their own advertising, and decided upon their own capital improvements.

The basic administrative problem for National Dairy, then, has been the formation of an effective central headquarters. From the start, the

[59] The reports of Armour & Company (Illinois) were less full than those of Swift. The most important are those of 1945, inside back cover, and that of 1949, pp. 4–5, which describes the changes made in that year. Some additional information was available in *Fortune*, Vol. 3 (April, 1931), 49 ff.; Vol. 9 (June, 1934), 58 ff.; Vol. 51 (May, 1955), 129 ff.

[60] The data on National Dairy Products Company came from its annual reports and from *Fortune*, Vol. 46 (Dec., 1952), 144.

duties of the central staff have been to provide specialized services and advice. These services have been steadily enlarged and today include, among other activities, research, quality control, merchandising advice, and personnel and management training. In 1949 the duties of the head-quarters' staff were more specifically defined with a grouping of these service units into an Executive Management Staff, which was given the task of assuring "coordination and teamwork among our subsidiaries."[61]

More difficult was the formation of an effective top executive unit. After 1928 major policy-making, supervision, and coordinating functions, which had at first been handled by a board made up almost entirely of the heads of major operating subsidiaries, were given to a smaller executive committee. In 1942, in direct response to the increasing complexities of wartime demands, an important change was made. The executive committee was enlarged to include a number of "outside" directors, all but two of whom were elected to the board that year. Many of the coordinating and possibly supervisory duties of the executive committee were given to a new operating committee, which consisted of the heads of leading subsidiaries, who also seem to have had charge of groups of smaller subsidiaries in their regions. As the "inside" members of the executive committee were also on the operating committee, they could now rely on the latter as well as on the headquarters staff and "outside" directors for assistance in policy planning and executive action. Such assistance may have been essential, since several of the executive committee are also heads of subsidiaries and so must have other duties besides overall company planning and supervision.

If National Dairy is a good example of an evolving management structure, United Fruit Company provides a typical picture of a static one. From the first, even before the merger of 1899 created the modern company, this Boston-managed firm was primarily concerned with one product—bananas—and with achieving a completely integrated unit from plantation to consumer.[62] In the first decades of the twentieth century the company did develop holdings in Cuban sugar and Costa Rican cocoa, which could be easily fitted into its integrated, banana-oriented organization. As the major operations in the organization were quite distinct from each other and as successful growing and banana marketing depended on changing local conditions, the different functional units had from the beginning considerable local autonomy. The growing areas were divided into large geographical units, each with a staff of specialists and each, in turn, being subdivided into smaller regional units. The marketing of bananas, handled

---

[61] The annual report of the National Dairy Products Company for 1949, pp. 6–7. The name, Executive Management Staff, appears to have been dropped in 1952.

[62] The United Fruit Company story comes from Charles W. Wilson, *Empire in Green and Gold* (New York, 1947), supplemented by its annual reports.

by the Fruit Dispatch division, was also done along regional lines through branch offices in the major rail and port centers in the United States and abroad. The growing and marketing as well as transportation departments were headed by vice presidents whose offices were in the Boston head-quarters.

Besides managing their own departments, these men, assisted by the heads of the staff departments, carried on top-level coordination of their activities with the president and his office. In what time they still had available they formulated current company policy and future plans. Although the company has long recognized the need for generalists in its top executive positions, it has done little to train such officers, nor has it made the necessary changes in the organizational structure to make such training possible. The only significant development in the company's organization since World War I has been the expansion of its coordinating and service departments. By the end of the 1920's these included the research, communications, advertising, public relations, personnel, and medical departments. As only limited attempts have been made at diversification, either in the development of by-products or the growth and marketing of tropical fruits and foods besides bananas, sugar, and cocoa, there has been little obvious external pressure on the United Fruit Company to make changes in its overall operational structure.

The Tobacco and Liquor Companies

Even more than United Fruit, the large tobacco companies concentrate on one product. Whether they came into being by mergers or whether they were small firms grown large, their organizations have always been functionally departmentalized and highly centralized. The largest, the American Tobacco Company, today as was the case well over a generation ago, has vice presidents in charge of purchasing, manufacturing, marketing, finance, and advertising.[63] The only change during the past generation has been an increase in the size of the vice presidents' staffs. The purchasing department, for example, has added an assistant vice president in charge of purchasing domestic leaf and another for Turkish leaf. The manufacturing department also acquired two assistant vice presidents, while sales have been divided between a vice president in charge of western markets and one in charge of eastern markets. The senior vice presidents thus have more time to join with the president in executive committee to carry out the necessary coordinating, supervising, and policy-making functions.

The administrative structures of the other two leading tobacco com-

[63] The information about the American Tobacco Company came mostly from its annual reports with a little additional data from *Fortune*, Vol. 14 (Dec., 1936), 97 ff.

panies, R. J. Reynolds Tobacco Company and the Liggett and Myers Tobacco Company, are much the same as American's.[64] They have smaller top staffs, however, and no cigar division. On the other hand, like American, they remain family dominated firms. Where the American Tobacco Company has had in its top management two generations of Hills, Liggett and Myers has had two of Toms and the third company two generations of Reynolds.

The administrative history of Distillers Corporation-Seagrams Ltd. parallels that of the three tobacco companies, while that of Schenley's, the second largest distilling firm, follows quite a different pattern. Seagrams, started in 1928 as a merger of two Canadian firms, expanded its operations into the United States in 1933 with the repeal of the eighteenth amendment.[65] It grew fairly rapidly in the 1930's and early 1940's, but concentrated this expansion almost wholly on the acquisition of whiskey distilling and marketing firms. Aside from whiskey, it makes some gin, has a small by-product unit which produces dried cattle grain, and a new subsidiary, the Pharma-Craft Corporation, which manufactures drugs and toiletries on a small scale. Because of its predominant concentration on whiskey-making and selling and because its top management has from the beginning been dominated by one family, the Bronjmans, there is little reason to anticipate changes in this highly centralized, functionally departmentalized management structure.

The other leading distilling company, Schenley Industries, Inc., has since the end of prohibition stressed product diversification. In the 1930's, while concentrating on domestic whiskey, it became the American distributing agent for Bacardi rum and for many of the best-known European wines and liqueurs.[66] Then, between 1942 and 1945 it purchased the Roma Wine Company, the Blatz Brewing Company, two Puerto Rican rum concerns and two other wine firms. Moreover, during the war it began long-scale manufacturing of industrial alcohol and, more important for postwar operations, penicillin, penicillin products, streptomycin, and a variety of pharmaceuticals.

With this expansion the firm's management has become increasingly decentralized. Its major operating subsidiaries are divided along both functional and product lines. Schenley Distillers, Inc., operates the distilleries and most of the bottling plants except those in Pennsylvania and Maryland, which are run by Joseph S. Finch and Company. The major

[64] The generalizations on both companies are based on their annual reports. *Fortune*, Vol. 3 (Jan., 1931), 45 ff.; Vol. 18 (Aug., 1938), 25 ff., are good on the R. J. Reynolds Tobacco Company.

[65] The data on the Distillers-Seagram Ltd. are from its brief annual reports.

[66] The Schenley story is also from the annual reports. *Fortune*, Vol. 13 (May, 1936), 99 ff., provides some more information. Other important subsidiaries of Schenley Industries, Inc., are Canadian Schenley, Ltd., and Ron Carioca Distilleria of Puerto Rico.

share of the marketing is handled by the Schenley Distributors. Wine, however, which is manufactured under the auspices of the parent company in California, is distributed by the C.V.A. Corporation. Schenley's Import Corporation, Schenley's International Corporation, and the Louisville Cooperage Company handle other important functions, while all beer operations are conducted by the Blatz Brewing Company and pharmaceuticals by Schenley Laboratories, Inc. The central staff offices continue to grow, particularly the sales staff, and appear to play as important a role in coordinating the operating units as in providing them with services. After a change of command in 1952, the top supervisory and policy-making group was enlarged and its functions seem to have been more carefully defined. The annual reports and articles written about Schenley, however, do not indicate clearly the duties and functions of the company's large number of vice presidents, the degree of autonomy given the heads of the operating units, or the specific duties of the central staff and executive offices.

Summary: Market-Oriented Firms

The Schenley experience, like that of the other food, stimulant, and marketing firms, emphasizes the point that growing complexity of operations is the major stimulus for decentralizing operations. Its experience is also a reminder that such complexity does not necessarily result from increasing size alone. Schenley's operations, for example, are certainly more complex than those of the larger Seagrams concern or, for that matter, of the still larger tobacco companies. And when complexity turns a management to decentralization, the history of these companies indicates again how the orientation of the autonomous units varies with the nature of their business. Still, whether the organization of these food, stimulant, and distributing firms is articulated along regional, product, or functional lines, its basic structure has much in common with that of decentralized companies in other American industries.

SUMMARY AND CONCLUSIONS

After this examination of the administrative history of fifty of the nation's largest industrial firms, the historian can report categorically that this relatively new type of decentralized, overall management structure has become a dominant one. Since the First World War both highly centralized, functionally departmentalized operating companies and loosely federated holding companies have reorganized their administrative structures so that operations are handled by autonomous management units whose work is coordinated and supervised by a central unit consisting of a staff of specialists and an executive office of generalists. This change has resulted from the growing complexity of operations and the administrative problems raised by such complexity. For some firms these pressures resulted from the development of new lines of products and new markets or from significant changes in existing markets. This has been particularly true for the chemical and electrical firms, but also for some rubber, automotive, oil, marketing, food, and liquor firms. For others, and this has been especially characteristic of the oil, food, and paper firms studied here, the growing complexity and resulting decentralization came as these companies expanded operations into different and diverse regions of the nation and the world. For a few automotive, oil, and non-ferrous metals firms, the change was primarily a response to an increase in the size of their operations. Finally, the firms that have retained the old centralized structures are those that still stick largely to the making and selling of one major line of products. The experience of the non-ferrous metals firms suggests that there may be a correlation between lack of competition, slow growth, and administrative conservatism.

For most of the companies that made the change, the new complexities came in times of prosperity and in an expanding economy. The first major administrative reorganizations to set up decentralized structures were made in the 1920's, and the largest number of them came in the 1940's. Important reorganizations took place during the years of the great depression but, except for those in some of the large oil firms, they more often led to tightening rather than decentralization of top management's control over day-to-day operational decisions.

It does seem significant that decentralization did not become widespread before 1920. Before the First World War nearly all large industrial companies concentrated on the processing and marketing of one major line of closely related products. Often, too, where the company was formed by a series of mergers motivated primarily by a desire to control price and production, the men managing the merged properties continued for some time to consider their chief function to be that of setting price and output quotas rather than that of coordinating operations to meet the demands of a changing and expanding market. In the 1920's swift urban and suburban growth enlarged and altered markets, particularly the consumer markets. The opening of new sources of raw materials in the United States and abroad extended the operations of the vertically integrated companies. Rapid changes in the techniques and technology of manufacturing and marketing emphasized even more the need for flexible administrative structures. Finally, just before and after World War I, companies like duPont, Union Carbide,

United States Rubber, General Electric, and Westinghouse began an extensive program of product diversification and systematic research and development which made their existing administrative organizations obsolete.

The problems encountered in changing to the more flexible decentralized structure reflected the way a company's business had expanded and changed. For the firm that expanded by new plant construction and the purchases of smaller companies, the most serious initial problems involved the creation of effective autonomous operating units. For the company that came into being after a series of mergers, the primary concern, aside from rationalizing its extractive, processing, and marketing units, was the formation of an effective central coordinating, supervising, and policy-making unit.

The form and functions of the central and operating units that were created to answer these problems also varied with the basic nature of the firm's business and the manner in which it had grown. Where its business remained that of processing and marketing a comparatively few closely related products, the major operating subdivisions were organized along functional lines—a separate, self-contained unit for each of the major processes in the progression from obtaining raw materials to reaching the consumer. Where marketing became the most complex part of a business, as was the case of some distributing or food firms, the major units were often set up on regional lines. Finally, where a firm's business was based on a broad technology (chemical, electrical, or automotive engineering) which produced a large number of products for widely varying markets, the self-contained operating units were organized around products or groups of products.

So also did the nature of the business affect the size, organization, and duties of the central coordinating, supervising, and policy-making unit and of the central service staff. In the functionally decentralized organization, both the top management group and the central service departments remained comparatively small. The staff officers appear to have been even more concerned with coordination than with providing services. The small senior top management group often included some men who were more operating specialists than policy-making generalists. In regionally decentralized firms, the central staff units put more emphasis on supplying services to than in coordinating the efforts of operating units, while top management was usually relieved of the day-to-day operating decisions. Finally, the firms whose operating units were defined along product lines had the largest central offices. In these cases the service departments, while playing an important coordinating role, were most concerned with providing services to both the operating divisions and the top management group. The latter usually consisted almost wholly of men who had little to distract them from focusing on the overall company view. Such central offices had much in common with those devised by Standard Oil (N. J.) and

Standard Oil of California and used between 1937 and 1950 by the United States Steel Corporation. However, such units which supervised and made policy for regionally integrated as well as for functional and product subsidiaries were given larger coordinating roles than those in product decentralized firms.

Although increasing size, diversity, and complexity of operations have been the primary cause for administrative reorganization they have in no way guaranteed it. Too often managements have failed or refused to recognize that growth or qualitative changes in producing and marketing required administrative readjustment. In many of the firms studied here necessary reorganization came only after the retirement and occasionally not until the death of a powerful executive or dominant group of managers. Until the retirement of Elbert H. Gary, Gerard Swope, the elder Henry Ford, Willard Dow, Harry F. Sinclair, Sewell Avery, K. T. Keller of Chrysler, Orlando Weber of Allied Chemical, Harold McCormick and Addis E. McKinstry of International Harvester, and E. T. Stannard of Kennecott, the firms they had long managed were unable to make the essential administrative adjustments required by growth and changing external conditions. In 1955 a number of the most highly centralized organizations among the top fifty industrial firms were those still dominated by men well beyond the normal compulsory retirement age. This was true of the management of Firestone, Goodyear, Anaconda, International Nickel, Alcoa, Seagrams, A. & P., Bethlehem Steel, and Republic Steel. Moreover, most of these companies continued to concentrate more than their competitors on the single line of products their managers had produced when both they and the company were younger. As these veterans leave the scene many of their firms will undoubtedly make significant changes in their management structures.

It may be safe to say, therefore, that while the causes for administrative reorganization were the development of new products, shifts in established markets, and expansion of the overall economy, the timing of these changes has been greatly influenced by the turnover of top management personnel. Of course, a crisis or semicrisis created by overproduction or by sudden contractions and, occasionally, by rapid expansion of markets did force changes on a well-established top management. And if it resisted or failed to adjust to the new situation, that management sometimes was replaced. But, except for crisis, age was the primary reason for changes in the top management. Nevertheless, several large corporations did make basic organizational changes before the coming of a crisis and without requiring a major change in the top command. Some of the most significant innovations were made by relatively young men who might have managed their organizations in the old way with a more than fair assurance of continuing profits.

The fundamental innovations in the major variations of decentralized administrative structures existing in large industrial concerns all came in the 1920's. The first and by far the most significant was that engineered by Irenee and Pierre duPont in 1921. The two brothers created simultaneously for the duPont company and for General Motors the organization that is still the model for companies decentralizing their operations along product lines. Since more and more companies are turning to product diversification as an answer to a number of their business problems, this type of structure will undoubtedly become even more widely used than it is today. What the duPonts did for the multi-industry firm, Walter Teagle and his Standard Oil of New Jersey staff did for the ·integrated, single-industry concern. Moreover, besides innovating in functional decentralization, Teagle pioneered in the creation of a central unit which could effectively coordinate and supervise a number of huge vertically integrated subsidiaries as well as functional and product-defined autonomous operating units. The final innovation, that of regional decentralization, was initiated by General Robert Wood in 1929. Although it has for obvious reasons not been widely adopted by industrial concerns, the Sears, Roebuck organization has been copied in the decentralization of large financial firms, particularly the insurance companies.

These innovations are among the most notable in the long history of large-scale organization. The creation of a new overall administrative form before a major external crisis or internal change of command takes place is, historically, an impressive achievement. Even the most imaginative efforts in the creation of government and military administrative structures, such as those of Alexander Hamilton's formation of the executive branch of the American government or Elihu Root's reorganization of the Army, came after periods of change and crisis. Moreover, there are few cases in history where men in power have consciously and willingly delegated a large number of key decisions and responsibilities. Prior to the communications revolution of the nineteenth century, military, church, government, and business bureaucracies permitted local managers a wide range of decision-making. But this was largely because of the limitations of technology and not because of the specific desire of the top command. Once the technological limitations of communications and control were overcome, the trend was to centralize more and more decisions in the top office.

The recent innovations in the administrative organizations of large business firms may be reversing this trend. This shift to decentralization is undoubtedly easier for a business than for a government or military organization because the nature of business operations provides the central headquarters with more readily available criteria for continuous evaluation of the performance of operating units. But also, business decentralization may have been successful because the type of structures the duPonts, Wood, and Teagle created defined more clearly and more realistically than almost any other administrative organization yet devised the role and functions of the staff specialist, the operating commanders, and the top policy-making and controlling officers.

Mabel Newcomer

9

Professionalization of Leadership in
the Big Business Corporation [1]

Interest in the "professionalization of business management" has grown in recent years among both the sociologists and the economists. There is general agreement that such professionalization is developing rapidly, and the evidence usually presented is the growing number of chief executives of our larger corporations, at least, who are salaried managers trained for the job by long experience in the field, and perhaps also by formal schooling, in the art of management. This much is well established. But while there is an expanding literature on the appropriate training and qualifications of the business leader, few studies have been made of the actual training and qualifications of business executives, the extent to which professionalization can be said to have taken place, and the implications of such professionalization for the future conduct of business—and more particularly its implications for the control of big business.

This paper attempts to make some small contribution to our knowledge in this field. It presents part of the findings of a larger study I have made of the origins, training, and experience of the top executivès in our large corporations, shortly to be published by the Columbia University Press.

The study is limited to the presidents and board chairmen of large nonfinancial corporations for three different business generations—1900, 1925, and 1950. The test of size used is assets, and the study covers all nonfinancial corporations listed in *Moody's Manual of Investments* with assets in excess of $75 millions in 1950, $50 millions in 1925, and $25 millions in 1900. These amounts are roughly comparable in terms of the purchasing power of the dollar for the three periods. In addition, a sample of smaller corpora-

[1] This paper was presented at the joint session of the Sheraton Group and the American Historical Association, New York, 28 Dec. 1954.

tions has been included for each period. These smaller corporations are, however, still large in absolute terms, the 1950 group having assets in excess of $50 millions. The number of corporations exceeds 200 in each of the earlier periods and is over 400 in 1950. The number of officers is more than 300 in each of the earlier periods and nearly 900 in 1950.

I am limiting myself here to discussion of (1) the tests of professionalization of top business management, (2) the extent to which professionalization appears to have taken place in the big nonfinancial corporations, as indicated by these tests, and (3) some of the implications of such professionalization.

The first test of professionalization is the extent and kind of formal education. The American tradition of "rags to riches" has assumed only the sketchiest kind of formal schooling; and the self-made businessman has often scorned a college education as a waste of time at best, and at worst a real handicap. One top executive, himself a Harvard graduate, comments that the Harvard student is "taught to 'get by' on his exam and then forget," and that after such training it is difficult, if not impossible, to teach him thoroughness and sustained effort. And another writes that when the college graduate enters the business world the first thing he has to learn is that "seventy per cent isn't passing."

The fact is, however, that big business not only tolerates the college man; a college degree is increasingly the ticket of admission to jobs with big corporations. It is true that the representatives of large business corporations who descend upon the college campuses every spring are looking for engineers and scientists, lawyers and accountants, and not for top administrators. But the fact remains that the great majority of chief executives are college men. Three-fourths of the 1950 executives of my study had some college education, and for those appointed after 1943 the proportion is four-fifths. Two-thirds of these recent appointees have a bachelor's degree, and one-fifth have pursued graduate study. Most of this latter group are engineers and lawyers—sometimes both—but they include a small number of Ph.D.s, M.D.s, and men with advanced degrees in business administration.

The proportion of big business executives with college training is estimated to be approximately 12 times the proportion found in the entire male population of their age group. In view of the wide variation in the ages of these executives this comparison cannot be exact. For the entire male population I have used the proportion of males 18 to 21 years of age enrolled in college in 1910, the census year nearest that in which the median age of the 1950 executive group was 20.

The 76 per cent of 1950 executives with some college training is much higher than the 51 per cent found for the 1925 group and the 39 per cent found for the 1900 group; but even in these earlier generations the proportion of college men among the business executives is nearly 10 times that for the male population of their age groups. In other words, whether because of or in spite of a college education, a disproportionate number of college trained men are reaching the top executive position and have been doing so throughout this 50-year period.

When the *kind* of university education that the executives have had, or should have, is considered, generalizations are harder to make and defend. The actual educational experience of the 1950 executives is widely varied. Nineteen per cent of the 540 university graduates among the 1950 executives had law degrees, LL.B.s and J.D.s, and 32 per cent had first or advanced engineering degrees. These two professions combined account for just over half of all college graduates. Some of the remaining group majored in economics, accounting, and various business courses, but the proportion that had highly specialized training in this field appears to be small. The nature of their undergraduate courses in these fields usually cannot be identified by the kind of degree they earned, but the very fact that degrees in these subjects are not as regularly differentiated from the A.B. degree as those in law and engineering is in itself indicative of the fact that the training in business and economics is not as well defined or as specialized as that in law or engineering. Only 3.5 per cent of the 1950 business executives with college degrees had advanced degrees in business administration, as compared with 7.6 per cent with advanced degrees in engineering and 9.8 per cent with advanced degrees in law.

This should not be taken as evidence that professional training in law and engineering are more suitable for executives than professional training in business administration itself. The graduate schools of business administration are still too young to have turned out any large number of graduates among the age groups now in top positions in big business. Also, there is some evidence that within the official group from which the chief executives are likely to be chosen there are more engineers and lawyers than professional business administrators. The corporations have turned to the universities and colleges for promising young engineers, lawyers, and scientists in the lower ranks. They have not sought promising young general administrators at that level. And when the time comes to choose a new president or board chairman, it is engineers and lawyers—not general administrators—who predominate among the vice presidents from whom the choice is most frequently made.

It seems probable that the graduate training in business administration as such is more suitable than graduate training in some other profession, although there is still greater diversity in the nature of this training than in that for the older professions. The consensus among the executives themselves and the authorities on administration is that specialized training, whether in law, engineering, or some science, is not as useful as a more general education. And while most do not appear to object to *advanced* training in business administration they stress the importance of a *general* education at the undergraduate level.

The best test of a suitable education for business administration is not the number of top executives who have been trained in the different fields, since the corporations have been relying on training on the job for their top executives rather than on their formal schooling. And as long as they require large numbers of engineers at the bottom for operations and production, a disproportionate number of engineers is going to get the administrative experience which leads to the top.

The best test of a suitable education would appear to be, consequently, the relative success of top executives who have had different kinds of training. In an attempt to throw some light on this question a comparison has been made of the education of the top executives in rapidly growing corporations and corporations that have remained fairly static. All industrial corporations with assets in excess of $75 millions in 1950 were used for this comparison. The fast-growing corporations have been defined as those whose assets multiplied five times or more between 1925 and 1950. The "static" corporations are those whose assets actually declined or did not double during this period. Very few of this group had a large enough increase in assets to offset the increasing cost of replacement of assets. Change in asset values is not in itself an adequate test of success, but it is at least an objective measure which bears some relation to success. The officials of the corporations included in this study were the presidents and board chairmen who held these offices for at least three years at some time between 1925 and 1950, and who should, in consequence, have had some responsibility for their companies' expansion or failure to expand. The number of officials is 119 for the fast-growing corporations, and 138 for the static corporations.

A slightly larger proportion of the officials of the fast-growing corporations had college degrees than was found for the officials of the static corporations—51 per cent as compared with 48 per cent.[2] But the more striking difference lies in the proportion with specialized degrees—particularly in law. Only 6.8 per cent of the officials of the fast-growing corporations had law degrees as compared with 14.1 per cent of the officials of the static corporations. There were likewise more engineering degrees among the officials of the static corporations although the difference here is too small to be dependable. And whereas 30.5 per cent of the officials of the fast-growing group had relatively unspecialized bachelor's degrees, only 19.3 per cent of the officers of the static corporations had such unspecialized degrees. Such evidence as this comparison affords, then, appears to support the contention that the broader education is better. However, the relatively small number of cases and the limited value of the assets test suggest caution in accepting these differences as conclusive evidence of the superiority of a general education in this field.

[2] The fact that the proportion for both groups is smaller than for the 1950 officials as a whole is due to the fact that this comparison included many older officials whose term of office ended before 1950.

While the debate continues as to the amount and kind of formal schooling that is desirable for training executives, it is training on the job that the corporations are really depending on. Increasingly top executives are chosen from the ranks of the companies' employees. For the 1900 group of executives 59 per cent had no previous history with the corporations, and only a fraction of these outsiders was selected for administrative success in other companies. For the 1950 executives, on the contrary, only 23 per cent had no previous history with the corporation, and most of the outsiders—18 per cent of all officials—were selected for successful administration in other companies.

The change is due primarily, although not entirely, to the fact that the 1900 corporations were comparatively young. Only 29 per cent were as much as 20 years old at that time. Large numbers of them were still in the hands of their founders or the founders' heirs. Also, high office was something to be bought and sold in the stock market along with a controlling number of shares. But whatever the reason for the change, it is true today that the new corporation president is expected to have had many years of successful administrative experience, whether in his own corporation or elsewhere. His formal schooling may have contributed toward his success in the lower ranks, but it is too far behind him to be given much weight in the factors that lead to his final selection for top office.

Most of the authorities on qualifications for top administrators stress the importance of experience with general administration. They deplore the choice of specialists, whether the specialist be vice president of sales, the treasurer, or an engineer in charge of production. They favor the choice of men with experience as top executives of smaller companies, on the assumption that experience as a general administrator is more important than knowledge of the special problems of the individual corporation. The officials responsible for the selection of future presidents and board chairmen, on the contrary, tend to select from within—and therefore to select specialists. They recognize the need for breadth of training. But they attempt to meet this need, not by looking outside of their own organization but by selecting promising young officials from within and giving them special training. Some companies deliberately move these prospective top executives from department to department so that they will learn the business as a whole; others send them to the short training courses offered for executives by a number of universities; still others offer training programs of their own. But however the training is accomplished the fact that it is provided is recognition of the need for professional standards.

Another indication of increasing professionalization of business management is the almost universal acceptance of the principle that the job should be awarded on merit. The proportion of chief executives who inherited the office from other members of the family declined from 30 per cent to 15 per cent between 1900 and 1950 among those large business concerns old enough to be inherited—i.e., those more than 20 years old. And even the inheritors are expected to have given long and reasonably competent service. The growing dispersion of stock ownership makes it increasingly difficult for the heirs to enforce their claims, and the loyalty of the directors is more likely to be to the corporation and to the stockholders as a whole than to the founder's family. Substantial stock holdings may lead to a directorship but they give little if any claim to the presidency. This is not to say that favoritism plays no part in the final selection, or that the search for talent—whether inside or outside the corporation—is always as extensive as might be expected in view of the importance of the job. But neither is the office awarded lightly. Some show of merit there must be. Also, while the executives continue to come from wealthy families in disproportionate numbers, there is a declining proportion from such wealthy families—36 per cent in 1950 as compared with 46 per cent in 1900.

Still another indication of increasing professionalization of business management is the attitude of the executives themselves. A recent investigation of highly paid business executives in California showed not only that the majority worked overtime, but that these were happier than the group who kept more regular hours. They were definitely interested in their jobs and worked overtime because they liked what they were doing. It is true that the compensation of our top business executives ranges considerably higher than that in most professions. And this, too, is an important incentive. But there is general agreement that the principal attraction lies in the interest of the work itself.

Finally, it is apparent that a professional code of business ethics is developing and is receiving wide acceptance. I have no quantitative data to prove this, but illustrations can be cited. For instance, a number of top executives of 1900 held important government positions at the same time. Today, the top officials are expected to give full time to their business position, and if they leave it—as they must—when they accept high government positions they may not even retain their stockholdings in the corporation they formerly headed. Any such close alliance between business and government is viewed with misgivings. Also the presidency of a large company was used all too often, at the beginning of this century to make a quick profit for the president himself, even though such financial manipulation might leave the corporation bankrupt. Today the small stockholders' rights are usually protected by the top officials. They even urge the stockholders to participate personally in stockholders' meetings, and to interest themselves in other ways in the company's affairs. The man who, after spending the major part of his working life with one corporation, is rewarded with the presidency, has a loyalty to the organization that is hardly less than the pride of the founder. And he tends to think in terms of the welfare of the corporation itself. Nor is his concern limited to the company and its stockholders. The general welfare is recognized, not only in public statements but with increasing frequency by appointing representatives of the general public to the board of directors. And while one may take exception to Secretary Wilson's statement that what is good for General Motors is good for the country as a whole, at least it shows recognition of the fact that the general welfare must be reckoned with. Not even the most obtuse of today's top executives is likely to be caught expressing sentiments such as those in the remark attributed to W. H. Vanderbilt, "The public be damned."

These changing standards are in part the result of government restrictions. But these restrictions are the reflection of a changed public attitude which the majority of officials appear to accept. Many officials are even convinced that these standards are in the long-run interest of business itself, and they participate actively both in formulating and in enforcing them.

Summarizing the evidence that the leaders of big business are developing a profession of business administration, it should be noted first, that wealth and family position have declined in importance as a way to the top; second, that the amount of formal education expected has increased; third, that increasingly long years of experience are required before being entrusted with top positions; fourth, that the officials themselves are for the most part completely absorbed in their work; and, fifth, that a professional code of ethics is emerging.

Too much should not be claimed for this, however. Wealth and family position are still important, and the nature of formal education for administration has not been standardized to the extent that it has been in law, medicine, and engineering, for instance. And most of the officials with a professional education have obtained it in another profession than that of business administration. To that extent it is a vicarious profession. No specific examination or degrees are requirements for entrance into the profession; and long years of faithful service may be an acceptable substitute for well-rounded training and experience. Also, the code of ethics, while undoubtedly developing, is still somewhat amorphous.

Turning to the apparent reasons for this development toward professionalization of business administration, the important ones can be quickly enumerated. The increased size and age of our leading corporations have brought separation of ownership and control. Very few really large family corporations remain. Within the past few months, for example, steps have been taken to make a public offering of the stock of both the Ford Motor Company and the Campbell Soup Company. These are among the very few large corporations still under family control. The management control which necessarily results from dispersion of ownership tends to become a kind of self-perpetuating trust, with promotion from within, and— when possible—expansion from its own profits, thus freeing itself from the outside control of the bankers. Many corporations today have predominantly, or completely, inside boards made up of full-time officers of the company. And it may be noted, incidentally, that the record of the inside boards is better than that of the outside boards, although this is contrary to the accepted principles of administration. The interest of these lifetime employees of the company becomes identified with the interest of the corporation itself, and—one step removed—with the interest of the multitude of stockholders. This leads to more emphasis on training for what has become a highly skilled, lifetime job. The sheer size of the hundred million or billion dollar corporation makes dilettantism unthinkable. The stakes are too large.

One of the consequences of control by salaried professional managers, instead of investors, is that the pressure for immediate profits is lessened. The managers can afford to take a long view. This often means using a large share of the profits for expansion, which contributes to production on the one hand, and, by increasing equity capital, reduces the risks of failure on the other. It may even lead to continued production when the business outlook is uncertain. General Motors announced publicly last spring that they were betting $1 billion on prosperity. In other words, they were launching a $1 billion expansion program in the face of a business recession. It has been suggested that the engineers, who so often reach the top, will be more interested in production than in profits, and will not tolerate the "conscientious withdrawal of efficiency" which Veblen associated with the big businessman. On the other hand, a lifetime devoted to working up slowly in one department of one corporation cannot be depended on to develop breadth of vision or the imagination and daring that are associated with progress.

The professionalization of business, as far as it has developed, has not been planned. The fact that the top executives have been trained in other professions than business administration is, alone, evidence of this. Again to quote Veblen, "industrial experts, engineers, chemists, mineralogists, technicians of all kinds, have been drifting into more responsible positions in the industrial system and have been growing up and multiplying within the system, because the system will no longer work at all without them."[3] And there is still much to be done before business administration as a profession can achieve the prestige of engineering, law, or medicine. Much of its present prestige comes from financial rewards and power rather than from the skills required.

Nevertheless, it seems quite possible that the professionalization of big business will in the long run make an important contribution toward solving the so-called problem of big business. We have tolerated the giant

[3] Thorstein Veblen, *The Engineers and the Price System* (New York, 1921), p. 44.

corporation in this country, even while we have feared it, because mass production is efficient. It is usually given a large part of the credit for our high and rising planes of living. Consequently, we have been half-hearted in our enforcement of the antitrust laws. And we have continued to hope that big business could be controlled for the public good, rather than destroyed. Professionalization of leadership in the big business corporation appears to offer one possible route to this end. The critics used to talk about the "heartless and soulless" corporation. Some of them today are discovering the "corporate conscience."